HOW TO THINK LIKE A
MILLIONAIRE

HOW TO THINK LIKE A
MILLIONAIRE

The Success Secrets of
Ten Millionaires

CHARLES-ALBERT POISSANT
AND CHRISTIAN GODEFROY

Thorsons

Thorsons
An Imprint of HarperCollins*Publishers*
77–85 Fulham Palace Road
Hammersmith
London W6 8JB

The Thorsons website address is: www.thorsons.com

© Editions Libre Expression, Canada 1985

First English language edition
© Thorsons Publishing Group 1989

First published by Thorsons 1989
This edition 2001

7 9 10 8 6

Charles-Albert Poissant and Christian Godefrey assert
the moral right to be identified as the authors of this work

A catalogue record for this book
is available from the British Library

ISBN 0 7225 3105 2

Printed and bound in Great Britain by
Omnia Books Limited, Glasgow

CONTENTS

INTRODUCTION

For some mysterious reason or other, the rich have always fascinated ordinary people. We, too, have admittedly fallen prey to their magic spell. We decided, however, to lift the veil of mystery surrounding them, to discover the secrets of their wealth, and how they came to build their empires. Our initial idea was essentially quite simple. We began with the basic premise that success cannot be attributed to fate (even if luck does occasionally have something to do with it), but to the sound application of very specific principles. Lo and behold, this theory of ours was confirmed beyond all expectation. Each of the men we researched put certain broad principles into more or less deliberate application (more rather than less, shall we say).

Of course, some of them enforced these rules of thumb differently and more rigorously than the others. Nevertheless, each of them had his own 'speciality', putting more emphasis on one specific principle, which ended up becoming his 'trademark' or personalized success formula. Ray Kroc, for example, the world-famous hamburger millionaire, represents the most amazing example of persistence against all odds. He became successful only after the age of 50, at a time when most people normally think of retiring. In his eyes, perseverance was so vital that he unhesitatingly placed it above talent and even above genius.

Paul Getty, one of the richest men in the world, believed that business success depended mainly on knowing how to direct human activity. This millionaire oil baron was undoubtedly a leader of men. All of his closest secrets, which influenced his entire life and which he disclosed in a kind of spiritual legacy, will be revealed throughout this book. Each character in this gallery of wealthy men championed one major recipe for success, and so a study of their lives will therefore shed light on the enigmatic art of being successful.

Each area of life, be it music, business, medicine, or law, has its own rules and regulations which make it into an art or science. These professions each have their own masters or experts, people who have refined their art or skills to the utmost. When we wish to learn or perfect something, we automatically turn to them for guidance and we use them as role models. We can of course learn the piano or advanced calculus on our own. This task, however, would be a very long one and relying on a teacher speeds our learning up. Consequently, the aim of this book is to offer you the wisdom of the greatest financial teachers of all time. It will help you avoid making blunders and running into obstacles, and it will enable you to get rich more quickly and easily!

SELF-MADE MILLIONAIRES

There are two categories of wealthy men. The first are those commonly known as the 'inheritors', meaning those who were born with silver spoons in their mouths and who started out in business already armed with a generous nest egg. This class of millionaire is not without interest in its own right. However, it is obviously much easier to get going in life when you have pockets stuffed with a couple of million dollars, since this can generally be made to flourish with a bit of sound advice.

The second category consists of those often referred to as 'self-made men'. Unlike the first group, their prosperity owes nothing to the chance of birth. They are therefore much more interesting for the purpose of our study, because these men started out in life with no more advantage than the rest of us. The details of their biographical sketches, which you are about to read, prove this beyond a shadow of a doubt. Their childhoods were generally rather commonplace, often poor, and sometimes miserable. At school many of them were notorious dunces. Yet, each one of them at a crucial moment in their lives decided to take their fate into their own hands, and, enlightened by a book, the advice or example of a friend, or by a powerful sense of intuition, they set out one by one to get rich.

Socrates, the Greek philosopher, unceasingly moaned about the weakness of his own nature. Yet, he came to realize that man is perfectible. Mankind can always improve himself. Similarly, his capacity to grow richer, no matter how small that may seem, can also be perfected. Man's ability to uplift himself can develop at any moment in life.

In fact, no matter how old you are or what your circumstances may be, you could very well have reached the critical stage that will change your life. All you have to do is to stay alert and receptive. The secrets contained in this book can help you reach the same decisive turning point which brought wealth to these 10 men.

We have chosen these self-made men from a wide variety of different fields so that you can see it is possible to succeed in any activity. Of course, it was impossible to find 10 men to cover the full range of businesses. Nevertheless, the qualities they demonstrate and the principles they adhere to are applicable to all kinds of enterprise, and our aim is to help you apply the same qualities and principles and to equip you for similar success.

Our gallery of millionaires, as you shall see, is made up of men whose names you are probably very familiar with. In fact, several of them are so famous that their names have become household words. These men are: Henry Ford, Conrad Hilton, Thomas Watson, Ray Kroc, Soichiro Honda, Walt Disney, Aristotle Onassis, John Rockefeller, Paul Getty, and Steven Spielberg.

THE EXTENT OF THEIR WEALTH

How much *exactly* are these men worth? Paul Getty once remarked that anyone who can estimate the size of his fortune is not really rich at all. The men we have studied and analysed are incredibly wealthy. It is impossible to know exactly *how* wealthy they are because they own such complex portfolios of shares, and the value of these continually fluctuates. In addition, for financial reasons, most wealthy men tend to be discreet about the empires they have built up. Many of them become obsessive about privacy and carefully avoid any kind of publicity.

The best example of this tendency (which, in the case of Howard Hughes, turned into a genuine phobia), is Paul Getty. In 1957, the prestigious American magazine, *Fortune*, published a survey of the richest men in the world. Paul Getty came out on top. Until then, Getty had always managed to remain anonymous. The public knew nothing about him. In fact , one story has it that when a former classmate of his from college ran into Getty long after he had become a multi-millionaire, he asked him who he was working for!

In spite of their attempts to keep the extent of the fortunes secret, we know that the wealth of these men is enormous. There are, of course, even richer men in the world, for example, OPEC magnates whose daily incomes run into millions. But since they are not well known, we felt that their example would be less interesting. What is fascinating about the 10 men we have selected is that they have proven beyond a shadow of a doubt that the 'American dream' is a reality, that it *is* possible to start from scratch and acquire a colossal fortune through hard work and determination.

Although most of the men we discuss are American, the secrets of their success apply anywhere in the world. If we had studied millionaires of other nationalities, we would undoubtedly have reached the same conclusions. All our research confirms the theory that the principles behind success are universal. Englishmen such as Richard Branson, Robert Maxwell, Terence Conran and Elton John became rich by applying the same formulas as their American counterparts.

Although most of these 10 men rarely talked about the money they made, they were happy to discuss the philosophy behind their success. Many of them have written their memoirs, leaving behind a spiritual legacy. Those who did not write about themselves generally opened up to reporters during in-depth interviews, or allowed their closest associates the opportunity to learn their philosophies. This made our task a lot easier. When one of these men explains his recipe for success, we sit up and listen. It goes without saying that advice like this is priceless.

Joseph Kennedy, the father of John F. Kennedy was once asked by a student doing a survey why he was rich. He coldly replied, 'I'm rich because I have a lot of money.' Joseph Kennedy was worth over $360 million, yet his lips were sealed when it came to explaining how he had accumulated this vast amount. Fortunately, the 10 men we studied were not so secretive and were happy to explain their strategies so that other people could benefit.

WHAT THIS BOOK CAN DO FOR YOU

There is an old Chinese saying that 'a journey of a thousand miles begins with one step.' By deciding to read this book you have just taken the first step towards becoming rich. The crucial point about this book is that it offers exactly what you are looking for. Not everyone in the world is cut out to be a millionaire. We would all like to be one, but not everyone is ready to make the necessary sacrifices. It goes without saying that those who did manage to become billionaires were workaholics and very often sacrificed some of the ordinary pleasures of life. Yet, everything in life is a matter of choice. The purpose of this book, therefore, is not only to help you clarify the options open to you so that you can discover what you really want, but also to help you achieve your goals.

DOUBLE YOUR INCOME IN A YEAR

Many people dream of doubling their incomes. That would not necessarily mean becoming rich, but being better off, being able to afford a few more luxuries than usual, take holidays more often, change cars every two years, and

so on. This book will teach you how to go about making
more money.

Perhaps, like thousands of others, you are unemployed
or dissatisfied with your job. Again, this book will come
to your rescue. Despite what you may think, despite the
'hard times' we are going through (that oft-repeated, age-
old fallacy, as we shall see further on), despite unemployment and inflation, you *can* find the ideal job you dream
of — faster than you ever believed possible. In spite of
the fact that most people presume you can't always do
everything you want to in life, you will be able to find
a career that will truly satisfy you. It's your right, after
all. And, as we explain, it's a duty!

Do you dream about becoming very, very rich, being
able to join the Millionaires' Club? Why not? It's perfectly
legitimate and quite possible. The Millionaires' Club isn't
a closed circle. It's simply up to you to walk in and sign
up. Every year in Europe and North America, thousands
of people go beyond the million dollar mark. This book
will help you become one of them, probably much sooner
than you would expect. We live in exciting times. The
world is continually changing, and new needs are consequently being created. Anyone with a little initiative can
make a million.

Perhaps your dream is to get that raise or promotion you
know you deserve, but which has somehow eluded you.
You are probably surrounded by colleagues, some possibly less talented and qualified than you, who are effort-
lessly climbing up the corporate ladder and are being
generously compensated for their efforts. Here you will
learn how to play the game better. You will learn how
to make use of strategies which will get you what you
want, and what you deserve, both at work and at home.

If you are already well off and would like to increase
your capital assets, the ideas in this book will also help
you. You are obviously already applying some of the principles outlined here since you are already quite successful. But these formulas for success will allow you to go
even further. By reading this book and following the
guidelines, you will profit from the experience of 10 of
the richest men in the world. You will be able to multi-
ply your potential and wealth. These rich and famous men

will become so familiar to you that you will always be able to turn to them for advice (a step we recommend you to take in your day-to-day business dealings). When faced with a particularly thorny problem, you could ask yourself, 'What would Onassis have done in this case?' or, 'How would Conrad Hilton have solved this financial problem?' or 'How would Rockefeller have decreased these overheads?'

A man sitting on a giant's shoulder sees further than the giant himself. The advice you will pick up from the 10 men you will shortly read about will help you reach unequalled heights. Your vision of life will become broader. You will be able to see further. You will become a bigger person.

'Give me a point of support', said Archimedes, referring to a lever, 'and I will lift the world.' To make a fortune, you need leverage. Yet very few people know what that means. You will find out in the next few pages and you'll discover that you won't be the only one making use of it. The 10 richest men in the world will be there with you, all pushing down together and helping you to lift a mountain of gold!

APPLYING THE PRINCIPLES
OF WEALTH

Before you begin reading the first chapter however, a few words of warning are necessary. You will find advice on setting up a business and developing what is commonly termed 'entrepreneurship'. This is not meant to encourage you to drop everything you are doing and set up your own business. Unfortunately, not everyone is cut out for this. You need a certain type of personality and you must feel a real need to go out on your own. If you feel this urge, then you probably already have the basic qualities of an entrepreneur. This book can be a guide. Otherwise, this book will allow you to improve your material assets considerably, without compromising your basic security.

We suggest that you sit down and start by reading this book from cover to cover. You will find all of the chapters useful. They have been designed as a step-by-step method, so it is essential not to skip any chapters.

After going through it once, re-read it and underline important or relevant points in pencil. Refer to it when in doubt or faced with problems, or simply to refresh your memory from time to time.

Just one more thing before you get down to reading this book. Some of the words of advice will appear original and surprising, others will seem commonplace. Don't let appearances deceive you. These men never gave up repeating them, and, above all, never ceased applying the principles they discovered. The success they achieved depended on them. You should do the same if you want to improve your financial status. So, don't be put off by the apparent simplicity of some of these golden rules. Take some time to think them over. Are you applying them already? Are they really part of your life and working habits? This is the best frame of mind to be in when you begin reading this book.

WHERE DO I START?

THE MAJOR PREREQUISITE FOR BECOMING RICH

'Where do I start?' is the question most people ask when they think about making money. They may simply want to increase their income or they may want to become out and out millionaires, depending on their personal ambition. But where *do* you begin?

Believe you can get rich

At first glance, this statement might come across as a cliché, but take time to stop and think about it for a while. Our education, society, and intellectual conditioning, are all unfortunately more pessimistic than optimistic, and lead us to believe that wealth is meant for others, but not ourselves. How often does someone tell you not to waste your time on pipe dreams, that you have to be 'realistic'? Because most people think like this, success always seems reserved for the fortunate few and wealth seems to be an exclusive club. That is just not true. If affluence is an exclusive club, it is because it seems to be so in the minds of people whose attitudes bar their own entry. In fact, every wealthy person started out believing that one day they would be rich and famous.

Sit back and think about this for a moment even though, as we warned you earlier on, this idea may at first seem obvious. You will be amazed by the ideas that pop into your head. Don't be afraid to analyse those thoughts more closely, it will help you understand what barriers you may be putting between yourself and success.

You must completely convince yourself that not only is it possible for you to become as wealthy as you would like, but also that *it is easy*, much easier than you had ever dreamed possible. In fact, dozens of opportunities appear to you out of the blue every day. Profitable ideas flash through your mind, but you always seem to let them slip away or never do anything concrete about them. In the following chapter, we will discuss the art of self-suggestion, which will help you discover how to develop your powers of intuition as well as the financial sixth sense that has enabled so many people to make their fortunes. You already have these qualities, but you are probably not yet aware that they exist and so you haven't learned to develop and exploit them.

Another principle goes hand in hand with the first observation. You'll probably find it surp.ising, yet it is true.

Succeeding is no harder than failing

For most people, failure has become a way of life. Failure is a hard habit to break; after all, our social conditioning has given us low expectations. But in order to get rich, we have to accept that success is basically no more difficult than failure. It's simply a different kind of mental programming, and one which our subconscious mind sees no reason to object to, since it views work and effort as both one and the same thing. Reflect on this for a minute. Doesn't failure involve a highly complex combi-

nation of circumstances? Consider what it takes to mis-
fire every time you attempt to do something, to miss out
on perfect opportunities, to go out of your way to avoid
meeting the people who can help you climb the ladder
of success, to consider every single idea you get useless
when it could actually lead to something worthwhile, and
to repeatedly go through the motions that lead to defeat.
You have to agree that it is quite an achievement to fail,
and yet the subconscious mind sees no difficulty in accepting defeat as natural. In the following chapter, we shall
analyse in detail the vital role that the subconscious has
to play in success.

To help you understand exactly what we mean, here
is a brief analysis of the reasons, or, rather, excuses, used
by people who don't believe they can get rich.

EVERYTHING WAS MUCH
EASIER IN THE GOOD
OLD DAYS!

How many times have you heard this same old, worn-out
excuse? For some people, it has become a sort of personal
creed. They justify their inertia with it and, in their eyes
anyway, make allowances for their failure. This pathetic
excuse is proven wrong every day of the year. Every day
in the United States, 40 people on average become first-
time millionaires. No fewer than 15,000 Americans
become millionaires every year. In Europe, these figures
are slightly lower, but they are equally spectacular. Just
think about those figures. Besides, if 15,000 people
become millionaires in the United Stated every single year,
how many people do you think pocket half a million or
a quarter of a million dollars?

And yet, people keep repeating that it isn't easy nowadays, what with unemployment, inflation, and huge multi-
national companies covering every market. This is another
fallacy that statistics expose. In 1950, 93,000 small businesses were created in the US alone. In 1984, the number had risen to 600,000. These companies obviously

created millions of new jobs and a great deal of money for the owners.

The claim that things were easier 40 or 50 years ago must have been heard by successful men, not only after they had made their fortunes, but also when they were just starting out. Fortunately, this dim view cannot have made much of an impression on them.

Paul Getty once confirmed to an audience of young people that he would love to be in their shoes so that he could start all over again, and show that becoming a millionaire is always possible.

Becoming rich is not only possible today, but it is actually easier than it used to be

---

This means that all those that succeeded in the past would be just as successful today, if not more so. As we shall see further on, success depends less on outside circumstances (in free societies, anyway) than on mental attitude and strength of character. As a matter of fact, society is changing so rapidly nowadays that huge fortunes, which would have taken decades to build in the past, are now being made within a few short years. Did you know, for example, that Apple Computer Company had an estimated capital of over $1,700,000 after only seven years, and that its co-founder, Steven Paul Jobs (who held seven million personal shares in the company), was only 27 at the time! The figures speak for themselves; they prove that it is still possible today to make these dreams come true.

I'M TOO YOUNG!

There is an old saying that 'A youth with a single aim in life arrives early at the harvest'. The example of Steven Jobs proves that becoming a millionaire before the age of 30 is possible. Paul Getty got his first million at the age of 23. Steven Spielberg, brilliant director of *Jaws, Back to the future* and *ET*, became a billionaire when he was only 35 years old! There are countless examples of people who made their fortunes early in life. Youth must never be considered a drawback. In fact, it is more often than not an asset. Lack of experience can be compensated for by boldness, daring, instinct, or originality.

Lack of experience, however, does hold many people back. Everyone is aware of that annoying vicious circle: to get experience you need to have a job; but to get a job you need experience. But not all employers share this vision of things. Many of them trust young people and are willing to give them a chance. Several companies prefer training their employees themselves and are prepared to overlook their lack of experience. To all of you wishing to set up your own businesses but lack experience, history shows that most wealthy men learned as they went along, starting out just as inexperienced as you are now.

I'M TOO OLD TO GET RICH!

Did you know that Ray Kroc, the creator of the McDonald's franchise, was over 50 years old when he began making money? Surprising, isn't it? And yet, if he had given up when he was 45, or if he had stopped believing in his lucky star, not only would he never have become famous, but he would certainly never have become rich. His example, which we will discuss in detail further on, is an encouragement to anyone who thinks that after a certain age they have no chance of success. Sometimes even people who are still young consider that they are already too old to succeed. They seem to have the impression that there is only one boat out in life, and that they missed it!

In his autobiography, Ray Kroc writes:

> People have marvelled at the fact that I didn't start McDonald's until I was 52 years old, and then I became a success overnight. But I was just like a lot of show business personalities who work away quietly at their craft for years, and then, suddenly, they get a break and make it big. I was an overnight success all right, but 30 years is a long, long night.

Max Gunther, in his book, *The Very, Very Rich, and How They Got That Way* makes an interesting point about the relationship between age and success. He says:

> It turns out as a general rule, that highly successful men tend to bloom later. The success drive, whatever it may be, may exist in them during their school days but somehow doesn't find expression in the school society. They tend to be quiet kids at best, academic flops at worst. Not until the third decade of their lives — the decade between age 20 and 30 — do most of them begin to show signs of being more than ordinary men. Some even remain semi-dormant until the fourth decade.

There is a lot of wisdom in what these two men have to say, and we will expand on that in the following chapters. Ray Kroc's confession is clearly an endorsement of persistence, and it explains one of the fundamental secrets of success — that in any successful achievement, nothing happens by chance. A spectacular success story very often follows directly in the wake of a failure, or a series of failures. As we shall see, this is what almost always happens. The fact is that the flops preceding someone's rise to fame and fortune usually go unnoticed and are quickly forgotten. The same goes for the lengthy, backbreaking preliminary work. Therefore, we get the false impression that people's fortunes were made overnight.

Max Gunther's book shows not only that success can come late in life, but that many successful men displayed no early signs of being destined for fame and fortune, having often been considered 'slow learners'. A survey carried out by Napoleon Hill on thousands of wealthy men established that most of them started making money only after the age of 40. So, those of you who haven't made your fortune yet, don't despair! It could be that you are about to start reaping the benefits of your earlier efforts.

But isn't illness or disability an obstacle to success? Of course, it may be to a certain extent. But let us go back to the example of Ray Kroc. When he finally became a success he was an ailing, but persistent businessman. He says:

When I flew back to Chicago that fateful day in 1954, I had a freshly signed contract with the McDonald brothers in my briefcase. I was a battle-scarred veteran of the business wars, but I was still eager to go into action. I was 52 years old. I had diabetes and incipient arthritis. I had lost my gall bladder and most of my thyroid gland in earlier campaigns. But I was convinced that the best was ahead of me.

Before telling yourself that you are too old to succeed or that your health problems are too serious, re-read this quote at least one more time. Ray Kroc died at the age of 75, having been fully active right up to the day before his death. Work doesn't kill. Idleness, on the other hand, is often deadly; people who take early retirement often die younger than those who keep working. The fact remains that many men and women begin a second or even a third career, sometimes the most successful of all, late in life. So never believe for a minute that you are too old. Don't put your future behind you. No matter how old you are, live each day as if it were the first day of the rest of your life. Seen in this perspective, age becomes a secondary factor. Your years of experience, even in some of the things you may have failed at, will be priceless to you.

Do not put your future behind you

There is an inspiring passage in the international best-seller, *The Greatest Salesman in the World*, which illustrates this point.

I will live this day as if it were the last day of my life.
And what will I do with the last precious day of my existence? First of all, I will seal it up in a bottle so that not a single drop seeps into the sand. I will not waste a single moment of this day, complaining about my past miseries, past defeats, or past torments, since doesn't good always come out of adversity?
Can fallen grains of sand make their way back into

a sand glass? Can the sun rise where it sets? Or set where it rises? Can I erase my past mistakes or correct them? Can I heal yesterday's wounds and become healthy again? Can I be younger than I was yesterday? Can I cancel the hurtful words that were uttered, the blows that were given, the suffering that was inflicted? No! Yesterday is dead and buried forever and I will never think of it again.

I will live this day as if it were the last day of my life.

I HAVE NO CAPITAL!

How often have we heard *this* objection? It seems to be a major obstacle for many people who are hoping to set up their own businesses. And yet, did you know that the 10 men examined in this book had barely a penny to their names at the beginning of their careers? (Aristotle Onassis' family was rich, but he never profited from their money. Getty inherited almost half a million dollars from his father, but he was already a millionaire by the time he was able to get his hands on it. In any case, if you compare this amount to the immense fortune he amassed, it is fair to say that he started out with practically nothing.) And yet, a lack of cash was not a drawback for these men. Some of them, such as Conrad Hilton, did start out with a nest egg of £1,000 or £2,000. But these days most people can save at least that amount of money. The fact is that the experience of not only the world's wealthiest men, but thousands of millionaires, proves beyond a shadow of a doubt that money doesn't count in the beginning. What does count is having a good business idea and a positive mental outlook, two points we will come back to later on.

I'M NOT EDUCATED

With only a few exceptions, such as Paul Getty, who graduated from Oxford, the rich men we studied did not have university educations. In school most of them were even considered 'dunces'. Some of them developed such an aversion to school that it stayed with them for the rest of their lives. Thousands of men have managed to get rich without the benefit of higher education. However, even though they were not 'educated' in the traditional sense of the word, they did acquire an in-depth knowledge of the industry in which they made their fortunes. We shall come back to this distinction later on.

Along with inadequate education, people often bring up their lack of talent or intelligence. We advise you to put up a serious fight against these thoughts. Everyone in the world has at least one talent, one passion, one hobby that can become profitable if used correctly. We shall see how later. As for your intellectual potential, never make the costly mistake of believing that you are not smart enough. You are simply not making efficient use of your brain power. Each human being has considerable potential, but only exploits an infinitesimal part of it. The rich have simply learned how to put their inner powers to good use. They developed the ability to use resources that are accessible to every one of us. In his book *The Money-Makers*, Dominique Frischer agrees wholeheartedly with us regarding the intellectual capacities of successful men. Here is what he has to say about this:

> Because of modesty perhaps, none of them owns up to having a superior IQ or describes himself as a highly gifted individual prevented from becoming a universally acclaimed genius purely because of an unlucky stroke of fate. Not one of them pretends to have a methodical kind of intelligence, combined with the intellectual rigour picked up in universities, to explain his success. All of them, however, speak of possessing an instinctive or more irrational quality — intuition.

In *What They Don't Teach You at Havard Business School*, Mark McCormack relates the following story which, besides being funny, illustrates how pointless it is to develop an inferiority complex.

> There is an old tale of two friends who met on the street after not seeing each other for 25 years. One, who had graduated at the top of his class, was now working as an assistant branch manager of the local

bank. The other, who had never overwhelmed anyone with his intellect, owned his own company and was now a millionaire several times over. When his banking friend asked him the secret of his success, he said it was really quite simple. 'I have this one product that I buy for two dollars and sell for five dollars,' he said. 'It's amazing how much money you can make on a 60 per cent mark up.

McCormack concludes by saying:

> I do not have an innate prejudice against intellect, intelligence, or, for that matter, graduate degrees, but they are not substitutes for common sense, people sense, or street smarts.

The same cannot be said for all the rich men we studied. Some of them did have a prejudice against university diplomas. Soichiro Honda, for example, left school when he was quite young, but took university courses to increase his knowledge in certain areas later on in life. He never received a diploma, however, since he refused to sit for the exams, believing that the work he was doing already provided him with the real tests of life. In the light of his spectacular rise to success, one of his teachers nevertheless admitted that Honda was the greatest oversight of his teaching career. Honda couldn't care less about diplomas, and wrote in his autobiography that a diploma was less useful than a cinema ticket, since with a ticket you could at least enter a cinema and spend an entertaining evening, but with a diploma you were not even sure of being able to enter life!

Thomas Edison left school before he was 16 years old. His teacher, whose name is long forgotten, was absolutely convinced that his young student didn't have a brain in his head. Yet, Edison became one of the world's greatest inventors. Had he believed his teacher's assessment, not only would his destiny have been radically different, but all of humanity's as well. Had it not been for Edison, you might be reading this book by candlelight! Edison had a hard head, so the story goes, and his mother believed in his talent. This is unfortunately not the case for everyone. Many people have had their lives literally spoiled by unkind and totally unjustified remarks from a teacher or relative.

Each of us can easily develop a personality which will set us on course for success, and in the next chapter we will explain how we can mould the subconscious and condition ourselves to succeed.

DO I NEED INBORN TALENT TO BECOME RICH?

Many people talk themselves into believing that they don't have what it takes to change their lives. They justify — and unfortunately accept — their unsuccessfulness by convincing themselves that they were simply born unlucky, whereas others were born to be rich. Poverty seems to be a family tradition, an inherited trait like the colour of one's hair or eyes, which is passed down from generation to generation. It is true that it's sometimes more difficult for people whose family have always been poor to imagine that one day they could become rich. The image we get of ourselves and of life in general is often tinged with pessimism, and the role models that surround us are not always very inspiring. Nevertheless, many rich men came from very poor families. One of history's wealthiest actors, Charlie Chaplin, spent his youth wandering around the streets of London. The humiliation of poverty and early contact with the harsh realities of life have in many cases spurred people on to achievement. They have experienced what is commonly known as creative frustration.

The ability to make money is not inborn. It can be learned. It can be acquired. Paul Getty remarks on this in his book *How To Be a Successful Executive:*

Don't misunderstand me. In no way am I trying to imply that I think that businessmen are born and not made. I'd be the last person in the world to advance any such theory, for I have my own example and experience to indicate that the opposite is probably true. I most certainly was not a born businessman.

Quite to the contrary. I showed no early urge or drive
— or, for that matter, talent — to be a businessman.

This confession is surprising, coming from a man destined
to be the wealthiest man in the world. His sincerity is
undeniable. There is not a hint of coyness or false modesty
in it. And, if the richest man in the world admits to never
having had a natural bent for making money, then an initial lack of talent is not necessarily a disadvantage. If a
man with no innate talent can accumulate such a vast fortune, how far can someone go who is convinced he has
exceptional natural abilities?

I DON'T HAVE THE ENERGY
IT TAKES

This is also a very common excuse. Yet, every action we
take requires a minimum amount of energy, especially of
psychic energy. Low vitality inevitably breeds low motivation. This appears to be an inescapable vicious circle. But,
all it takes is a tiny spark to ignite the resources of energy
which lie dormant in everyone. The potential energy we
all have is enormous. In certain people, it simply hasn't been
aroused yet. It is hibernating, waiting to be activated. This
is the only difference between those who succeed and
attract money and those who fail or experience only moder-
ate success. In the next chapter, we will discover the key
to awakening latent energy and describe the art of developing willpower, motivation, and inner strength. All of these
qualities can be achieved more easily than you realize.
Developing them is essential, however. To be successful
or wealthy, everyone has to develop a lot of energy. The
extent and speed of your prosperity is directly proportional
to the amount of energy you have.

I'M AFRAID OF FAILING

Of all the fears, that of failing is the most powerful and,
unfortunately, the most widespread. This anxiety is

paralysing. Often deeply-embedded within us, it results from past failures, a lack of confidence bred by our parents without realizing it, and enforced by general pessimism about life. This fear, which is sometimes expressed quite overtly, is most often unconscious and is subtly disguised. People will therefore never admit that they are afraid of failing in their attempts to get rich. Instead they will skirt around the issue by insisting that you mustn't build castles in the air or that only fools believe in the nonsense contained in 'get-rich-quick' books. These people are paralysed by the fear of failure, or by pure and simple fear, and are usually champion excuse-makers. If they only thought about it for a minute, they could probably get very rich by writing a bestseller called *How To Find a Good Excuse*! They have family obligations; they don't have the time; they already have enough problems at work as it is, and so on and so forth. If they are out of a job, they have no hope of ever finding one because there are so many people out there just like them, but more talented, more experienced... They must have been born under an unlucky star... But, if they had contacts... If their boss would only notice them... If somebody could help them get started... If they could hit upon a good idea... If they didn't have so many financial worries....

The list could actually go on forever. Excuses such as these are symptoms of that common disease 'excusitis'. This is an extremely prevalent affliction which characterizes that other devastating illness: the fear of failing.

Obviously, if you never try to do anything, the chances are you will never fail. But then, you aren't very likely to succeed either. Success does not miraculously appear out of the blue. It is always the result of concrete action or a positive mental attitude. In fact, most successful men have experienced failure at one point or another in their lives. Did you know that Thomas Edison had to make a thousand attempts before perfecting the incandescent light bulb? Did you know that Abraham Lincoln lost 18 elections before becoming the President of the United States? We aren't singing the praises of failure, but we do believe that every personal defeat can be an education in itself, at least if it is accepted with an open mind.

After all, setbacks are inevitable. Failure, as we shall see in Chapter 2, is often the result of faulty mental programming.

WHY HAVE YOU FAILED UP TO NOW?

One of the reasons underlying an individual's paralysing fear of failure is that he has already met with failure, or at least has the distinct impression of having been unsuccessful in everything he has ever undertaken. Each new setback has reinforced this feeling and contributed to undermining his self-confidence. These experiences often end up turning him into a kind of permanent loser in life, a personality trait that is in itself the source of failure. People start with one flop on their hands, then see themselves as losers, which in turn leads inevitably to more aborted attempts. These failures reinforce their loser mentality, which becomes so powerful that it becomes second nature to them. They are no longer aware that it is responsible for their behaviour. They end up believing that life in general is a series of hard knocks, defeats and frustrations. Those who don't share this point of view are hypocrites or imbeciles. Negative forces are undeniably powerful, hypnotizing the vast majority of people. This results in unhappiness and poverty. Yet, there are a circle of fulfilled individuals totally in control of their destinies — the happy few. The truth is, it is completely up to you to join this club. In a sense, this book is your initiation to becoming a fully-fledged member of this circle of people who magnetically attract all the wealth life has to offer.

Why have you failed until now? Perhaps because deep down in your subconscious you have wanted to fail. If the success you are entitled to has always managed to slip through your fingers, ask yourself whether you feel you can get out of this syndrome or whether fate has permanently condemned you to mediocrity. In the chapter focusing on how our minds function, we shall learn how to conduct this self-analysis. So, no matter what results you come up with, don't worry about it. You should reassure yourself that, in the conscious mind, no programming is irreversible. Even the strongest, most powerful negative programming can be changed. Quickly. Completely.

We have just reviewed some of the different reasons that prevent you from believing that you can get rich, but there are even more, of course. However, you have to tell yourself that all these seemingly plausible and valid reasons are only flimsy pretexts or excuses.

You will probably be surprised at the inner resistance you put up. There is a very specific reason for this: within each of us, repressed, of course, in successful people, there is a force which prevents us from perceiving the reason for our failure and poverty. Certain people seem to hypnotize themselves by endlessly repeating that there's no way they can make it, that they're unlucky, that they'll be poor for the rest of their lives. In the chapter on the subconscious, we will clearly demonstrate the power of words and the inner monologue that most people engage in as well as how to make the best use of this power.

Now take a pen and write down the list of excuses that have prevented you from being successful up to now. It is vital to be perfectly honest with yourself. The first stage is absolutely essential. It is basically a way of wiping the slate clean of all your old beliefs that wealth is difficult to gain. You have to doubt everything systematically, just as the French philosopher and mathematician Descartes did before establishing the principles of modern philosophy.

THE LIST OF EXCUSES

Now that you have banished your old prejudices from your mind and believe you can grow rich (a conviction that will grow stronger as you read this book), you are ready to learn another basic principle. Once again, it will probably appear trite at first and you might wonder why on earth we have chosen to highlight a statement as obvi-

ous as this one. But wait. Suspend your judgement for a
while. Here is this principle:

Your situation will not improve if you do nothing about it

Most people live with the idea that everything will magically work out all right, or that they will somehow end
up being free of their money problems. What they are basically expecting is a miracle. They might get a 5 or 10 per
cent raise if their bosses feel so inclined. If they are unemployed they have a vague hope that someone will come
and offer them a job on a silver platter. What do most people do when they need money? Some borrow it, which
doesn't solve their problems. On the contrary, they then
find themselves in even deeper water. Others wait
patiently, and 'tighten their belts'. Instead of adapting
their income to their needs, they adapt their needs to their
meagre income. You will soon understand that you not
only can, but *must* adapt your income to your needs.

Instead of trying to bend the world to fulfil their dreams,
people limit their dreams according to the world's 'constraints'. This passive wait-and-see attitude, meaning let's
see if this miracle happens, is typical of many people's
outlooks. The extraordinary popularity of the football
pools is evidence of this type of mentality. In short, your
situation will not get any better on its own. You must take
action, adopt precise measures, and change your attitude.

Don't forget: your situation will not magically improve on its own

---

To improve your financial situation, to track down a job if you are out of work, to get a rise in salary, to double your income, to become a millionaire (why not a billionaire), you must passionately want an improvement in your life. This must become your complete obsession.

An overriding desire for wealth is essential when it comes to attracting money. Furthermore, the following equation always holds true: the degree and speed of a person's success are directly proportional to the intensity and constancy of his desire to succeed. Remember those two words well: intensity and constancy. Napoleon once said, 'Whatever we constantly and ardently desire, we always get.' He knew what he was talking about! All great men have been, above all, men of determination and will-power. They craved success more than anything else in the world. For them it became a kind of obsession until they reached their goals, no matter which obstacles seemed to block them.

Many people fail in their attempts to get rich, but still honestly desire an improvement in their lives. The reason for this is that they have mistaken wishing for really wanting. Incidentally, wishful thinking is much more common than really wanting something. A wish is weak, changeable and passive. It doesn't yield to concrete action. It isn't strong enough to eliminate procrastination. Really wanting something is a spur to action. It doesn't tolerate delays. It bypasses obstacles. It gives us wings to fly on. If you have fallen short in every attempt you have made to get rich, ask yourself this question: did you mistake wishing for really wanting?

One day a wise man's disciple asked him what it took to obtain wisdom. The sage led him to a river and plunged his head under water. After a few seconds, his anxious follower began struggling, afraid that he was going to drown. But the wise man continued to hold his head under water. The student started struggling even harder. Finally, the wise man let him go just before he would have drowned and asked him, 'When your head was under water, what did you want most?' 'To breathe,' the frightened boy answered. 'Well, there you have it. This is exactly how much you must want wisdom.'

This analogy applies perfectly to wealth, especially for

anyone wishing to become very rich. Life gives you what
you sincerely want. If you content yourself with a mediocre situation, you will never get out of it. No one will
miraculously come to your rescue, giving you a million
dollars or an ideal job from the goodness of their heart.
If all you want is a slight improvement, you won't get any
more, if you get anything at all.

Many millionaires had difficult, impoverished childhoods. They felt humiliated by their inferior social status.
Their desire to rise above poverty and never to be penniless again was so intense that it helped them become
wealthy.

Their dissatisfaction and frustration became highly
productive. It can work like this for you. Besides, if you
are now reading this book, it is because you are not perfectly satisfied with your situation. This is nothing to be
ashamed about. On the contrary, there is something
intensely motivating about dissatisfaction. Only feeble-
minded or wise men are perfectly happy. Since we have
not yet reached this state of contentment, we should not
be afraid to bring our dissatisfaction out into the open.
It is perfectly legitimate to aspire to a better situation.
The dreams you carry and nourish in your heart are part
of you. They are actually the most noble part of you —
your ideal. So, don't be ashamed of discontent. Dissatisfaction fuels your dream. But your dream must not
become vague, irresolute, or stagnant. Make it fuel in turn
the action you will take.

In the name of 'rationality' (which basically means being
passive, cowardly and defeatist), many people abandon
their dreams much too quickly. We rarely
dare to give our dreams the chance to come true because
of all the reasons, or unfounded excuses we listed earlier
on, and because our education and the society we
live in have accustomed us to denying ourselves what we
want most.

The great French writer Balzac, who lived out his liter-
ary dream to the very end, wrote: 'I belong to the opposition called "life" .' Anyone who stops dreaming, anyone
who ignores his most intense yearnings has become one
of the living dead. Don't let this happen to you. Be part
of the opposition called 'life'! Change your existence by

daring to live out your dreams to the full and letting yourself be carried away by them.

This philosophy may appear somewhat naïve to you. And, to a certain extent, we admit that it is. Yet, without naïvety, without the innocence of dreams, nothing great would have been created in this world. Ford would never have invented the automobile; man would not fly; motion pictures would never have been created. The examples we could give could go on forever. A serious outlook, rationality, and cynicism are the greatest obstacles to success. Don't get us wrong. We are not preaching in favour of extravagant, free-for-all behaviour. The truth is, however, that at the root of every great discovery and exceptional success story lies a dream, a desire. Rational thinking and seriousness followed shortly thereafter. It is vital never to put the cart before the horse. We must begin by dreaming and listening to our hearts' desires.

To sum up, there are three initial conditions to fulfil in order to grow rich:

---

1   Believing you will get rich

2   Becoming aware that your situation will not change magically if you do nothing about it

3   Passionately desiring an improvement in your life

Having faith, as we stated above, is the first prerequisite for success. You must believe that you can attain success and wealth. You must believe in yourself. Self-suggestion is an invaluable tool for building confidence and it is just as useful when the time comes to put your faith in a pet scheme of yours or in your plans for becoming rich.

Why is it so necessary for you to believe in your plan? The reason is simple: If you don't believe in it, you will never convince anyone else to believe in it. Furthermore, success never comes out of the blue, and the obstacles you will have to overcome, the difficulties you will inevitably meet, and the sustained effort you will be forced to make will need a good dose of faith to lead you to success. In your current endeavours or future plans, be they individual or collective, you could even establish the following behavioural principle: if you don't completely and honestly believe in what you are about to do, don't do it, otherwise you will fail. Success requires total commitment. Unless you believe in your plan, no matter how solid it is, you will not know how to use your energy. Once you discover the laws governing the mind you will understand why. When you don't fully believe in something, the codes you are programming into your subconscious are false, vague, and often contradictory. The results will reflect this faulty programming. Partial conviction leads to partial success, and that means partial failure. Doubt is reflected in poor results.

All successful people have learned to banish doubt from their minds and have tremendous faith both in themselves and in their plans, despite any opposition they may have faced. The person who undoubtedly exemplifies this principle the most is Henry Ford. He dreamed of a self-contained eight cylinder motor, but all his engineers concluded that his scheme was impossible. 'Do it anyway,' insisted Ford. Ford was stubborn and the faith he had in his motor, later to be called the V-8, was unshakeable. A year passed and his engineers' efforts were still fruitless. And yet, one day, the solution to this 'unsolvable' problem was discovered. Ford's entire life illustrates that the power of faith leads straight to success.

HENRY FORD'S MAGICAL FAITH

Henry Ford was born on July 30, 1863 in Dearborn, Michigan, USA. His father was a farmer and didn't see any reason for his son to continue going to school. In fact, when Henry finished primary school, his father judged that he would be more useful on the farm, instead of wearing out the seat of his pants on a school bench. As a result, Ford was soon introduced to the hard manual labour of farming. 'Even when very young', he relates in his autobiography, 'I suspected that much might somehow be done in a better way.' Ford's practical mechanical and engineering genius, and his vision of machines replacing the manual work had united man and animal under a single yoke for millenniums, was already beginning to blossom. His dream was to take shape a few years later.

The first things Henry Ford remembered owning were odds and ends of metal, which he always converted into tools. He recalled that, 'In those days we did not have the toys of today; what we had were home made. My toys were all tools — they still are! And every fragment of machinery was a treasure.' While other boys of his age spent their days playing in the fields, Henry occupied most of his time in a small workshop that his father had given him permission to set up in a shed on the family farm. With a few modest tools, this child was preparing his future.

THE TURNING POINT IN HIS LIFE

When he was 12 years old, Henry Ford had an experience that was to transform and direct his life.

> The biggest event of those early years was a meeting with a road engine about eight miles out of Detroit one day when we were driving to town. I was then 12 years old... I remember that engine as though I had seen it only yesterday, for it was the first vehicle other than horse-drawn that I had ever seen... The engine had stopped to let us pass with our horses and I was off the wagon and talking to the engineer before my father, who was driving, knew what I was up to... It was that engine which took me into automotive transportation. I tried to make models of it, and some years later I did make one that ran very well, but from the time I saw that road engine as a boy of 12 right to today, my great interest has been in making a machine that would travel the roads.

This chance encounter was obviously a decisive turning point in this young man's life. The idea of building a machine that would travel the roads was going to haunt and obsess him from then on. Yet, there is often an enormous gap between getting an idea and putting it into action, and that frightens off the majority of people and condemns them to inaction. Ford was not the type to let himself be disheartened by potential hurdles. His philosophy involved just the opposite, and his formula was:

Interesting work is easy and I am always certain of results

Henry never managed to summon up much interest in farming. 'I wanted to have something to do with machinery,' he explains. When he was 17, his decision was made (in fact, it had been made long before): he would become a machinist's apprentice for the Drydock Engine Works. His father strongly disapproved of this, since he naturally viewed his son as a good strong back for his farm. He gave his son up for lost. America, on the other hand, had just found one of its greatest industrialists.

Back then it took more than three years of thankless work to become a machinist. Ford completed his training in less than a year, by which time he had a complete understanding of mechanics 'Machines are to a mechanic', he writes, 'what books are to a writer. He gets ideas from them, and if he has any brains he will apply those ideas.'

Ford's dream had rooted even more deeply after his apprenticeship, and his genius was about to come into its own. His idea of creating a self-propelled vehicle had never left him. The important point is believing that where there's a will there's a way, even though it might seem impossible at first.

Henry Ford believed that there were several ways. For a while he thought of using steam, but abandoned this idea after two years' work, realizing that it would lead nowhere. Ford devoured every scientific magazine he could get his hands on, since he wanted to know as much as possible about his field. This compensated for his few years of formal education. There was talk in these magazines of new machines, especially one called 'Otto', the 'silent gas engine' — a predecessor of the motor car. These magazines also mentioned the possibility of one day replacing illuminating gas with fuel formed by the vaporization of petrol. These discoveries were greeted as curiosities, a kind of sci-fi projection into the future, but not as innovations that would eventually revolutionize the living and working habits of millions of people. All the experts and specialists agreed on one point: petrol would never replace steam to make an engine run. But a young man living in a small Michigan town believed otherwise.

Ford went back to his family farm after leaving his job at Westinghouse, where he had worked as a specialized mechanic. His workshop now occupied almost the entire shed. His father even offered him some land, on condition that he gave up his damned machines. But Ford kept going.

When I was not cutting timber, I was working on the
gas engine — learning what they were and how they
acted. I read everything I could find, but the greatest
knowledge came from my work.

Far from giving up his idea of one day seeing a self-
propelled machine come to life in his workshop, he was
steadily working towards making that dream come true.
Farm life still did not agree with his basic temperament.
Inventions alone filled his mind, and manual labour never
managed to stir his imagination. So, when he was offered
a job as an engineer and machinist at Detroit Edison Company, he had no trouble accepting and left his family farm
for the second time. He was destined never to go back.
He set up a workshop behind the small house he had
rented in Detroit. After coming home from the factory,
he would spend hours every evening working until late
at night his petrol engine. 'Interesting work is never hard
and I am always certain of results,' was the motto he had
created for himself. His efforts and perseverance were
not in vain. In 1892, when he was 29 years old, 17 years
after having seen that famous road engine and having
vowed that he would one day achieve his dream, he put
the finishing touches on his first automotive engine. It
took 17 long years and countless sacrifices before he
finally achieved his goal. Genius, so they say is infinite
patience. Success also demands patience. Those who are
tempted to give up after a few months or a few years
should be encouraged by this man's tenacity.
The residents of Detroit were probably as surprised by
the sight of a young man straddling this first petrol 'buggy'
as they would have been by visiting extraterrestrials.

It was considered to be something of a nuisance, for it
made a racket and it scared horses. Also it blocked
traffic. For if I stopped my machine anywhere in
town a crowd was around it before I could start up
again. If I left it alone even for a minute some
inquisitive person always tried to run it. Finally, I had
to carry a chain and chain it to a lamp post whenever
I left it anywhere.

Between 1895 and 1896, Ford drove his car no fewer than

1000 miles, constantly submitting it to all sorts of tests to enhance its performance. He finally sold it for $200.
  Ford had no intention of stopping after his first successful achievement, but wanted to go further, much further.

It was not at all my idea to make cars in any such petty fashion. I was looking ahead to production, but before that could come I had to have something to produce. It does not pay to hurry.

During this time he continued working for the Detroit Edison Company, but he encountered a lot of scepticism about the future of his petrol engine. He was finally offered a promotion and a substantial raise in salary. But this presented a problem. If Ford wanted this position, he would have to give up his research on petrol engines and devote himself entirely to electrical energy, which was predicted to become the only power source in the future. In short, he was being asked to give up his dream. In exchange, he was being offered material security and a guaranteed future. Most people would have jumped at this offer. After all, a bird in the hand is worth two in the bush. Most people's need for security is so great that they would be prepared to sacrifice their most precious dreams for it. It didn't take Henry Ford long to make up his mind. He preferred trying his luck and devoting himself to realizing this dream: the mass production of petrol-propelled vehicles. Once again in the history of mankind, one man was going to prove that he could prove the scepticism of an entire nation unfounded. 'It was make or break,' said Henry Ford.

I RESIGNED, DETERMINED NEVER AGAIN TO TAKE ORDERS

On August 15, 1899, Henry Ford left the Edison Company, completely penniless. He now had to prove wrong the assumption that the automobile was a rich man's plaything. No 'serious' businessman in Detroit would have invested a penny in such a risky venture. People are generally reluctant to accept a new product, particularly when it seems unnecessary. So, Henry Ford did not have an easy task; he was basically proposing to create a new need.

Nevertheless, Ford managed to persuade a few enterprising businessmen to back him in the construction of petrol-propelled machines, and founded the Detroit Automobile Company. He became its chief engineer, and for three years the company built cars more or less resembling the first one Ford had designed. However, his company never sold more than six or seven cars a year. Ford's idea was to produce a sturdy, well-built car for the general public, whereas his associates' only concern was to churn out custom-made cars and make as much money as they could. A conflict inevitably grew between Ford and his backers.

In March 1902, Ford handed in his resignation and withdrew from the Detroit Automobile Company. He wrote: 'I resigned, determined never again to take orders.'

This bitter experience, however, had not destroyed Ford's convictions. It did teach him a simple principle, however: to make a fortune, you have to be independent and have your own business firmly in hand.

> It is nice to plan to do one's work in office hours, to take up the work in the morning, to drop it in the evening and not have a care until the next morning. It is perfectly possible to do that if one is so constituted as to be willing through all of one's life to accept direction, to be an employee, possibly a responsible employee, but not a director or manager of anything.

Henry Ford had the firm intention of being part of this second category of individuals and was now going to use all of his time to lay the foundations of his empire on his own. What he still lacked, however, was the publicity necessary to make people aware of his product. Car racing was about to change all this.

At the time, people were especially interested in seeing which motor car was the fastest. Consequently, many builders took up the challenge because the winner was ensured enormous publicity. Ford considered the races an excellent opportunity to display the power of his engines to the world. So, in 1903, he designed two vehicles that were specially built for racing and called them '999' and 'Arrow'. Ford won the race by half a mile. Everybody now knew that Ford built the fastest cars. Spurred on by his success, Ford decided to gamble everything by founding the Ford Motor Company. He became its vice-president, chief engineer, chief mechanic, floor supervisor, and managing director. His reasoning was simple. It was better to strike while the iron was still hot. His triumph had given him great publicity. He had to take the plunge. It was now or never. He rented a bigger workshop and got down to work with the help of a few associates.

Ford had the edge over his competitors from the very beginning. They were unconcerned about the weight of their vehicles, believing in fact that the heavier the vehicles the more expensive it could be. Ford did not share this philosophy. The car he was going to design (the Model A) was the lightest that had ever been built until then. As a result it was faster and more economical. In a single year of operation the Ford Motor Company sold 1708 automobiles, proving him right that it was possible to market a car for the general public. As a result of his resounding success, competitors began sprouting up by the dozen. Ford paid no attention to them. His ideas were fixed and furthermore, they were realistic. He believed that few people would be bold enough to launch their own products, and that they would simply continue to copy his. Ford always told himself: 'Why not do better?' And that's exactly what he resolved to do.

Ford's Business boomed, and his cars were soon reputed to be the most solid and dependable ever built. In the second year of production, Ford forged ahead once again by introducing three new models (Models B, C, and F) and soon had to think of finding another factory to accommodate his flourishing company. He built a three-storey factory, allowing him to increase his production volume even further. After only five years of operation, the Ford Motor Company had 1,908 employees on its payroll, owned its own factory, and was producing 6,181 cars a year which were sold both in America and in Europe.

The little boy who had once seen a road engine and sworn that he was going to build a self-propelled machine had realized his dream. He had become a millionaire. Yet, Henry Ford was not a man to say, 'I'm successful; I now earn a lot of money. Now is the time to stop.' Instead he said:

> I can entirely sympathize with the desire to quit a life
> of activity and retire to a life of ease. I have never
> felt the urge myself but I can comprehend what it is
> — although I think that a man who retires ought to
> get out of business entirely. There is a disposition to
> retire and retain control. It was, however, no part of
> my plan to do anything of that sort. I regarded our
> progress merely as an invitation to do more . . .

Ford's production now reached the magical number of 100 cars a day and some of his associates started believing that Ford's delusions of grandeur would lead him straight to bankruptcy. In the world of finance, many even went so far as to predict that at this rate his company would soon burst at the seams, saturating the market. During a board meeting, one of the stockholders asked Ford if he believed he was capable of maintaining this output. To this he replied that one hundred cars a day was only a trifle and he hoped before long to make a thousand a day. He then added:

> If I had followed the general opinion of my associates
> I should have kept the business as it was, put our
> funds into a fine administration building, tried to
> make bargains with competitors that seemed too
> active, made new designs from time to time to catch
> the fancy of the public, and generally have passed on
> into the position of a quiet, respectable citizen with a
> quiet, respectable business.

But Henry Ford saw much further than this, and his vision was much, much bigger.

Ford had done a lot to lighten the weight of his vehicles, but the materials existing at the time did not seem to allow him to go further in this area. But 'a lucky stroke of fate', which was probably a manifestation of his sub-conscious, came to his rescue. During a race Ford was attending, a French car was wrecked. After the race, as if guided by a sixth sense, Ford went on to the track and collected some metal debris from the car, which had seemed faster than all the others. He wanted to discover which alloy had been used to build it. He picked up a lit-tle valve strip stem, which seemed both light and highly resistant. It wasn't at all like the materials known at the time. 'That is the kind of material we ought to have in our cars,' thought Ford. However, no one he knew could identify this alloy. After having had it analysed, he learned that it was vanadium steel. Since no foundry in North America knew how to cast it, Ford was obliged to send for someone from England capable of producing it on a commercial basis. Later, thanks to a small factory in Ohio, he was able to find the means to cast it in America. So, once again, his alert mind and tireless search for new knowledge had put him several paces in front of his nearest competitors.

Pursuing his desire to build a truly 'democratic' auto-mobile, Ford began designing a new model which would become a legend in automobile history: the famous Model T. Ford was about to change the lives of millions of peo-ple by turning the car into a consumer product, or rather, a necessity.

In the spring of 1909, Henry Ford announced to his board of directors that, from then on, the Ford factory was going to manufacture a single model, the Model T. He even added, 'Any customer can have a car painted any colour that he wants so long as it is black.' It produced an uproar. Until then, cars had always been considered a luxury item, a kind of special 'toy' that only the well-off could afford to buy. There seemed to be no advan-tage in building only one model, especially an inexpen-sive one. Besides, there were still very few paved roads and petrol was rare. Ford's confidence in his car was so great that he cheerfully rebuffed every one of these objections.

The task facing Henry Ford was not going to be an easy one. Even the most serious experts warned him that this venture would ruin him and that he was making a serious mistake. Ford also had to deal with the resistance of bankers, with whom Ford had never had a very smooth relationship. But Ford saw things in a different light:

> I refuse to recognize that there are impossibilities. I cannot discover that any one knows enough about anything on this earth definitely to say what is and what is not possible... If some man, calling himself an authority, says that this or that cannot be done, then a horde of unthinking followers start the chorus: 'It can't be done.'

For Henry Ford, the word 'impossible' did not exist in the English language.

Besides marketing his new 'democratic' model, Ford revolutionized the automobile industry. It was to be a cottage industry no more. Assembly-line methods enabled him to reach a level of production unequalled until then. His factory soon became too small and Ford had a immense industrial complex built, which soon employed over 4,000 people and produced 35,000 Model Ts a year. Yet, in spite of this, the press never stopped predicting that Ford would break his neck, that the man who would be king would soon find himself a pauper.

Henry Ford was one of the first to create a mechanized assembly-line system. By this very fact, he became the father of industrial robotics. According to him, it was necessary to bring the work to the worker and not the other way around. This vision of things was going to upset the entire notion of productivity and human labour. His factory was to become the most modern in the world. Body parts suspended in mid air by enormous hooks were sent to assembly in the exact order assigned to them. The results were astonishing. The 10 hours it normally took to assemble all the motor parts were reduced to five because of the assembly line. This small time mechanic's idea was visionary, and his famous Model T became such a success that Ford began opening up factories throughout the world. Ford factories were soon building 4,000 cars a day. When he died in 1947, Henry Ford, who had never worried about money, except to finance his dream, was a billionaire, which in those days was an astronomical feat.

Ford Motors never stopped growing. By 1960 it was considered the second largest enterprise in the world. By 1970, the company employed 432,000 people and had a wage fund of $3.5 billion!

'Everything is possible... Faith is the substance of things hoped for, the evidence of things not seen.' This succinct and deeply optimistic formula concludes Henry Ford's autobiography. These last words are a kind of spiritual legacy, and the fact that he spoke of faith is not at all by chance. All of his life and work are proof that, for a person motivated by unshakeable faith, everything is possible.

HOW TO FIND
WEALTH

For most of us, the way to get our hands on that 'money tree' seems like a well-guarded secret reserved for the chosen few. The most common mistake we make is looking outside for what we should find inside of us. Money is no exception. Just as the source of true happiness lies within each of us, so money also comes from within. Money is the result of a very specific mental attitude. Call it what you like: the mentality of the rich, of millionaires, or of successful men. Money is the outward manifestation of an inner focus, of thoughts being steered towards a specific target. Unfortunately, most people are unaware of this. The major principles we will examine in the following chapter all lead to a higher, universal truth — that the mind is capable of anything. Genuine wealth is, above all, a state of mind — a state that has taken form in the lives of the rich. We must begin by being rich in mind before we can become rich in life.

Wealth is a state of mind

Gaining a clear understanding of the subconscious is fundamental. It is all very well to tell people that they must believe in success and fortune, and want it passionately. Yet, most people are paralysed by bad experiences. In addition, they appear totally incapable of cultivating what Nietzsche called 'the will to power'. It is not at all easy to demand action and firmness from someone who is irresolute, passive, and unmotivated. By discovering the mechanisms and power of the subconscious mind, however, anyone can overcome this obstacle. So, let us examine the subconscious mind, the source of man's greatest personal and material wealth — the one and only place to look for the money that grows on trees. Soon you will learn how to tap into it at will.

THE GOLD MINE WITHIN YOU

IT'S ALL A QUESTION OF ATTITUDE

Man is the creator of his own happiness or misery, a fact that cannot be doubted by anyone who has studied the laws of the mind, even superficially. This maxim probably isn't new to you. Some of you may have greeted it with scepticism, while others of you may believe in it wholeheartedly. Nevertheless, there aren't many people who have thought it over carefully or measured the full extent of its consequences.

The lives of the rich men we examine reveal that each one of them made full use of his subconscious mind to become wealthy. The key to success ultimately lies in the proper use of the subconscious mind. 'Why?' you might ask. The reason is that both the means to make money and the outside circumstances affecting us are so varied and personal that it would be impossible to propose a sure-fire winning formula. Besides, no miracle recipe exists. It would be too simple. What does exist, however, and thousands of brilliant success stories testify to this, is a positive inner attitude.

Many books deal with the secrets of real estate, the stock market, management, and so forth. These books are obviously invaluable reference tools. But the advice they ladle out, no matter how precise it is, is, inevitably, always general. Pretending otherwise would be naïve and dishonest. In fact, however instructive a book claims to be, it will not tell you whether you should accept a job that comes your way, bid on a house, or invest in a particular money making proposition. Each case is unique. Even if your preliminary studies are very comprehensive, there are always imponderables in any scheme. Any analysis will be inadequate. We're not saying that it's unnecessary. On the contrary, improvisation and rashness are usually inadvisable. What we do mean is that there are times that your analysis can go no further. This is when a person's sixth sense, what some people also call 'business sense', 'luck', or 'intuition', comes into play — the result of positive mental programming and a well-utilized subconscious mind. This is what makes the difference between a successful and an unsuccessful person.

WHAT IS THE SUBCONSCIOUS?

We have all at some time or other heard talk about the subconscious mind. Its existence is now accepted in all scientific fields, although its final definition is still a matter of dispute. We have no intention of engaging in a long theoretical or historical analysis here. Let us simply state, without getting bogged down by theoretical details, that the human mind can be divided into two parts: the conscious and the subconscious. The most common image used to illustrate the importance of the two parts is an iceberg, the small visible part being considered the conscious mind, the submerged and much larger part, the subconscious.

In fact, the role the subconscious has to play in our lives is much greater than we believe it to be. It is the seat of our habits, complexes, and the limitations of our personalities. No matter what we think, the subconscious — not outside circumstances — is responsible for an individual's wealth or poverty.

The subconscious can be compared to a computer. It blindly and infallibly executes the programme fed into it. Every individual is programmed whether he knows it or not, and most people are programmed negatively. Given that the subconscious is phenomenally powerful, a person who has been programmed in this way will unfortunately never be successful or wealthy.

HOW IS THE SUBCONSCIOUS PROGRAMMED?

As long as an individual remains unaware of the laws of the mind, he will stay ignorant of his own programming. This is the case with most people, for a very simple reason. Mental programming takes place very early in a person's childhood, at an age when his critical sense is still undeveloped. He naturally accepts all suggestions from the outside world. These suggestions, the program's data base, so to speak, come at first from his parents and teachers. They become engraved in his young mind, which is as impressionable as a piece of soft wax. A single word can often blight someone's life or at least weigh him down for a long time to come. This word may have been said without malice, but its effects can be disastrous. As for examples, there are plenty to choose from. A pessimistic mother, oppressed by misery, will tell a child she considers too impulsive or absent-minded, 'You'll never get rich,' or, 'You'll never get anywhere in life,' or, 'You'll be a loser, just like your father.' These remarks are recorded in the child's subconscious, becoming part of his mental programming. The subconscious, whose power is almost limitless, will do its utmost to execute this programme, making the child fail over and over again. The most tragic thing of all is that this person can spend his entire life unaware that he is the victim of negative mental programming.

HOW A FEW WORDS CAN CHANGE YOUR LIFE

You might be sceptical about the effects of an apparently insignificant word or phrase, but words are extremely powerful agents. A declaration of love, a piece of bad

news, a word of congratulation, all have an impact on our
inner state. And what is most astonishing is that these
words, which are actually suggestions, as we shall see further on in this chapter, do not even have to be true for
the mind to accept them. Let's say your boss congratu-
lates you on the job you have done. Perhaps he is not
really all that satisfied with it, but since he knows that
you are having marital difficulties, getting divorced, say,
he judges it best not to reproach you. His words of
encouragement, although insincere, raise your low morale
and revitalize you. This is only one example among many
of the power words can have.

The authors of that remarkable book, *In Search of Excellence*, recount an experiment that illustrates the principle of the power of words even when those words are
untrue.

The old adage is 'nothing succeeds like success'. It
turns out to have a sound scientific basis. Researchers
studying motivation find that the prime factor is
simply the self-perception among motivated subjects
that they are, in fact, doing well. Whether they are or
not by any absolute standard doesn't seem to matter
much. In one experiment, adults were given 10
puzzles to solve. All 10 were exactly the same for all
subjects. They worked on them, turned them in, and
were given the results at the end. Now, in fact, the
results they were given were fictitious. Half of the
exam takers were told that they had done well, with
seven out of 10 correct. The other half were told they
had done poorly, with seven out of 10 wrong. Then all
were given another 10 puzzles (the same for each
person). The half who had been *told* that they had
done well in the first round really did do better in the
second, and the other half really did do worse. Mere
association with past personal success apparently leads
to more persistence, higher motivation, or something
that makes us do better. Warren Bennis, in *The
Unconscious Conspiracy: Why leaders can't lead*,
finds ample reason to agree: 'In a study of school
teachers, it turned out that when they held high
expectations of their students, that alone was enough
to cause an increase of 25 points in the students' IQ
scores.'

The results of these experiments are food for thought. The subjects' subconscious minds had been influenced by the falsified results. It is this and this alone which radically improved one group's performance and weakened the other's.

A little further on, the same authors advance the following theory as a result of this experiment: 'We often argue that the excellent companies are the way they are because they are organized to obtain extraordinary effort from ordinary human beings.' What applies to business applies equally to individuals. This is why it is so astonishing that seemingly unexceptional people achieve such extraordinary results. Their secret: a well-guided subconscious mind.

Each individual is programmed. Parents, teachers, and friends are programming agents who are often clumsy and harmful, using negative words without realizing the impact they have. There is also another very important programming agent: the individual himself. All of us have our own inner monologues. We repeat to ourselves: 'Things aren't going very well, are they?' 'I'm always tired,' 'Why am I not succeeding?' 'I'm overworked,' 'I'll never find a job,' 'I'll never get a raise,' 'I'll never be rich,' or 'I'm not talented enough.' These negative, pessimistic thoughts that you more or less consciously repeat to yourself are all suggestions that influence your subconscious or reinforce its current programme. Needless to say, these thoughts must definitely be driven out of your mind. Let's see how.

IT'S NEVER TOO LATE TO GROW RICH

It is reassuring that proof exists showing that no programme is irreversible. Just as we can modify or revamp a computer programme, we can completely overhaul our personalities, which are moulded in the subconscious mind. Experiments carried out on many subjects have demonstrated that it generally takes thirty days to set up a new programme.

How can we acquire a personality that will magically attract success and trigger favourable circumstances? We can rely on a wide variety of methods currently available, which are based on self-suggestion. These methods often carry different names. Some authors speak of the Alpha method, others of psycho-cybernetics, mental programming, positive thinking, or self-hypnosis. All of these techniques are basically valid, yet, each is a variation or adaptation of an astonishingly simple method developed by a French pharmacist, Emile Coué. His discovery was accidental. One day, one of his clients insisted on buying a drug for which he needed a prescription. Faced with this client's stubbornness, Emile Coué thought up a trick. He recommended a product to him that was ostensibly just as effective, but which was actually a sugar-pill. The patient came back a few days later, completely cured and absolutely delighted with the results. What was later to be called the placebo effect had just been discovered!

What had happened to this patient? Well, it was basically the same phenomenon that had occurred in the experiment in *In Search of Excellence,* except that the magical effect of words, of confidence and of the subconscious had acted on the physical, rather than intellectual level. This subject was cured by his confidence in the pharmacist and in the medication, as well as by the mental certainty that he was going to get well.

It didn't take Emile Coué long to realize the significance of this experiment. If a word could cure an ailment, what could it do to someone's personality? In the next few years he developed an extremely simple formula which has been applied throughout the world and has improved the lives of thousands of individuals. Why self-suggestion? Since Coué couldn't stay at each patient's bedside, or stay in contact with him, the patient could cure himself using his own chosen formula.

Here is the formula Coué developed:

Every day, and in every way I am getting better and better

He advises people to repeat this formula aloud in a monotone voice about 20 times a day. Countless variations have been developed. You will soon be able to concoct your own according to your needs and personality. The effects it produces are astounding. This general formula embraces all aspects of existence and has limitless possibilities. It must be repeated on a daily basis. Repetition is the golden rule of self-suggestion. We must literally flood our subconscious with this saying. A new programme will set in little by little, and a new personality along with it. Negative reinforcement will give way to positive reinforcement, enthusiasm, energy, boldness, and determination. Don't get put off by the apparent simplicity of this method like several of Emile Coué's contemporaries, who refused to believe that such a simple technique could be effective. Remember, your negative programming is intent on survival. Practising this method threatens its existence and will overcome any scepticism.

Every day, and in every way I am getting better and better

The rich men whose lives we delved into did not always use these formulas explicitly. And yet, faced with adversity, each of them subconsciously resorted to them. The principles outlined in their biographies are proof of this. Whether confronted by problems or on the threshold of a new adventure, each of them had learned to condition or programme himself by repeating that he was going to be successful, that no obstacle would short-circuit his attempts.

Ray Kroc, whom we mentioned earlier on, revealed in his autobiography that a large part of his success was due to a personalized variation of self-suggestion.

I learned how to keep problems from crushing me. I refused to worry about more than one thing at a time, and I would not let useless fretting about a problem, no matter how important, keep me from sleeping. This is easier said than done. I did it through my own brand of self-hypnosis. I may have read a book on the subject, I don't remember, but in any case I worked out a system that allowed me to turn off nervous tension and shut out nagging questions when I went to bed. I knew if I didn't, I wouldn't be bright and fresh and be able to deal with customers in the morning. I would think of my mind as being a blackboard full of messages, most of them urgent, and I practised imagining a hand with an eraser wiping that blackboard clean. I made my mind completely blank. If a thought began to appear, zap! I'd wipe it out before it could form. Then I would relax my body, beginning at the back of my neck and continuing on down: shoulders, arms, torso, legs, to the tips of my toes. By this time I would be asleep. I learned to do this procedure rather rapidly. Others marvelled that I could work 12 or 14 hours a day at a busy convention, then entertain potential customers until two or three o'clock in the morning, and still be out of bed early, ready to collar my next client. My secret was in getting the most out of every moment of rest. I guess I couldn't have averaged more than six hours of sleep a night. Many times I got four hours or less. But I slept as hard as I worked.

Ray Kroc's technique is preceded by physical relaxation. Physical and mental relaxation go hand in hand. Furthermore, in a state of relaxation our brain waves slow down and the subconscious is much more open to suggestion.

There is obviously a broad range of relaxation techniques available on the market. If you already know one, so much the better. If not, here is a very simple one.

HOW TO RELAX

Lie down on the floor or in bed, or seat yourself comfortably in an armchair. Close your eyes. Inhale deeply about 10 times. Then relax each separate part of your body, beginning with your feet and going up towards your head. This technique, by the way, is popularly called 'autogenic training'.

Once you are feeling very relaxed, start repeating your suggestion. Emile Coué's well-known formula is excellent for obtaining results in every aspect of your life. But you can also work on more specific elements. In order to apply the principles we will be discussing, you will have to develop certain qualities. In fact, with this method of self-suggestion, you can transform your personality and become the person you have always dreamed of being. Make an outline of the qualities you would like to have or perfect. To help you do this, here is a list of the basic characteristics shared by most of the rich and famous. Millionaires are usually:

• Tenacious	• Confident
• Enthusiastic	• Imaginative
• Energetic	• Diligent
• Bold	• Positive
• Intuitive	• Astute
• Persuasive	• Dependable
• Authoritative	• Daring

Choose the qualities you lack or need to work on the most. Work on one at a time, starting with your weakest point. You will see how much stronger you will be just by eliminating one of them.

A simple way of making up your own formula is by varying Emile Coué's famous one. You could select one of the qualities listed above and say to yourself, 'Every day, and in every way, I am becoming more and more enthusiastic,' or 'Every day, and in every way, I am becoming more and more energetic.' Create your own suggestions. Choose simple words that are the most familiar and evocative to you. Write your suggestions down on paper. The simple act of writing a suggestion down will have a great impact on you, giving your thoughts more power and authority. It becomes a concrete action. It is the springboard for the action you will take, the starting point of your personality change. Never lose sight of your suggestions. Re-read them often. They will soon be part of your life. The old person within you will be replaced by a younger one who will fulfil your aims and guide your actions. Here are a few other basic rules for making up your own suggestions. Experience has shown that, to be fully effective, suggestions must be:

● **Brief** If they are too long they will not be effective.

● **Positive** This is absolutely essential. The subconscious works differently from the conscious mind. If you say, 'I'm not poor any more,' the word *poor* might be retained since it is the key word. It could have the opposite result. Say this instead: 'I'm becoming rich.'

● **Gradual** Some authors state that we must formulate our suggestions as if we already had what we desired. This could be counter-productive, however. Our conscious mind sees a contradiction here. Mental conflict may arise which might compromise the positive results of the suggestion. So, if you repeat 'I'm rich,' or 'My job is perfect,' your mind will naturally sense the inconsistency here, especially if you are broke or out of work. It would be better to say, 'I'm getting richer day by day,' or 'I'm getting a perfect job.'

These formulas will guarantee you success. One way of avoiding conflict is by repeating key words without any verbs. One of the most powerful word associations you could use is the following:

Success — wealth

Repeat these words over and over. This is the goal you are now aiming for.

Here is a powerful variation of Emile Coué's formula. It is a little longer, but if you like it, it will accomplish marvellous things for you.

> Every day, and in every way, things
> are getting better and better and
> I am growing richer in every
> area of my life

Even a mechanical and barely convincing repetition of these words has some effect. However, the more emotion and feeling you put into your suggestion, the better the results will be. If you want something with every ounce of your body, mind, and soul, your dreams will be realized. Thomas Edison once said that years of experience had taught him that any man who wants something so badly that he will gamble his future on one roll of the dice is sure to win.

The 10 wealthy men examined in this book put all of their hearts into their endeavours and their desire to succeed was fuelled by unwavering passion. Be bold enough to imitate them. Don't be afraid to listen to your heart. Start programming yourself today. There is enough power to transform your life and make you wealthy in this chapter alone, yet no one can make you rich but yourself. No one can repeat these formulas for you. Your first step should therefore be to repeat the formulas you have chosen.

YOU'LL NEVER GET RICH IF YOU CAN'T PICTURE YOURSELF RICH

Everyone who wants to become rich must convince himself thoroughly of this. Similarly, anyone who sees himself as nothing but a lowly employee and who cannot imagine ever being able to scale the corporate ladder will stay in this position for the rest of his life.

The result of all inner programming is called your 'self-image' in psycho-cybernetic terms. Despite our conscious efforts to create a self-image, each of us has only a vague idea of the one we actually project. We have an even more vague idea of the role self-image plays in our lives. It is important to understand this since people are what they believe themselves to be. Everything in your life, including your degree of wealth, is directly proportional to your self-image.

You must therefore give serious thought to the premise that the greatest limitation man can impose on himself is the one created in his own mind. Similarly, the greatest freedom he can enjoy is mental freedom.

How is your self-image created? Well, it follows the same process as your mental programming, since your self-image is a faithful reflection of it. In fact, it is the conscious part of your mental programming. As we stated previously, most individuals are unaware of the impact that self-image has on their lives. Their self-images are basically shaped by two primary sources: the external world, including parents, teachers, friends, and acquaintances, and the inner world, namely, the thoughts that they have.

Man's greatest limitation is the one created in his own mind

Stop and analyse this principle for a minute or two. It could very well start you on the road to a totally new life. How do you picture yourself? Do you believe that you could easily double your income within a year? You don't? Rest assured, life will prove you right, since this belief has been programmed into your subconscious, whether you realize it or not. You have given your mind a command — a negative command. You have entered a limit into your subconscious and it will put everything into motion to run this programme as best it can. Your subconscious is very powerful and has a vast memory bank at its disposal. The problems it will come across to prevent you from doubling your yearly income will be formidable. It is therefore just as hard for you to fail as to succeed. It is just as easy for you to succeed as it is to fail. In the following chapter, we will discuss the importance of goals. Now that you are aware of the mechanisms of the subconscious, you know that an objective is simply a specific programme that you enter into your subconscious. By the way, do you know what you must base your goal on? The answer might surprise you. Despite certain outside factors that will inevitably come into play here, you will automatically establish your goal according to your self-image.

> ## We always establish our goals according to our self-image

First of all you might say to yourself: 'I want to increase my yearly income by £5,000.' That's good. It's legitimate and absolutely possible. It will most likely enhance your lifestyle significantly, even if the Inland Revenue grabs a large chunk of it. But why did you limit yourself to £5,000? The reason is simple: the image you have of yourself is of a person who can only get £5,000 richer in a year. We don't mean to dismiss this goal in any way. We could have chosen £2,500 or £50,000. This figure is arbitrary, chosen merely for the purposes of demonstration, but you must ask yourself what is 'reasonably' preventing you from increasing your income even more substantially? There isn't one valid constraint. Do you know how much Steven Spielberg earned in 1982 after ET had been released? Over one million dollars a day! Now you can see that your goals are limited only by the mind.

Therefore, the starting point for growing rich and surpassing yourself is to expand your self-image, or better yet, remould it. A new self-image will produce a new goal, and a new goal will result in a new life for you. This appears simple, but it is constantly being confirmed.

All rich men pictured themselves rich before achieving their dreams

No matter how poor they were at the beginning, no matter how little education they had, no matter how few contacts they enjoyed, all of them pictured themselves rich before making their fortunes. All of them were convinced that they would one day become millionaires. Life answered their dreams in accordance with their self-image and the faith that they had in their success.

To try to discover your self-image, tell yourself, for example: 'I'm going to be very rich.' Now analyse your reactions. Remember, there is an exact ratio between your ego and what life offers you. You can change it at any time, however, according to your aspirations. In the beginning, when you begin reprogramming yourself and shaping a new self-image, you will see that you will inevitably be influenced by your old image. This is completely normal. Change takes place in gradual stages.

Create your own self-image. Nothing is easier. Rely on the method we exposed earlier on. Here are a few formulas that you can use. Later you will add your financial goal, setting a precise amount and a deadline for reaching it. We will explain how to do this further on.

- 'I'm getting richer day by day.'
- 'I'm going to find an ideal job that will satisfy all my needs.'
- 'Life is putting the people who will help me improve my financial situation directly in my path.'
- 'I'm going to meet the ideal partner.'
- 'I'm going to find a way to double my yearly income.'
- 'All my abilities are getting better, allowing me to increase my income.'
- 'I'm going to keep going until I succeed.'
- 'It's easy for me to reach all my goals.'
- 'I'm going to find the situation that will help me perfect my qualities and talents.'

When creating your own formulas (if those we have recommended don't suit you) don't impose limitations on yourself. Don't be afraid to be bold when setting your objectives. The potential you have is extraordinary. Develop it. People who become wealthy are not ostensibly any different from you. The mental limits they set for themselves are simply unlike your own. The amounts they earn in an hour might impress you. But do you think it impresses them? Generally not. Their earnings are the result of a highly ordinary, normal mental programme for them. It can be the same for you. Ray Kroc once said, 'Think big and you'll become big.' As we are about to see, his entire life clearly reflects this fundamental principle.

RAY KROC

> I have always believed that every
> man creates his own happiness
> and is responsible for his
> own problems

Ray Kroc was born in 1902 in Oak Park, a neighbourhood on Chicago's West Side. His father, Louis, was a technician at Western Electric Union. His brother Bob, who was three years his junior, became a doctor specializing in endocrinology, as well as president of the Kroc Foundation, a philanthropic organization. But, unlike Bob, Ray was not particularly attracted to studying. He preferred action. To make ends meet, his mother, Rose, gave piano lessons at home. Ray, of course, learned to play the piano, and it was a skill he would find very useful later on in life.

Ray Kroc's business acumen developed very early in life. After having spent a summer working in his uncle's pharmacy and saving every penny he earned, he and two of his friends opened up a music store. With an initial investment of $100 each, they rented a tiny office space to sell musical scores and harmonicas. They were forced to close after only a few months, however, because business was bad. Kroc had nevertheless acquired his first taste for business, and this failure was useful as it helped confirm his vocation in life.

The United States had just entered the war at about this time. Bored with school, Ray decided to leave at the age of 14. He did not feel that what he was learning there would be of much use to him. He lied about his age and enlisted in the army. He trained as a Red Cross ambulance driver, but the war ended just as he was about to leave for France.

Ray Kroc went back to Chicago to look for work. He got a job as a haberdashery salesman. That was his first step in the world of sales and where he discovered the secret of being a good salesman. His career soon came to a dead end in this small company, so Kroc left and got a job as a pianist in an orchestra which was popular in Michigan at the time. Here he met Ethel, the woman he would marry several years later.

Think small and you will
stay small

Shortly after marrying Ethel in 1922, Ray began searching for a more stable job. He quickly found a job in sales at Lily Tulip, a paper-cup firm. Ray sensed that there was a huge market for paper cups. The flair for business he had displayed even as a youth was going to serve him well throughout his career.

> Paper cups were not an easy sale when I hit the streets with my Lily Cup sample case in 1922. Paper cups... were more hygienic, and they eliminated breakage and losses through unreturned take away orders. Those elements became the principal points in my sales story. I was green as grass, but I sensed that the potential for paper cups was great and that I would do well if I could overcome the inertia of tradition.

Ray's sixth sense nevertheless allowed him to conquer this resistance, a normal or at least frequent phenomenon when it comes to any new product. He foresaw extremely lucrative marketing possibilities in paper cups. 'I was convinced', he said, 'that if you thought small, you stayed small, and I had no intention of staying that way.'

During this period, Ray worked to a frenzied self-imposed schedule. By 7 a.m., sample case in hand, he was already pounding the Chicago pavements looking for orders and new markets. At around 5 p.m., when most people were going home from work, Kroc would go to Chicago radio station where he was the official pianist, music being broadcast live back then. His day ended at around 2 a.m. How did he survive? He was no stronger physically than most people, but he had learned to develop his resistance.

> My secret was in getting the most out of every minute of rest. I guess I couldn't have averaged more than six hours of sleep a night. Many times I got four hours or less. But I slept as hard as I worked... I hated to be idle for a minute. I was determined to live well and have nice things, too, and we could do so with the income from my two jobs.

Kroc's paper cup sales kept on growing, boosting his self-confidence higher and higher. In the spring of 1925, Ray reached as far as he could go as a Lily Tulip salesman and got permission to take five months off without pay. A few days later, Ray Kroc energetically cranked up his Model T Ford and took to the road. Florida was hundreds of miles away.

Where there's not risk there's no pride in anything you do, so there can be no happiness in it

---

Back then, Florida was considered a new land of opportunity, an El Dorado, in a manner of speaking. Miami was full of fortune seekers when Ray Kroc arrived there after an exhausting ten-day car trip. It didn't take him long to find a job with W.P. Morgan & Son selling real estate along Las Olas Boulevard in Fort Lauderdale. His work consisted of finding rich clients eager to buy Florida property. Ray soon excelled in this job and even received a superb Hudson sedan driven by a chauffeur, a bonus given to the 20 best company salesmen. Not bad for a 23-year-old! This bonanza didn't last long, however. Cover-page stories in magazines about the sale of Florida swampland quickly put a stop to the wave of prosperity that Florida was beginning to enjoy.

Back in Chicago, Kroc started working for Lily Tulip again. Race tracks, stadia, zoos, beaches, and pastry shops were all targets for his talent and initiative. From 1927 to 1937, Ray acquired new territories and increased his sales income. But one morning his boss called him into the office for an urgent meeting.

> 'Close the door, Ray, I want to talk privately with you.' (John Clark) told me how much he appreciated my hard work, how well the company thought of my production, but I would have to take a salary and expense cut. It applied to everyone, across the board.

This news was a great blow to Ray. He wasn't keen on the salary decrease, but it was his pride above all that had taken the blow. How could his boss treat his best salesman so arbitrarily?

> 'This is unacceptable, that I be put on the same basis with some of the people who are cost problems to the corporation. Those people — you know who they are — they're part of the overheads in this company. I'm part of the creative. I bring in money, and I'm not going to put myself in the same category with them.'
> 'Ray, listen a minute. I'm taking a cut myself.'
> 'Take it. That's your prerogative. Take it, brother, but I won't accept it. I will not.'

Having said this, Kroc resigned on the spot.

When Kroc closed the door behind him, Clark remained transfixed. Never before had he met such a determined man, nor such a talented salesman, and he had just let him slip through his fingers. Kroc's wife reproached him for acting so impulsively. But Ray didn't want to hear anything about it. His stubborn attitude paid off in the end, however, since his boss called him back shortly after. Kroc immediately accepted his profitable offer: an expense account that would make up for his 10 per cent salary decrease without causing envy among the other employees since it wasn't going against the company's general policy. 'I felt several inches taller when I left that office,' remembered Kroc. He hadn't budged an inch, and he was now reaping the benefits of his determination.

> I'm convinced that I'm a winner

In about the same year as this, Ray Kroc met Earl Prince, an engineer who was setting up a chain of ice-cream parlours called 'Prince Castle'. Ray was his paper cup supplier. Ray figured that this business had a lot of promise. Kroc's own affairs had never been so good, either. In fact, he now had 15 salesmen working for him. However, growing conflicts with his boss concerning the company's future and the way he stimulated his salesmen were beginning to get on his nerves and sap his enthusiasm. Kroc therefore jumped at the chance to become Prince's partner when asked. He was of course sacrificing a lucrative job, but the future and new challenges attracted him even more. He was only 35 years old and he had just spotted a good deal. Prince has just developed the 'Multi-Mixer', a six-pronged gadget for making milkshakes. Kroc would be its exclusive marketing and sales agent throughout the country and Prince would manufacture them. They also decided to split the profits 50/50. No agreement could have been more equitable.

> For me, this was the first phase
> of grinding it out — building
> my personal monument
> to capitalism

In 1936, Kroc took off to conquer new markets, carrying a sample case that weighed 50 pounds! Business did not go very smoothly in the beginning. Restaurants did not see any reason to switch from their traditional mixers to the one Ray was selling, even though it was a multipurpose appliance. Furthermore, the First World War was making it hard to get the copper necessary to manufacture the Multi-Mixer. Kroc was forced to shelve this appliance and spent his time selling powdered malted milk. As soon as the war ended, Kroc immediately took up where he had left off and the Multi-Mixer business was soon brisker than ever, especially because of the new food chains. Kroc never stopped looking for new markets and attended all the conventions organized by restaurant owners and dairy associations. In 1948, he reached a sales record of 8,000 Multi-Mixers. This record was only the first step.

'You are going to eat the best hamburger of your life without having to wait or leave a tip'

Two of Ray's clients were the McDonald brothers, who operated eight Multi-Mixers, a rare feat at the time. Since these appliances could each make six milk shakes simultaneously, this meant that they must have had a great many customers. On a business trip to Los Angeles, Ray Kroc finally saw the McDonalds' restaurant for the first time in his life. Extremely impressed by it, he realized that before him was a potentially great business opportunity. However, he was quite taken aback at first by the nondescript appearance of the restaurant. It was a small octagonal structure, located on a plot of land measuring barely 200 square feet. All in all, it looked like any other roadside café. Since it was close to lunchtime, Ray parked his car nearby to get a better view of what was going on. He couldn't believe his eyes at first: the staff were all dressed in white with matching paper hats. They marched past him, carrying bags of potatoes, cans of meat, buns, and soft drinks from a warehouse back to the restaurant. He had a remarkable sense of the order, discipline and efficiency with which the restaurant was run. The car park was soon jammed with cars and people were already lining up at the counter. Kroc joined the queue, which kept growing longer and longer and was very impressed.

The same afternoon, Kroc returned to the restaurant, hoping to have a chat with the McDonalds. He got an appointment for that very night, having firmly decided to get to know everything about them. He learned that Maurice and Richard McDonald had worked as prop men in a Hollywood film studio for several years until 1932 when they decided to set up their own business, and bought a movie theatre. It didn't work very well and in 1937 they convinced a real estate owner in Santa Anita to help them build a drive-in restaurant, an increasing trend in California at the time. This type of restaurant was becoming more and more popular, and some owners even made their waitresses wear roller skates and costumes. California was, and still is, the cradle of American culture!

Starting out with no idea of how to run a restaurant, the McDonalds quickly picked up what they needed to know from one of their employees who had been a cook in a steakhouse. Their small restaurant was to be the prototype of thousands of restaurants which Ray Kroc was going to franchise. The menu was limited: hamburgers, french fries, and soft drinks. Everything was prepared by assembly-line methods, each production stage being carried out with a minimum of time, effort and cost.

That night back at his hotel, Ray Kroc thought about what he had seen and heard during the day. There was nothing he could do to keep his imagination from bubbling over with ideas. This is what he wrote about that night: 'Visions of McDonald's restaurants dotting crossroads all over the country paraded through my brain.' The next morning, Kroc's plan of attack was ready. He would go and see the McDonald brothers, offering to set up a chain of restaurants similar to theirs all across the country. They would increase their profits and Kroc would maximize his Multi-Mixer sales, a deal both parties would benefit from. Strangely enough, Kroc was primarily interested in increasing his Multi-Mixer sales.

'We don't need any more problems than we have already in keeping this place going. More places, more problems. It'll be a lot of trouble,' Dick McDonald objected. 'Who could we get to open them for us?'

'Well, what about me?' Kroc replied.

On the plane back to Chicago, the air hostesses would surely never have guessed that Ray Kroc, a rather ordinary-looking passenger who was not only suffering from diabetes and arthritis, but had also had his gall bladder and part of his thyroid gland removed, would one day become one of the most powerful food magnates in the world. Kroc kept glancing at his briefcase, gripping it tightly as if it contained millions of dollars. As a matter of fact, it contained a genuine gold mine: a contract freshly signed by the McDonalds and giving him the right to build McDonald franchises throughout the United States. It also contained a clause stipulating that all the buildings had to be identical, that is, following the blueprint designed by their architect for their newly constructed restaurant. Furthermore, the name McDonald had to appear on each building. All the menus had to be uniform and any modifications whatsoever had to receive prior written approval from the brothers. The contract offered Kroc 1.9 per cent on the gross sales of any franchised store, but Kroc had to reimburse 0.5 per cent to the McDonalds. The contract also mentioned that Kroc would be granted $950 for each franchise he set up, an amount helping to cover his expenses. Each license granted to the franchisees would be valid for 20 years. Kroc's contract with the McDonald brothers was good for only 10 years, but was later extended to 99 years.

As soon as he got back to Chicago, Ray started looking for land to build the first McDonald's restaurant on. With the help of a friend, Art Jacobs, who would later become his associate, Ray dug up a small lot that seemed to fulfil all of the conditions. Most of Ray's friends thought it was sheer lunacy to get involved in a business selling cheap hamburgers.

Ed MacLuckie, one of Kroc's friends, was the only one who encouraged him and got interested in this scheme. Kroc had no problems convincing him to become the manager of his first restaurant. Thus, in 1955, armed with the advice of Hart Bender, the brothers' manager, Ray Kroc opened his first McDonald's restaurant in the Mid-West. But the Californian-style building their architect had drawn up was poorly suited to the Mid-West, especially in winter. Kroc had numerous arguments with Maurice and Richard McDonald over the changes he wanted to bring to the building to suit each different geographical location, but both of them refused to sign the letter of agreement as stipulated in the contract.

Preparing the french fries also caused Kroc problems. Even though he had learned the brother's recipe by heart, he couldn't manage to get the same taste as the marvellous fries he had eaten in California. The success of his enterprise depended on being able to offer the same standards of quality and taste in hundreds of restaurants. Kroc finally solved this problem by having a ventilation system built in the basement which would speed up the curing process of the potatoes. Potatoes taste much better as they dry out, and as the sugar changes to starch. The McDonalds kept their potatoes in wire-mesh bags open to the desert breeze and were using a natural curing method without knowing it. While taking care of the restaurant, Kroc continued selling Multi-Mixers, which paid his restaurant's rent and his employees' salaries. He dropped in early each morning to lend a hand. 'I've never been too proud to grab a mop and clean up the toilets. . . .'

A year after the first McDonald's opened up, three other franchise outlets sprouted in California, and during the last eight months of 1956, eight new restaurants were already flourishing in different states across the country. Selling Multi-Mixers had allowed Kroc to examine several thousand kitchens in all sorts of restaurants, and this experience was now helping him to manage his new franchises. Ray Kroc's experience is a good illustration of the 'spin-offs' and the 'extra-mile theory' we shall be discussing in the following chapters. All of his efforts during these first few years would soon allow him to make a fortune.

One of Kroc's main objectives during this time was to

create a network of restaurants known for their quality, service, and cleanliness. 'If I had a brick for every time I've repeated the phrase *QSC and V* (Quality, Service, Cleanliness and Value), I think I'd probably be able to bridge the Atlantic Ocean with them.' A philosophy such as this demanded a permanent training scheme for all the franchise owners and managers.

To foster the growth and expansion of his restaurant chain, Kroc got the idea of convincing real-estate owners to rent their land to him on a subordinate basis. In other words, they would take out a second mortgage so that Kroc's team could go to the bank and negotiate a first mortgage. Kroc had no problems convincing them since it didn't take them long to realize that their empty lots could bring money in. This was when McDonald's finally started becoming profitable. Kroc also developed a monthly payment system for the franchise-holders, which allowed him to pay off the mortgages, cover expenses, and make a profit. Kroc received a fixed fee or a percentage of the restaurant's sales, whichever was the highest. After a while, this formula started bringing in substantial revenues. Ray Kroc had barely touched the tip of the iceberg!

> I believe in God, in the family
> and in McDonald's, but at work
> this order is reversed

Kroc then got down to surrounding himself with key men, including accountants, lawyers, financial advisers, etc. 'Much of the success of my organization has been a result of the kind of people I have picked for key positions.'

A few years later, faced with the rapid expansion of the McDonald's chain, Ray Kroc increasingly felt that he had a sound business on his hands. The only fly in the ointment was that it wasn't really his! He was bound to the McDonalds by contract. It became obvious that if he wanted to become truly rich and to expand his chain to match his dreams, he would have to get rid of the obstacles in his way. He had to buy back his contract. This is what he set out to do.

After a long discussion with his main financial consultant regarding the best negotiation strategy for a buy-back, Kroc opted for a direct approach and telephoned Dick McDonald to ask him how much he wanted for it. Two days later when the brothers mentioned their price, Ray Kroc, flabbergasted, dropped the phone. It literally took his breath away. They wanted $2,700,000!

This was a huge amount then and now, and one Kroc simply didn't have, especially as he had just divorced his first wife.

'We'd like to have a million dollars apiece after taxes, Ray,' Dick explained. 'We've been in business for 30 years, working seven days a week, week in and week out, and we feel we've earned it.'

How on earth was he going to get his hands on such an astronomical amount of money? The next morning Kroc gathered his team and a few days later, John Bristol, a financial adviser from Princeton University, was hired to find some backers. Bristol eventually found the necessary amount. The final cost of this transaction rose to $14,000,000 and Kroc's budget forecasts indicated that it would take until 1991 to reimburse it all. Yet by 1972 the total amount was paid back. Kroc had made a slight miscalculation — he had based his forecast on the 1961 sales, unable to foresee, despite his usual optimism, that his restaurant chain would grow as quickly as it did.

Ray Kroc had taken his first major step on the road to riches. But the game was far from being won. Kroc faced several administrative and legal battles, and had to prove that he was a great manager. The expansion of the McDonald's empire was phenomenal. In 1977, when Ray Kroc published his autobiography, McDonald's owned 4,177 restaurants in the United States and 21 overseas. Since then, the success of his chain has continued. Total sales now exceed $3 billion.

The policy Kroc imposed on his licensees was to account every single detail of the day-to-day operations. Cooking time was determined to the minute and controlled by machine The hamburgers had to be a precise size and weight. Hamburgers which were not sold 10 minutes after being cooked were to be thrown out. Staff rules and regulations were extremely strict, affecting not only their uniforms, but their hairstyles and manners. The employees had to greet their clients with a smile and look them straight in the eye. There were numerous and often subtle ways of cutting costs. For example, the staff handed out salt, pepper, and condiments only when the clients specifically requested them.

As soon as Ray Kroc bought his contract back from the McDonalds, he imposed a rigid policy on all his licencees, which explains a large part of his success. His attention to detail was legendary. It is often a series of minute and seemingly banal details that can make or break you in business. This preoccupation is the result of experience, and of a constant search for improvements.

The 10 men in this book spent their lives paying attention to details that others would have scorned. Ray Kroc, for one, was taken for a fanatic because he was so particular about detail, particularly cleanliness.

> I was always eager to see... my McDonald's! But sometimes the sight pleased me a lot less than other times. Sometimes Ed MacLuckie would have forgotten to turn the sign on when dusk began to fall, and that made me furious. Or maybe the lot would have some litter on it that Ed said he hadn't had time to pick up. Those little things didn't seem to bother some people, but they were gross affronts to me. I'd get screaming mad and really let Ed have it. He took it in good part. I know he was as concerned about these details as I was, because he proved it in his own stores in later years.

Ray Kroc worked till the end of his life, spending all of his time looking for good locations for future restaurants. The McDonald Corporation purchased a plane, which he used in his hunt for sites close to schools and churches.

Despite the crippling pain in his hip, Kroc continued travelling and going into the office. Given the kind of man he was, suffering was surely better than idleness. Towards the end of his life, someone reproachfully told him that it was easy for him to talk about success since he already had several million dollars stashed away somewhere. 'So what!' retorted Kroc. 'I can still only wear one pair of shoes at a time.'

GET RID OF YOUR MENTAL BLOCK

Creating a new self-image inevitably entails making a clean sweep of the old one. Yet, everybody puts up fight, attempting to resist this change. One of the most common, deeply embedded and harmful mental blocks is the idea that 'money is dirty'. This notion manifests itself in different ways and is generally a subconscious one. People will tell you that it is unhealthy to want to get rich, and that those who wish to improve their lot in life are unscrupulous capitalists and vulgar materialists. These ideas are the vestiges of a puritanism. An aversion to money, however, is often hypocritical. People malign the rich, but secretly envy them. It should nevertheless be noted that attitudes are gradually changing, even though certain prejudices remain.

Another common hang-up is fear of going against family background and upbringing. Not everyone suffers from this, of course. We have already seen that the frustration and humiliation bred by poverty have been catalysts for many fortunes, proving that humble origins do not condemn people to mediocrity and that poverty is not hereditary. No matter how shocking this may sound, poverty is in many cases a form of mental illness.

This is reassuring to some extent. If poverty is an illness, it can be cured. People can get out of it. There are no external conditions, constraints, or circumstances that the mind cannot overcome. Anyone who understands this truth can become successful and shape his present and future life to match his aspirations. Anyone who becomes aware of this fundamental law and applies it to his life can become whatever he wants to be. And nothing, absolutely nothing, can stop him. Circumstances will bend to his wishes.

THE TRUE SIGNIFICANCE
OF MONEY

The view that money is dirty and that people deny their origins by raising themselves above their family expectations is indeed a deplorable one. The idea that anyone who has monetary ambitions is a mean-spirited capitalist is completely misguided. Apart from the money people inherit or win by chance in lotteries or at the races, what does making a lot of money mean? Money which has been earned honestly is simply a recognition of services rendered. A rich man is therefore one who has provided services to many people and has been justly rewarded for them. This is what most of those who scorn money forget when they condemn it. Henry Ford accumulated millions and millions of dollars. But what did he offer in exchange? Thanks to his patience, genius, and determination, this uneducated man, the laughing-stock of his peers, made mankind take a giant step forward. Can you imagine life nowadays without cars? Of course not. Furthermore, Henry Ford helped create thousands of jobs. His fortune is a symbol of public recognition, the just payment for services rendered. Ford was perfectly aware of the real value of money, and that awareness taught him the surest way of getting it. When a man asked him one day what he would do if he lost his entire fortune, he answered without batting an eyelid that he would think up another fundamental human need and meet it by offering a cheaper and more efficient service than anybody else. He went on to say that he would be a millionaire again within five years.

Finding a basic need and answering it with cheaper, more efficient service: this is how most rich people build their fortunes. We could establish the same equation for the 10 men we studied. Think of Walt Disney. He brightened the lives of thousands of children. Thomas Watson? His business genius allowed him to market IBM computers and to change our society. What would modern life be like without computers? Conrad Hilton? His hotel policy guaranteed travellers all over the world exceptional quality and comfort, and this earned him his fortune.

Those who criticize these men for having too much money should consider what they did for their fellow man in terms of products, services and employment. The recognition these men received was well earned.

What counts is the quality of the product or service. A single idea can lead to affluence. Putting it into operation, however, obviously requires more time and effort.

Rubik, the creator of the mind-boggling Rubik Cube, became a millionaire with a single idea. Which service did he offer the public? He amused thousands of people all over the world by making them rack their brains. And how much do you think the inventor of 'Monopoly' made in royalties?

Many people believe that money in itself is neither good nor bad. We, on the other hand, believe that money is the golden key of civilization. It is no coincidence that the richest countries in the world have also reached the highest cultural and scientific levels. The advantages of money are enormous, for individuals as well as for entire societies. So, get rid once and for all your medieval ideas that money is dirty, degrading, and evil. Naturally, we are not naïve enough to claim that money is a cure-all, but it does make life easier and it opens a lot of doors. The only danger is becoming a slave to it. Money is an excellent servant, but it is an autocratic master. What is most important is to integrate a positive view of money into your new self-image. It is your passport to greater freedom. You are entitled to it. Exercise this right. Get rid of whatever mental blocks you have about money. Until you do, you will never be able to grow rich. Be vigilant, however. This inhibition often comes disguised in insidious forms in order to escape your attention. While analysing your ideas, keep in mind the following principle: **There is no valid reason why you cannot become rich.**

PICTURE YOURSELF RICH ALREADY!

A picture is worth a thousand words, or so the saying goes. We have seen how to use verbal suggestions to change your self-image and to reprogramme your subconscious mind. These suggestions suit many people perfectly and are always effective. However, some people like to add guided imagery to them. Creative visualization can be a great help. We all use it every day in our lives. We think in images as much as in words. We constantly give in to what is popularly called 'daydreaming' or 'wakeful dreaming'.

We plan out our futures and evoke memories of the past, reliving them in images. Whether we know it or not, these images greatly influence our subconscious and help shape our personalities. In fact, they often mould our futures without our knowing it. If this is done in a positive way, there is nothing left to say. But since this imagery is generally not guided, it often has a negative effect on us. Constant memories of sadness or failure reinforce our negative programming. If we are pessimistic by nature, negative images permeate our dreams of the future, often fulfilling our expectations.

Mental imagery must therefore be steered in the right direction. Every day, make sure that the time you devote to reprogramming yourself is accompanied by creative visualization, or 'scientific dreaming' as some call it. Once you are relaxed, fill your mind with new and positive images. There is no limit to what you can do. Pretend that you already have what you are hoping for, and that your goal has already been reached. One of the reasons why this technique is so effective is that the subconscious is not governed by the same temporal rules as the conscious mind. In fact, time does not exist either in the subconscious mind or in dreams, which are its most easily recognizable by-product. There is no real past or future. It is like being eternally in the here and now.

This is why traumas experienced in early childhood can affect people for years, even when their rational minds understand that they no longer have to worry about the past. This is also why we can pretend that something is true. The subconscious mind doesn't distinguish between truth and pretence when it is dealing with images unrelated to time.

FILL YOUR MIND WITH THOUGHTS OF WEALTH

Your subconscious is like a vast field, governed, in a sense, by the 'Law of Sowing', meaning that what you sow, you will reap. This universal law, which brooks no exceptions, has also been called the 'Law of Compensation' by some authors. This law is to the mind what the law of cause and effect is to the physical world. Action breeds reaction. In the world of the mind, and so in life in general, thoughts and ideas are the cause; facts and events, the effect. Each thought that enters your mind tends to materialize in your life.

All your thoughts tend to materialize in your life

This why you must monitor your thoughts closely. If you continually think of your financial worries or never stop repeating that you can't make ends meet or that you might go bankrupt, you are entertaining thoughts that will show up in your life.

We certainly do not want to encourage recklessness. There is often a very fine line between lack of foresight and confidence, between optimism and brashness. We are not advocating a policy of burying your head in the sand like an ostrich, either. Difficulties and problems exist in any business dealing or enterprise. Nevertheless, the 10 men we studied, as well as hundreds of other millionaires, never let adversity defeat them. They no doubt saw the obstacles facing them, but their vision kept them going.

They were inspired by dreams, which they constantly kept aflame. Instead of picturing only drawbacks and problems, they focused on the means they had to tackle and overcome them. Most people have more imagination when it comes to conjuring up problems that will prevent them from realizing their dreams than when it comes to recognizing their chances of success.

In the world of the mind, ideas really exist. Even if they are invisible, they are as real as the book you are holding in your hands or the chair you are sitting in. This is not an attempt to be mystical or to throw sand in your eyes. It has been said that ideas govern the world. The power they have is phenomenal. It is therefore necessary to constantly fill our minds with thoughts of abundance, richness, and success. Each thought is a vibration, which, through some mysterious law of attraction, draws objects, beings and circumstances of a similar nature to it. The negative attracts the negative in the same way that the positive attracts the positive.

FOLLOW YOUR DREAM UNTIL YOU MAKE A FORTUNE!

Daydreams are often sneered at by 'down-to-earth' people who say that you have to look life squarely in the face and accept your fate, even if it leaves a lot to be desired. These are the kind of people who will systematically discourage progress and denigrate wealth, judging it to be vain and illusory. Yet, these resigned and unhappy individuals forget that there are two types of dreamers. On the one hand, there are daydreamers who make no attempt to turn their dreams into reality. On the other hand, there are 'realistic' dreamers, who believe in the creative power of the subconscious. All artists have a mental picture of their future works of art. All politicians start out with plans to change society. All of the 10 rich men began by dreaming of their future wealth. But their dreams did not stop there. They took concrete measures to make them come true.

Unfortunately, our educational system generally favour

the rational and strictly logical part of thought, neglecting or even scorning its intuitive and imaginative side. The right side of the brain has always been considered second best. And yet, nothing great has ever been achieved without an original dream. A dream is a kind of projection of our inner selves. What, in fact, is a projection or a project? By definition, it is a part of us that we throw forward. The greater we programme our self-images to be, the more grandiose our dreams will be. And the most surprising thing is that a dream, however bold it may be, is often more easily attainable than we believe.

THE LABORATORY OF YOUR MIND

There is a very simple technique used by businesspeople, artists and scientists to make use of the power of daydreaming. Just as photographs are developed in a darkroom, you must develop your dreams in a dark room. Sit or lie down in a room that you have made as dark and quiet as possible. Let images gradually flood your mind. Darkness and silence are particularly favourable for the growth of ideas and dreams because they put you in direct contact with your subconscious mind, which is essentially cut off from the outside world. It is important not to censure your thoughts, even if they seem far-fetched. This technique has been called 'brainstorming'. It can help you solve problems and discover a plethora of ideas.

YOUR SUBCONSCIOUS WILL LEAD YOU INFALLIBLY TO WEALTH

The power of the subconscious is equalled only by its wisdom. It never forgets anything. It is the perfect registry of our lives, recording each and every one of our gestures, words, and thoughts. Moreover, unlike the conscious mind, it never stops working. It works 24 hours a day. Filled with millions of events and ideas, your subconscious is a gold mine.

The only problem is that we often ignore it or don't dare to tap into it. But it's easy, and it's the best thing you could possibly do because all work without a good preliminary idea is pointless.

Your subconscious mind is the repository of thousands of ideas that could quickly make you rich. Yet, all you need is one. How do you find it? Learn how to converse with your subconscious. Send it a specific request, preferably at night before going to bed.

Earlier on we saw how important it was for your desires to be truly intense when you are formulating your suggestions. The same naturally goes for the requests you will send to your subconscious. The more vivid they are, the quicker they will be realized.

Rest assured, your subconscious will always provide you with the correct answer. The subconscious, if you remember, is where all our impressions, thoughts, and actions are registered. But what is more fascinating still is that it has access to information that we have never recorded, and therefore to things that we do not know about. This principle is illustrated in our own lives, if we think about it for a minute, as well as in the lives of the wealthy. Steven Spielberg once had a film project in mind as well as a scenario. All he needed was a producer, which is often the case in the field of motion pictures. One day, while he was on the beach, he 'accidentally' met a rich man who was ready to invest in young film makers. With the money Spielberg received from this producer, a total stranger to him, he was able to shoot *Amblin,* which was given an Honourable Mention at the Venice Film Festival and drew attention to him in Hollywood.

This is often how your subconscious solves a problem. You will meet someone 'by chance' who will help you put your plan into action. You will just happen to read a newspaper article or book or see a TV programme that will provide a clear-cut answer to something puzzling you or to a problem holding you back.

Those who remain unaware of or ignore this principle generally state that these happy coincidences are the result of luck or fate. Yet, in a world physically and mentally governed by the law of cause and effect, *fate does not exist*. The same goes for good and bad luck, which are actually the unexpected and often belated consequences of two things: our thoughts and previous actions. Anyone who adequately programmes his subconscious, that is to say, permeates it with positive thoughts of fame and fortune, and who tirelessly attempts to realize his dreams, will eventually reach his goal.

In a sense, we literally make our own good and bad luck. This is why we can say without hesitation that the people who learn and apply the laws of the mind and of success correctly can forge their own destinies.

If you start applying these universal laws today, you will soon discover that you are not creating your success alone. Your circle of family and friends and, at the same time, the strangers you meet will also contribute to your success. One example of this principle is the way Steven Spielberg got the idea for his first successful film *Duel*. It was not the result of long cogitations or intensive research. Far from it. One day his secretary suggested he read a short story in a magazine. When he read it, Spielberg was ecstatic. He knew immediately that he had found the idea he was looking for. Without his secretary, he probably would never have fallen upon this breathtaking story. But his subconscious was there, taking care of everything. Needless to say, 'lucky strokes' such as this one are commonplace in the lives of the rich. Not only does everything they touch turn to gold, but all the people they meet help them get richer. The same can happen to you. Make use of your subconscious mind. It is there to serve you.

We could go on and on about the unimaginable powers of the subconscious and the way to make use of it, but there are already hundreds of books devoted to this subject. In any case, you now possess the key principles that will allow you to succeed and enrich yourself according to your ambition and self-image. We shall now discover how to fulfil one of the capital requirements of success: *making the right decision.*

MAKING THE RIGHT DECISION

As we saw in a previous chapter, Henry Ford was a man of unshakeable faith and conviction, enabling him to conquer all the obstacles blocking his path to fame and fortune. Faith is one of the keys to success. A survey of the lives of several millionaires carried out at the request of the billionaire Andrew Carnegie allowed Napoleon Hill, the author of *Think and Grow Rich*, to state that the supreme secret of success is faith: the human mind can accomplish whatever it believes in.

Faith in yourself and in what you do is therefore vital. All successful people believe implicitly in their dreams. Nothing seems impossible to them.

Having faith is one thing, you will probably object, but how do you know whether you are putting it into a good idea and not making a disastrous mistake? Besides, even millionaires and seasoned businessmen make costly mistakes. Isn't it even more dangerous for someone just starting out? How do you know how to separate the chaff from the wheat? How can you decide what is possible or not? How can you find an idea, plan, or job that you can fully believe in? In other words, how can you develop the type of sound judgement that allows you to reduce, if not eliminate, mistakes?

We are constantly called upon to make decisions. This might involve accepting or looking for a new job, choosing a career, backing a project, or making an investment. Anyone wishing to survive and grow rich must make the right decision as often as possible. Is there a surefire method of developing this ability? Yes, there is!

This ability will help you discover what to believe in, which will enable you to be successful. Things that are too obvious rarely allow us get rich. If this were the case, everybody would be wealthy. Anyone who manages to make a fortune, while those around him wallow in mediocrity, tighten their belts and make do with what they have, is comparable to a clairvoyant amidst the blind. Unlike most people, successful people have acquired the capacity to perceive possibilities, even when things seem impossible. They see beyond the obstacles blocking their paths. They recognize the means that will ultimately lead them to victory.

Succeeding in business or in a career means walking a tightrope. A wrong move, while not necessarily fatal, does mean a temporary setback. We must therefore learn how to make right decisions more often than wrong ones. This means knowing how to say 'yes' when the time is ripe, 'no' when it isn't, and avoiding shaky business deals at all costs.

It is encouraging to note that most wealthy men do not believe that this ability is inborn, but that it can be acquired and enhanced, meaning that it is accessible to anyone who takes the time and energy to obtain and cultivate it. This chapter will explain how. Learning this fundamental skill is much easier than you would imagine.

The greater your capacity to see possibilities where others see only impossibilities and to make the right decisions, the more of an eccentric people will take you for. Most people tend to reject good opportunities when they knock at the door. Once you have ventured on to the road to success, do your best to ignore those who criticize you or throw snide comments your way.

The objections raised by the people around us, as well as by experts, are admittedly founded on 'rational' analyses. It is by cultivating our intuition that we can manage to see beyond 'logical' ideas. Besides, the secret of success lies in being able to distinguish between what is feasible and what is not, and in finding a vein of gold where others can't see it.

True, it would be naïve to claim that absolutely everything under the sun is possible. Some plans are simply not viable or would require too much time or energy. The best-seller *What They Don't Teach You at Harvard Business School* supplies an amusing example of this principle.

A dog food company was holding its annual sales convention. During the course of the convention the president of the company listened patiently as his advertising director introduced a point-of-sale scheme that would 'revolutionize the industry', and his sales director extolled the virtues of 'the best damn sales force in the business'. Finally it was time for the president to go to the podium and make his closing remarks.

'Over the past few days,' he began, 'we've heard from all our division heads of their wonderful plans for the coming year. Now as we draw to a close, I have only one question. If we have the best advertising, the best marketing, the best sales force, how come we sell less goddamn dog food than anyone in the business?'

Absolute silence filled the convention hall. Finally, after what seemed like forever, a small voice answered from the back of the room: 'Because the dogs *hate* it.'

Although this is an amusing anecdote, it proves that there are more possibilities than impossibilities. All you need to do is think of most inventions, for example. Did you know that when the Wright brothers were inventing their plane, scientific studies were undertaken to demonstrate that any body heavier than air couldn't possibly fly?

Soichiro Honda's life story exemplifies the same principle. His autobiography includes the following eloquent passage on this subject:

When I started manufacturing motorcycles, prophets of doom, who were sometimes my best friends, came to discourage me. 'Why don't you simply set up a garage? You'd rake in tons of money. There are lots of cars to repair all over the country.' I didn't listen to their pessimistic advice; so, beside my research laboratory, I started up the Honda Motor Company on September 24, 1948. It now covers the entire world.

Honda, a typical optimist, was able to see possibilities where others were blind, and to jump into action regardless of the negative arguments raised against his idea. Explaining his decision, he goes on to say:

> We were extremely poor, with our meagre capital of one million yen, but hard-working and very aware of the enormous risks we were taking. We were hoping to raise an industrial sector out of the doldrums at a time when the national industry lay destroyed before us. We were taking the absurd gamble of selling motorcycles when people were too poor at that moment to buy petrol and, if the economic situation got better, would later on surely want to own cars. We were flying in the face of even the most optimistic economic forecasts.

This is a clear illustration of the predominance of mind over matter and of optimism over pessimism. People with a positive mental attitude apparently tell themselves that things are never as bad as they look at first, and will always end up being even better.

One day during the Second World War, an American was taking a photograph of his young daughter when she asked him why they had to wait to see the pictures — a naïve, even absurd, question, but one which particularly interested her father. Her father was Edwin H. Land, an inventor who had already made improvements to the camera. His daughter's candid question started him thinking seriously about this matter. His reasoning was as follows: Someone who buys a pair of trousers or a car, or any commodity for that matter, can use it immediately after buying it. Why should it be any different in photography? Why should you have to wait days or even weeks to see the pictures you have taken? But would it be possible to develop photos in a tiny closed-off space in a matter of seconds when it normally took hours in a professional laboratory? All of Land's scientist friends told him his plan was impossible. Six months after his daughter's ingenuous question, the problem was resolved — in theory. On November 26 1948, the first 60-second Polaroid camera went on sale in Boston. As soon as the store opened, customers stampeded to get their hands on one of them.

A little girl's spontaneous remark instigated the invention of the Polaroid camera. Because children's minds are not yet filled with prejudices and preconceived notions, they have the ability to view things with a fresh eye and to see possibilities where rational minds see only impossibilities. In fact, genius has long been considered 'childhood revisited'. Prejudices have little or no hold on the minds of geniuses, who manage to hang on to their spark of originality, or at least find it again, through long and determined efforts. Traditional education is a handicap in a sense, as we shall see later on in this book. Excessive analysis, scepticism and an overly critical eye lead to mental stagnation and paralysis. Analytical studies are by definition interminable. Few of the men described here, except for Paul Getty, went to university. It was to some extent their 'ignorance' that helped them preserve their derring-do and enthusiasm, a point we shall have the opportunity to come back to.

> # The key to success is seeing possibilities where others see only impossibilities

This principle applies not only to inventions and large-scale enterprises, but to smaller endeavours as well. How often have you seen people raise their eyebrows at one of your seemingly impossible schemes? How often have you judged something unlikely or a job inaccessible to you before realizing that just the opposite was true? Because of 'rationality' or more often a secret lack of confidence, we give up our dreams, consoling ourselves with the thought that it wouldn't have worked out anyway. If you think this over for a minute, you will realize that this problem is intimately linked with our self-image. It is possible to categorically state that the better your self-image is, the more likely you will be able to see that a range of possibilities exists. There is a direct ratio between them.

It should be added, however, that many plans and ideas are neither feasible nor unfeasible, but somewhere between the two. What makes the difference between success and failure when putting them into action is the quantity and quality of the energy invested in them. They come to life and become viable through the sheer force of the vitality and thought put into them.

A person with a healthy ego is a powerhouse of energy and can easily tap into the unlimited reserves of his subconscious. Consequently, not only is he able to discern the positive side of things more easily, but his energy enables him to turn it to his advantage.

To gain a clearer vision of what is possible, expand your self-image

---

The major flaw of those who hesitate about carrying out a plan is trying to identify all the obstacles they could eventually run up against and ignoring the tools they have at their disposal to combat them — a paralysing, anxiety-producing attitude if ever there was one! Thus, the appropriate attitude to adopt is to look for all the reasons you are likely to succeed instead of conjuring up all the stumbling blocks you might face. You must, of course, weigh all the pros and cons. What happens in many cases, however, is that despite 10 favourable reasons, all it takes is one negative one to discourage people from trying at all. The reason for this is simple: most people are programmed negatively. Based on the principle of attraction, positive arguments, no matter how numerous they are, don't find fertile ground in a mind programmed negatively, whereas a single obstacle thrives there at once.

At this very moment, thousands of people are rejecting perfectly good ideas, plans, and dreams because a single negative idea has paralysed their judgement.

Naturally, it is extremely important to find out as much as possible beforehand about a proposed business deal, job offer, or plan. But remember, there are always imponderables in the end. Even the most detailed and sophisticated analyses will not dispel the unknown completely. Furthermore, studies undertaken by corporations and individuals alike often end up confirming their original ideas. Every scheme, admittedly, implies change and the need to confront the unknown. Psychological studies have demonstrated that people are frightened by unexplored territory and view change as a threat, or at least as cause for anxiety.

It is important, even essential, to know the facts before making a decision, but it should be recalled that facts must not take the place of intuition, an ability you must learn to cultivate. You must also discover how to interpret facts, for facts and figures in themselves do not constitute a conclusion. It is up to you to draw your own conclusion from the data you have collected.

DO IT NOW!

The fundamental weakness that ruins so many people's lives is procrastination. It goes without saying that time is often a vital component of any dream or scheme. An idea that came to nothing at any given time could be valid in six months or a year. A phone call might work wonders at one moment instead of another. Nevertheless, the best decision is to do it now. All wealthy people have shown the remarkable ability to make rapid-fire decisions. Even in matters involving big money, they acted much faster than we realize. All things being relative, you might object that the sums they were playing around with, considerable in the eyes of most common mortals, were a pittance to them. This is not the case, however. Their on-the-spot decisions were often made at the beginning of their careers, putting their entire fortunes, meagre back then, on the line.

One of those whose success largely depended on the ability to come to a speedy decision was Conrad Hilton. While still young, Hilton vaguely thought of becoming a banker. Heeding his friend's advice to check out banking possibilities in Texas, he went to San Francisco and

happened to see a hotel which he was thinking about buying. Years later, a reporter from *Nation's Business* asked:

> 'So . . . you looked at the books and decided this was a
> good proposition. Right?'
> 'I saw that it was much better than banking. I
> hadn't taken over the hotel 24 hours before I decided,
> "this is what I am going to do. This is my life".'
> 'Your mind was set from then?'
> 'Right there, I made up my mind. I didn't want
> anything else. That was in 1919. Certainly the banker
> raising the price $5,000 steered me off banking. But
> what really did it was going over there and seeing the
> bustle, having the owner tell me about all the business
> that he was doing, how the trains were coming in
> there at night and the money he was making. When
> he showed me the books, I figured that I could get all
> of my money back in one year.'

Notice that Hilton had made up his mind before the owner
had even shown him the books. This will surely rile all
those who advocate long feasibility studies! It should
nevertheless be mentioned that Hilton had seen the hotel
and been struck by its extraordinary opulence.

Hilton started out in business with the paltry sum of
$5,000, including $3,000 from his inheritance and $2,000
in savings. By purchasing this hotel, he was gambling
every penny he had. Making a decision out of the blue
like this is comparable to falling in love at first sight.
Besides Hilton, many of the others in this book
experienced this kind of 'instant love' throughout their
careers. It wouldn't even be stretching the truth to say
that they wouldn't make a decision without it. These men,
who were so persuasive when convinced of something,
never let their advisers, friends, or facts and figures
change their minds. Often they followed advice only if
it confirmed their initial ideas. It should be mentioned,
however, that their stubbornness did betray them at
times, making them lose a lot of money. Despite this, their
determination made them heed their inner voices, and this
was one of the determining factors in their success.

In the case mentioned above, Hilton had seen the small
hotel's potential rather than its current productivity. At

the same time he had a mental picture of how to make it produce a profit. This is how he explained it in the same interview:

> I saw, around the hotel, we were not getting what we should out of the space. So I changed it, and I have kept that as a rule throughout my life, to find out what is the best use I could make of space. You see, you can either lose your money or you can make it, depending upon whether you know what the public wants. You have to know that and give them the most space available.
>
> I figured out that customers at the Mobley [Hotel in San Francisco] could get food someplace else, and that they didn't need the hotel dining room. So we put beds in there. We were making no money on the food, and the rooms were in terrific demand. Today you might find that the best use of space is in a restaurant.
>
> Another thing was building *esprit de corps* among the help. We got all the employees together and told them that they were largely responsible for whether the guests of the hotel were pleased and would ever come back. I have done that throughout my life.

Hilton made snap judgements throughout his life, and his optimism and boldness were rewarded more often than not. Instead of harping on the obstacles preventing him from financing his schemes, he told himself that he would find a way around them. And he did!

The lives of these 10 men reveal that all of them at one point or another had to burn their bridges behind them, cutting off all retreat. This usually involved giving up a job offer without knowing what lay in store for them or investing all of their money in some venture of other. In either case, failure would be catastrophic. It was do or die!

Honda illustrates this principle in his autobiography. After having been a somewhat successful industrialist, he encountered technical problems so great that he had to hit the books again at the University of Hamasatsu when he was over 30 years old. He wasn't able to produce a piston flexible enough to function in an engine. Here is what he had to say about this:

Every morning from then on I went to school and, at
night, put everything I had learned during the day
into practice. I forced myself to be enthusiastic
because I had no choice in the matter. And yet, when
you put yourself in situations with only one
alternative, you get a new feeling of freedom: making
a decision that you can't back down from. A thousand
reasons crossed my mind to justify why I had to keep
on going. My friends and, above all, my father, but
also the employees working for me, all had faith in
me. I no longer had the right to turn back, and school
was the only way I had to overcome this situation, to
become a real engineer capable of doing engineering
jobs, to discover the theories behind my technical
intuitions and to put them into practice. I solemnly
told myself: 'If I give up now, everyone will die of
hunger.' And I pictured in my mind the poor, pathetic
people who depended on me.

Why is the technique of putting your back to the wall and
cutting off all your exits so effective? We have already
seen that you can submit specific requests to your subconscious and even give it orders to a certain extent. We
also mentioned that, to get a speedy response, your
desires, dreams, and ambitions have to be felt intensely.
By burning all your bridges behind you, your wishes
become much more imperative, thereby activating your
instinct to survive. This in turn produces results so great
that people, unaware of this principle, come to wonder
whether successful individuals are gifted with the ability to influence the outcome of events!

By making a snap decision and scorning the obstacles
he might possibly confront, Hilton put himself in a do-or-
die situation, cutting off all his exits, and results followed
almost miraculously. He, of course, started out with a positive mental programme. His subconscious was clearly
directed towards success. Moreover, he depended on his
intuition, an ability which is simply the special capacity
to enter into contact with a positive subconscious mind.
Besides, what else is a flash of inspiration, but a sudden
revelation of the subconscious which means that the
external object, opportunity or deal (in Hilton's case, a
small hotel) matches a specific type of programming

exactly? In other words, Conrad Hilton had programmed his subconscious to make a fortune. His conscious mind (whose power is limited, as we have seen) wanted him to buy a bank. He even had the opportunity and financial backing of a friend to do so. But his subconscious, which knew what was good for him, realized that he was destined to become a brilliant hotel operator and led him to that small hotel. His intuitive response was, as always, the conscious revelation of what was registered in his subconscious. This coincidental encounter between the subconscious and its external manifestation sparks excitement and enthusiasm.

This is why you will always be able to rely on your sixth sense as soon as you have learned how to programme your subconscious. This ability, the cornerstone of success, will increasingly develop as you learn how to make good use of this part of your mind. It will even become second nature to you in the long run. You will soon be able to command the most powerful computer of all — the subconscious mind. It will enable you to make faster and more reliable decisions.

Haste hinders good counsel, so the proverb goes. There is undoubtedly a grain of truth in this, and yet procrastination and slowness surely do more wrong than hasty decisions. If these 10 men erred on the side of excess, it was in making snap decisions. But that was how they got rich.

But how is it possible to know when to make a decision? How do you know whether you have examined the situation enough and have all the necessary facts at your disposal? The answer is to rely on your subconscious. Programme it by repeating: 'My subconscious immediately gives me the right answer.'

Sleep is the mother of counsel. Nothing rings truer than this old adage because we can easily contact our subconscious at night. So, sleep on your problem. Write all the facts you know about it, listing all the pros and cons. This might seem obvious to you, but this technique is invaluable for clearing up doubt. If the scale tips in favour of one side at first, your decision will be easy. If the pros and cons balance out, let your subconscious deal with it. It will come up with an answer — the right one!

WHY NOT TOSS A COIN?

You probably think this is a joke, but hang on a moment. This is merely a small trick to help you make contact with your subconscious. Of course, you must determine yourself what each side of the coin represents. Flip a coin right now. Keep a close eye on your reactions. If heads shows up, telling you to go ahead with your plan, and you are disappointed, it's probably because your subconscious doesn't really believe in it. If tails appears, it is a vital clue that you do not trust your plan and have already made up your mind without realizing it. There are four possible reactions in this game, two of which we have already described. In each case, analyse your reactions well. Don't consider the results you get as definite, but only as a means of helping you come to a decision. Experience has shown that this trivial little game often helps resolve a matter one way or another, usually for the better, especially when the pros and cons are split 50-50.

Let us add a further point: when the pros and cons balance out that evenly, it's perhaps a sign that your plan will run up against many problems or that it will not be completely successful. What is certain, however, is that the doubt persisting in your mind is a bad omen. It could eventually undermine your enthusiasm and faith. Since you only half-way believe in it already, the results you get will be in keeping with your expectations. We have already seen the importance that faith and enthusiasm have. If your plan doesn't fire you up enough, it would be best to discard it for another. The rich men in this book got involved only in projects they believed in 100 per cent, and they started out totally confident in their ultimate success.

Once you have learned how to make snap decisions and come face to face with a problem that makes you hesitate too long, beware. It could very well be the sign of an unsound proposition. This is another reason why speedy decisions are a good omen, even if the answer is 'no'. Making quick decisions is also knowing how to say 'no' quickly. This is not necessarily the product of a pessimistic mind, but only that not everything under the sun is valid, otherwise everybody would be a millionaire. However, if you systematically say 'no' to everything and never undertake anything for fear of making a mistake, it is an indication that you are poorly programmed.

Another reason why it is preferable to make hasty decisions is that good opportunities don't last forever. You must grab them while they're hot. New ones will of course knock at your door, but if you hesitate every time, you will miss out on every one of them. Hesitation can be fatal. You are not the only one in the race. If a sound opportunity crops up, remember that many others will see it too. Some of the vital facts will still be missing of course. But if you wait until you have your hands on all of them, chances are you will let the opportunity slip through your fingers.

This is what often happens to those who prefer analysing everything instead of trusting their intuition, the profound wisdom of their subconscious. Furthermore, proponents of long, in-depth analyses are inclined to forget that situations change all the time, and when they are finally ready to act, the facts they have are no longer relevant, thus their decisions are right off the mark.

In his autobiography, Lee Iacocca, who saved Chrysler from bankruptcy, makes an interesting point on this subject:

> Nothing stands still in this world. I like to go duck hunting, where constant movement and change are facts of life. You can aim at a duck and get it in your sights, but the duck is always moving. *In order to hit the duck, you have to move your gun.* But a committee faced with a major decision can't always move as quickly as the events it's trying to respond to. By the time the committee is ready to shoot, the duck has flown away.

Those who take too long to make up their minds often land in the same position as this clumsy hunter. As the old saying goes, 'Fortune favours the bold'.

TAKE A BREAK

We have just proved the necessity of making speedy decisions. Despite their boldness and daring, many success ful men have developed the habit of thinking things over one last time before taking the plunge. This 'time out' might last an hour, a few minutes, or even seconds. When you take this last-minute breather, go over all the arguments one by one. Verify the logic behind them and the way you arrived at your conclusion. Don't forget to write them down if you haven't done it yet. Writing is like using a developer in photography — without it, getting a clear picture is impossible. Then, set yourself a deadline and stop mulling your problem over. Tell yourself that in one hour, at exactly 3 p.m., for example, you will make your decision.

Better yet, sleep on it. Before falling asleep, go over all the facts and then hand them over to your subconscious to untangle. Your position will often be much clearer in the morning.

IS IT NECESSARY TO WAIT FOR THE IDEAL TIME?

The ideal time doesn't exist. It's a figment of the imagination of those who believe it exists. Most people make the mistake of waiting around for it. It's a perfect excuse, which people claim to be serious, well thought-out, the logical decision. Generally speaking, the ideal time is now. Right away. If you want to succeed, start today, this very minute.

STICK TO YOUR DECISION

One of the characteristic tendencies of the rich is that they stick to their decisions come hell or high water, regardless of everybody else's opinions, or of circumstances, obstacles, past failures or temporary setbacks.

Blindly adhering to your first option makes a lot of plans fall through. But sticking to your final decision is being logical with yourself and confirms your inner certainty that you have aimed right on target. Those who constantly change their minds will never be successful. Vacillation is a sign of a mental state gnawed by doubt. Since we have clearly seen that circumstances always end up duplicating our inner thoughts, there can be no question that doubt leads straight to failure. Consequently, success depends on two vital factors:

---

1 Making snap decisions
2 Sticking to them and jumping straight into action

HOW FAR SHOULD YOU STICK TO YOUR DECISION?

The principle of firmly upholding your decision is a general one, meaning that there are exceptions to the rule. Blindly adhering to a decision, come what may, implies that people never go wrong. Now, everybody, including the most astute entrepreneurs, makes mistakes and wrong decisions. It is therefore vital to be wary of being overly rigid and theoretical. We must learn to adapt to circumstances. One of the keys to success is finding the delicate balance between persistence and flexibility.

Sticking to your initial decision at all costs could be fatal to your success. But most people fail because they give up much too quickly.

An engineer called Mr Head had to do forty-three tests, spread out over three long years before he found a successful way of making a metal ski. If he had given up after his forty-second try, the metal ski would still have been invented and made someone a millionaire, but not Head.

Look around to see how widespread the tendency is to give up too quickly. What about you? How many times have you thrown in the towel after one or two failures? Have you ever persisted in what you were doing without getting discouraged after experiencing two failures in a row? All too often pride or a lack of self-confidence makes people give up too soon. Worse yet, they comfort themselves by saying that it was to be expected anyway. This does not mean that someone with a positive mental programme will not suffer defeat. All great success stories are punctuated with failures. The difference between positive and negative people is that the former will not let themselves be beaten down by their first blunders. If they don't succeed the first time, they always try, try again.

The lives of the richest men in the world have revealed a somewhat mysterious phenomenon. Life seems to have been designed as a test. When people have shown they could overcome obstacles and failures with unswerving calmness and faith, Life appears to lay down her weapons, in a manner of speaking, and fame and fortune appear, as if charmed by the strength of these people. Honda offered a similar observation in his life story:

> A company laboratory seems to be the best learning centre for mistakes! In fact, most researchers recognize that 99 per cent of the time they are dealing with hopeless cases. The modest percentage that survives this... is nonetheless enough to justify their efforts. Finally, I myself do not regret the thousands of times I have come home without a catch, having lost all of my bait and tackle. When days become this dark and gloomy, it means that the treasure I am looking for is about to be discovered. The great flash of light and hope that burst forth make me instantly forget my long hours of tedious work.

Napoleon Hill supports this opinion in one of his books, in which he relates that success often follows a resounding failure as if life wanted to reward the brave soul able to surmount such a devastating setback.

Determination, a quality absent in most people, is often generously rewarded. It must not, however, be confused with blind pigheadedness. The authors of *In Search of Excellence* conducted an experiment to illustrate the fact that we must watch out for dogmatism and stubbornness and learn how to adapt to circumstances (one of the secrets behind the success of the one hundred companies studied in the analysis).

'...If you place in a bottle half a dozen bees and the same number of flies, and lay the bottle down horizontally with its base to the window, you will find that the bees will persist, till they die of exhaustion or hunger, in their endeavour to discover an issue through the glass, while the flies, in less than two minutes, will all have sallied forth through the neck on the opposite side... It is their [the bees] love of light, it is their very intelligence, that is their undoing in this experiment. They evidently imagine that the issue from every prison must be there where the light shines clearest; and they act in accordance, and persist in too logical action. To them, glass is a supernatural mystery they never have met in nature; they have had no experience of this suddenly impenetrable atmosphere; and, the greater their intelligence, the more inadmissible, more incomprehensible, will the strange obstacle appear. Whereas the feather-brained flies, careless of logic as of the enigma of crystal, disregarding the call of the light, flutter wildly hither and thither, and meeting here the good fortune that often waits on the simple, who find salvation there where the wiser will perish, necessarily end by discovering the friendly opening that restores their liberty to them.'

It has thus been demonstrated that in business the ability to adapt quickly is one of the keys to success and that pragmatism and trial and error are better than idealism and dogmatism. But how do you know whether to persevere like the bees in the above-mentioned experiment or to change course to gain your freedom, your success? It would seem that the best, and possibly only, means is relying on a well-programmed subconscious. It will tell you when to keep at it, when to review your position, and when to adopt a plan better than your initial one. If you hit upon a short-cut to success after discovering new facts or following the advice of a friend, take it. You must learn to adapt your decisions to achieve even greater success. Making a new snap decision or changing your mind can often save a situation.

Mistakes will be made all the same. The best attitude to adopt with respect to blunders is the one shared by the 10 men described in this book. You must abhor making mistakes before the fact. However, you must not take for granted that you will make them before you do. This breeds passivity and submissiveness. You must accept them after having made them. This is what successful people do. Once again, TAKE ACTION! Regardless of the ever-present possibility of going wrong, the law of numbers favours those who make many attempts. The ideal situation would be to minimize the incidence of miscarried attempts. Successful ones will largely compensate for occasional flops whether you are searching for a job, starting up a company, or launching a product. Frankly, what is it to you if you get five doors slammed in your face when the sixth one opens up with an exciting prospect, offering you what you have been looking for all the time: the perfect job?

LEARN TO FORGET YOUR FAILURES!

One of the most indispensable skills to acquire on the road to riches is the subtle art of forgetting your failures and turning towards the future. Those who cannot do this are often paralysed by the spectre of past mistakes. They literally live in the past and fear the future. This is really too bad. They believe that because they failed once or twice or 10 times they are talentless or unlucky.

The rich all went through this, but it didn't stop them in their tracks. You must not look back or linger over the past. Life is ahead of you. Go for it!

LEARN FROM YOUR MISTAKES!

Each failure is a lesson unto itself. It has been said that people learn more from their failures than from their successes. They put themselves into question, analyse their ideas, methods and concepts, and benefit from this experience. There is no shame in making a mistake. What is generally a waste is making the same mistake twice. Straighten out your ideas about failure. If you have thoughtfully reasoned out why you failed, you will gain a clearer understanding of how to succeed. In this sense, each failure leads you closer to success. This is not only a paradox, but a truth, as witnessed by the experience of these 10 rich men.

One of the most articulate individuals on the decision-making process and one who had a remarkable success throughout his life was Paul Getty, the oil baron long considered to be the richest man in the world. The next chapter contains his life story, an almost perfect balance between thought and action. In fact, at the end of his fruitful existence, Paul Getty could have repeated the philosopher Bergson's motto: 'Act like a man of thought; think like a man of action.'

PAUL GETTY

Paul Getty, the son of George Franklin Getty and Sarah MacPherson Risher, was born in 1892. His father, coming from a poor Irish family, went through a poverty-stricken childhood and was forced at an early age to work for local farmers to support his widowed mother.

When George Getty was 12 years old, a rich uncle of his paid for his schooling in Ohio. A few years later, he graduated with a degree in science and became a teacher, a job he held for a few years. He was ambitious, however, a trait he was to pass down to his son. At the age of 27, he achieved a long-lasting ambition: he obtained a degree in law, graduating with distinction from the University of Michigan. Several years later, be became a magistrate.

According to some of Paul Getty's biographers, Sarah MacPherson Risher was the driving force behind her husband and son's fortunes. She was an ambitious and determined woman and urged her husband to give up teaching in favour of law, which was to be his first step on the road to riches. It would transform a small-time Michigan lawyer into one of the pioneers of the American oil industry. The year 1903 marked a decisive turning point for the Getty family, making it one of the richest families in America.

A client's legal problem sent George Getty to Bartlesville, Oklahoma. After settling this matter, he became infected with oil fever. Heeding the advice of a few oil drillers, he bought a 1,000-acre lot of land called 'Lot 50'. Drilling operations began soon after, and 43 wells were drilled. Of them, 42 were productive! George Getty then founded the Minnehoma Oil Company and firmly decided to devote himself exclusively to the search for 'black gold'.

Although Paul Getty was only 11 years old at the time, he remembered vividly until the end of his life the emotion he felt upon catching his first glimpse of an oil field.

> In retrospect, I think I was already — at some level — responding to the lure of oil. No, not to the business or profit aspects of petroleum industry operations, but to the challenge and adventure inherent in field operations, in the hunt — the exploration and drilling — for oil.

The young boy's encounter with this mysterious gushing force struck a passionate chord in him, sparking a challenge that he would shortly take up.

It was not uncommon to see him wandering around Lot 50, comfortably chatting with the professional drilling crew in conversations laced with oil-field jargon as if he were one of them. Although Getty learned quickly there, it was quite a different story at school. In 1906, his father, a strict man who was determined that his son would learn that money doesn't grow on trees, decided that a year at Harvard Military Academy would be the best medicine for him, teaching him the value of self-discipline.

Paul Getty later went to university, spending his summer holidays working as a roustabout on his father's oil leases. His father's only condition was that he be treated just like all the other labourers. He received the going wage, which was three dollars for a 12-hour day. Getty had to obey orders like everybody else. He adapted very quickly to rough living and working conditions and enjoyed them fully, unlike university life, where he had the impression of going nowhere!

Put off by the American educational system, which according to him stifled individual freedom, he left the United States in 1912 to study at Oxford. He spent a year there, reading economics and political science, two subjects which fascinated him. He graduated and finally returned to America with four career possibilities ahead of him.

On the one hand, his studies and personality inclined

him to become a writer. On the other, his passion for political science meant that he was interested in entering the US Diplomatic Corps. Furthermore, since the Second World War had just broken out, he had enlisted in the Air Force in hope of becoming a pilot. His fourth and, in his eyes, least appealing option, was to enter the world of business. On the advice of his father, who asked him to spend a year in business before coming to a final career decision, Getty returned to Oklahoma, but this time as a prospector. It was agreed that he would prospect for oil for $100 a month. His father would furnish the capital for the leases and they would split the profits 70-30, with the lion's share going to Getty Senior.

Months passed and nothing happened. Getty confessed later on that he had been tempted several times to drop everything. And yet, the idea of failure was something he simply could not tolerate.

> A hatred of failure has always been part of my nature and, I suppose, one of the more pronounced motivating forces in my life

In his autobiography, *As I See It*, he stated:

> It is not that I love success for its own sake. However, once I have committed myself to any undertaking, a powerful inner drive cuts in and I become intent on seeing it through to a satisfactory conclusion. In most fields of endeavour, I have been successful more often than not. When my efforts resulted in failure, I did everything possible to ensure that my mistakes were not repeated.

Towards the end of the year, an opportunity finally arrived. Having heard that an especially promising lease was up for auction, Getty decided to go for it. He thought up a ruse to outsmart his competitors, who were much richer than he was and just as determined to get their hands on this concession. He asked one of his friends, the vice-president of a local bank, to represent him at the auction and to bid for him without revealing his identity. The other contenders, automatically believing that he was standing in for a major oil company, didn't even bother to bid. Getty had won. He got the lease for the sum of $500 when it could easily have gone for $15,000!

The property known as 'The Nancy Taylor Allotment' spearheaded Getty's fortune. Spurred on by this transaction, Getty promptly formed a company to finance the drilling operations. His own lack of capital nevertheless forced him to make do with 15 per cent of the shares. Once he had hired all the drillers and labourers he needed, work began. Getty himself rolled up his sleeves and got down to work, sometimes putting in up to 72 hours without a break.

At the beginning of 1916, following months of tireless efforts, the hoped-for results materialized. The well began producing 30 barrels an hour, 700 a day. Henceforth, Getty's life was to be inextricably linked to this black gold.

Getty had instinctively adhered to a principle which would serve him well during his entire lifetime:

Recognize, seize, and take advantage of market opportunities

A series of new discoveries and profitable transactions soon followed, so that, by the end of 1916, Paul Getty had made his first million. He was only 23 years old!

Geology did not then have the status it enjoys today, and many experts scoffed at the idea that oil could be discovered by studying books or by relying on scientific methods. The popular notion was that you needed to be gifted like a diviner to smell oil out. Getty, however, threw himself heart and soul into studying geology. As a result, he stayed ahead of his competitors, activating a principle that can only lead to success:

Acquire solid background knowledge of your field while steering your thoughts and mental energy towards your goal

---

Strangely enough for a man just on the brink of his career, Getty decided to retire at the age of 24! He had become a millionaire and, believing that he could go no further, made up his mind to put an end to his oil adventure. He chose to lead a life of luxury in California. He quickly became a well-known figure in Los Angeles. In the eyes of several of his biographers, this murky period doesn't quite fit with his usual rigour, order, and self-discipline. So, at the end of 1918, it surprised no one that Getty became disgusted with the life he was leading and realized that he was wasting his time.

Getty nonetheless learned a vital lesson from his two wild and foolish years. From then on he knew that:

Money must be viewed purely as a means to an end

Imbued with this principle, he dived headlong back into work, determined to stick to his decision to the end. He was about to do battle on two fronts. He continued conducting joint ventures with his father, all the while financing independent enterprises with his own capital. Unfortunately, his first private venture failed miserably, and cost him $100,000. After buying an oil lease, he hired a contractor to oversee the drilling operations, since he was kept busy tending to his father's business affairs and by commuting back and forth between California and Oklahoma. When he discovered that the work was being neglected, Getty realized that he had made a serious mistake. He paid up his debts, swearing never to let that happen to him again. He later wrote:

> . . . whether operating in association with my father or on my own account, I acted as my own drilling superintendent.

> Another secret is never to delegate your authority in strictly administrative matters, 'If you want a thing done well, do it yourself,' said Benjamin Franklin. I do everything myself

Barely five years after his private drilling operations began, Getty's net assets were worth approximately $3 million, almost entirely reinvested in his oil leases. Getty had been right to apply these principles and become his own master!

Besides tripling his fortune in the 1920s and 1930s, Getty also got married. In fact, he went through five marriages and five divorces. He candidly confesses:

> How and why is it that I have been able to build my own automobile, drill oil wells, run an aircraft plant, build and head a business empire — yet remain unable to maintain even one satisfactory marital relationship?

In April 1930, tragedy struck the Getty family. George Franklin Getty, then aged 75, died following a heart attack. Paul Getty lost not only a father, but a friend and adviser as well. Since he already had his own fortune, his father left him only $500,000. All the rest went to his mother. George Getty's fortune was estimated at $15.5

million. Paul was nevertheless appointed President of Minnehoma Oil and Gas Company and of George F. Getty, Inc.

Unfortunately, after his father's death, Getty realized that his spirit of initiative, taste for calculated risks, ambition, and his desire to think big didn't fit in very well with his mother's conservative ideas regarding the future policy and direction of the Getty interests.

America was grappling with severe economic depression. Several oilmen had lost everything and many an empire came crashing down as quickly as it had shot up. The mere idea of expansion terrorized all but the shrewdest millionaires at the time. Even Getty's financial advisers urged him to liquidate everything, given the prevailing economic conditions. But Getty didn't see things that way at all. For him, the time was ripe for buying, not selling.

> # He had abiding faith in the future

So he bought. Right in the middle of the economic recession holding sway over the country, he began acquiring oil leases at cut-rate prices. His view was that:

> # Any businessman who goes against popular opinion must expect to be thwarted, scoffed at, and cursed. This is what made my fortune

Getty had one other major advantage over his competitors: he thought big!

This frame of mind led Getty to conceive the idea of a totally independent oil company, which would not only control the transportation and refining of crude oil, but also export the finished product. As such, he would no longer need to rely on middlemen to market his product and would increase his profits substantially. This is when he went searching for control of a refinery. One interested him in particular: the Tide Water Associated Oil Company. Yet, the company's top management systematically opposed his attempts to take over the helm. This was to be the beginning of a long battle. In 1932, he bought 1,200 shares of the company at $2.50 per share. Six weeks later he acquired an additional 39,000 shares, hoping that the board of directors of George F. Getty, Inc. and Minnehoma would support him in his struggle.

However, his expansionist views considerably worried Sarah Getty, who squarely refused to back him in his financial war and to reimburse the capital he had invested in the family firm. She even went so far as to oust him completely from all the Getty interests.

By then he had gone too far to stop. He decided to put everything into it. He founded his own company, transferring all of his shares from the family business into it. He then decided to do everything possible to acquire a controlling interest in Tide Water. This was when he learned that the real owner was Standard Oil, the financial giant created by Rockefeller.

> Had I known this originally, I would never have begun buying Tide Water shares, for a pigmy independent operator such as I could hardly stand a chance against one of the world's largest and most powerful major oil companies. But, by the time I discovered the truth, I was too deeply committed to withdraw from the fray.

Through sheer work and wily manoeuvres as well, David managed to outsmart Goliath. In 1952, after 20 years of constant financial wrangling, Paul Getty finally became the major stockholder.

Once committed I always try never to give up, but do my best to beat my opponent

This man's soaring rise seemed to have no limits. Getty now spent part of his time in Europe, overseeing his interests, which were beginning to span the entire continent. His dream of expansion and the global operations he intended to pursue made him willing to live out of a suitcase. He lived in hotels without ever bothering to unpack his bags, stuffed with his personal effects and working documents. His office was wherever his secretary opened his battered brown overnight bag. It was not uncommon for him to work for 12 hours a day, and he later admitted that he would sometimes work 14 or more hours a day.

In 1938, Getty temporarily set aside the oil industry and purchased the famous Hotel Pierre in New York City for $2,350,000, less than a quarter of its original worth. Getty also began investing in art and was soon to become one of the richest and most envied collectors in the world. He even built the Paul Getty Museum and wrote a treatise on art.

When the Second World War broke out, Getty tried to re-enlist in the army, but the authorities had figured out a better way for him to serve his country. Through his roundabout transactions concluded during his struggle to gain control over Tide Water, Getty had acquired the Spartan Aircraft Corporation, which manufactured aircraft components. This factory was so poorly run that most other manufacturers refused to have any dealings with it. Getty was therefore asked to spend the war years at the helm of Spartan and make it productive in order to support the war effort.

Getty fulfilled his duty with the same discipline he normally employed in his other business affairs, and within no time at all, Spartan was being praised by aircraft manufacturers for the quality of its products. The Pentagon even went so far as to send him a letter congratulating him on the magnificent job he was doing. During these few years, the factory space was increased sevenfold and the number of employees mushroomed from about 200 to 5,000!

At the end of the Second World War, Getty saw no other alternative but to get involved in the Middle East, rumoured to be fabulously rich in oil. Breaking into this new market, coveted by all major oil producers, was not going to be an easy task to accomplish. Getty nevertheless obtained the oil concession in the so-called Neutral Zone, a territory belonging to Saudi Arabia and which had been dismissed by most producers. There was of course a price to pay. He was forced to pay license fees of 55 cents a barrel, to reimburse 25 per cent of the profits to the government, and to respect all sorts of clauses affecting the Arab employees.

In the eyes of many, Getty was a fool for signing such a contract. Many people even predicted that he would lose all his money!

During the first four years of operation, it looked as though they had been right, since not a single drop of oil came to the surface. This lasted until 1952, yet, Getty didn't let himself get discouraged.

His sixth sense told him that the oil was there for the taking, just waiting to be discovered, sooner or later. His persistence paid off in the end. In 1953, drillers hit oil. Later, Getty continued to explore the interior of the Neutral Zone, discovering that the region was indeed phenomenally rich in oil. Getty's nonconformity and refusal to pay heed to the prophets of gloom and doom had allowed him to strike it rich once again.

Whatever else I may or may not be, I have never been a conformist, at least not in the sense that I consider conventional wisdom infallible. Quite to the contrary, I have often found that there is nothing more flawed and unreliable than conventional wisdom. This, it has been my experience, applies in all spheres of human endeavour.

While I have seldom if ever set out purposely and with malice aforethought to flout convention and demolish icons, I have never felt obliged to do this, that or another thing merely because it was what 'others' were doing

Paul Getty's anonymity persisted until 1957 when *Fortune*, the American magazine, published a list of the 10 largest fortunes in the United States. Getty came out on top. Newspapers got hold of this news and soon his name was on everybody's lips. He was called 'the richest man in the world'.

He belonged to that special set of exceptional human beings incapable of calculating their private wealth. He commented that if you could still calculate your fortune it was because you hadn't hit the fabulous billion-dollar mark yet.

How did Getty manage to become 'the richest man in the world' in the numerous fields where he exercised his business genius? What is this mental attitude, this secret that leads people to the pinnacle of fame and fortune? Getty revealed it to us in his own way:

> ## Whether you like it or not, there is such a thing as a millionaire's mentality

It's up to you to decide which category you want to be in. It's also entirely up to you to grab hold of your destiny, telling yourself that man, unlike any other living species, is endowed with a special privilege: the right to choose!

Paul Getty died at the age of 83 on June 6, 1976 at Sutton Place, his home in England. He left his beneficiaries the task of settling an estate worth over $4 billion!

In conclusion, remember this principle: the best decision you could ever make is to take action. Now. Success doesn't wait, and it shuns those who are afraid to grab it. Act now! All successful men have been men of action.

Some will object that this is precisely what paralyses them: they are not men of action. They are afraid of confronting the unknown, of failure, of taking risks.

The best remedy for fear is action

This is why you must not wait until you get rid of your fear of taking action. Act now, regardless of your fear. It will disappear while you are executing your plan. During this time, you will develop a new habit — a supremely important one: taking action. Thackery wrote these thought-provoking lines:

Sow a thought, and you reap an action; sow an action, and you reap a habit; sow a habit, and you reap a character; sow a character, and you reap a destiny.

THE BEST WAY TO GROW RICH

'I would have liked to have set up my own business, but I didn't have the talent or skills I thought it required.'

'My dream was to become a writer, but my father disapproved; so, I became a civil servant.'

'My job bores me to tears, but there's so much unemployment that I'd better not kid myself about finding a new one.'

'I used to dream of being a lawyer, but I didn't think I had what it takes to get through law school; so, I decided to do something else.'

How often have you heard avowals such as these, or variations on the same theme? How often have you yourself had similar muddled thoughts? Out of every 10 people, how many can boast of really enjoying their jobs? They are few and far between, in fact. Unfortunately, most people simply don't like what they do. The most tragic thing about all of this is that they are convinced that their hands are tied, that they will never be able to change their situations; in other words, that fate has permanently sentenced them to a life of mediocrity and drudgery.

If you find yourself in this position and dislike your job, which only frustrates you, think about the following question: don't you find it sad and even tragic that you will die without ever having done what you really want to do? Aren't you worth more than that? Don't you think that society has tricked and cheated you by preventing you from doing what pleases you?

Take a typical day in your life. You work eight hours, doing a job you hate, then sleep eight hours. This leaves you with another eight hours, eight miserable hours that you use to recover, trying to forget the frustrations heaped on you during your day. What kind of life is this? A pretty sad one, don't you think? And yet, you keep on doing it, believing you must.

This passive, fatalistic view is wrong. Nothing obliges you to keep working at a job you don't like. You can do something about it. There is a job for you that can impassion you as much as, if not more than, your current one. And you could start doing it right now. Immediately. This is not an empty promise. Why not get started as you read these words? Is life so poorly designed that it is meant to frustrate you constantly and deprive you of what you truly want? Impossible! Life is not that bad. It gives you exactly what your faith and self-image expect.

> # Life gives you exactly what you expect from it

What prevents most people from getting what they want is that they believe it is impossible. According to the principles stated previously, they get exactly what they expect from life: boredom, frustration, obstacles, and low incomes. People are what they believe themselves to be.

Think about your life as it is and especially how you picture it to be. If you are not doing what you would like to be doing (as can be normally expected), look back on your life. Make a list right now of six reasons supporting your belief that you cannot do what truly pleases you.

1 ....

2 ....

3 ....

4 ....

5 ....

6 ....

Now go over your list point by point and think about each reason you have written down. Are these obstacles really valid? Whatever they are (excluding a severe mental handicap or illiteracy, both improbable in this case, since you wouldn't be reading this book), there is no way that they can stand up to a serious and realistic analysis. Let us stress the word realistic, since people generally tend to accuse legitimate ambitions of being 'unrealistic'.

Denying our personal inclinations and ambitions normally begins very early in life. Yet, to be happy and self-fulfilled, we must be courageous enough to be ourselves. You have allowed yourself to be thwarted and have denied your inner self in the name of conformity for far too long. This is a mistake, but fortunately, nothing is irreversible.

As you analysed your list of reasons, you might have noticed that they are the same ones preventing you from getting rich. The relationship between the two is no coincidence. In fact, we can establish the following basic principle, which will probably surprise you: to make money, lots of it, you must first do what you enjoy in life. The reason is simple. If you don't enjoy your work, you cannot do it well: this is an absolute principle. When your heart isn't in something, you experience a drastic slump in energy and motivation. You inevitably come up with mediocre results or at least with a much poorer performance than if you loved what you were doing. It follows as a rule of thumb that your boss, associates, or clients, whatever the case may be, cannot be 100 per cent satisfied with what you accomplish.

If you are an employee, the chances are low that you will get promoted to a more interesting position or receive a substantial rise. If you are in business, the chances are high that your firm will not flourish. The monetary rewards you get will reflect this. When you receive poor compensation for your work, your motivation plummets and the quality of your work with it. It's a vicious circle!

Furthermore, people rarely work alone. If you hate your job, your enthusiasm is low, and you will drag your colleagues down with you. This is why one of the fundamental keys to success is to do what you enjoy doing.

Mark McCormack, the author of that excellent book, *What They Don't Teach You at Harvard Business School*, comments on job dissatisfaction, emphasizing this point:

> Boredom occurs when the learning curve flattens out. It can happen to anyone at any level of the corporation. In fact, it occurs most often in successful people who need more challenge and stimulation than do others.
>
> One of the sure signs of incipient boredom is knowing your job too well, or knowing all the right buttons to push. I simply will not allow this to happen to myself.
>
> I find that I am redefining my job all the time, taking on new tasks, or constantly creating new challenges for myself. If I reach some goal, either personal or corporate, that goal immediately becomes a step in the learning process toward another, more ambitious goal.
>
> This, I believe, is how people grow in their jobs and grow in importance to their company.

He then argues forcefully:

> If you're bored it's your fault. You just aren't working hard enough at making your job interesting. It is also probably the reason you haven't been offered anything better. Find out what you love to do and you will be successful at it.

When we declare that you must love your work, in no way are we suggesting that your ideal job will be devoid of frustration, disappointment, and problems. It won't necessarily be heaven on earth every day. But it's a little like true love. The deep bonds linking two people make them forget or overcome the short-lived dilemmas and obstacles that crop up along the way.

Some people don't really know whether they like their jobs or not. Admittedly, even the 10 wealthy men, who unanimously loved their work, went through temporary, but very real, periods of discouragement, depression and even self-doubt. If you want to find out if you really love your work, we propose that you take this little test, which is simple, but highly effective if you answer honestly:

If you won a million dollars, would you stay in your present job

---

If your answer is 'yes', congratulations! You obviously like what you do. Our 10 men would all have answered in the affirmative. Their lives prove that their work was their passion. They not only made a million dollars, but several hundred million...

When talking about the very rich, people who are poor and often hate their jobs to boot, often say: 'If I were in their shoes, I'd stop working and travel around the world.' They don't seem to understand that, even if money is an important consideration in the lives of the rich, what really goads them into action is loving their work and constantly desiring to do new things, to take up new challenges, and to face new risks.

This is why the rich rarely take holidays. True, their numerous obligations often preclude their taking time off, but the real reason is that work is their passion. For them, working is a pleasure, a leisure activity. This is also why they often work late into the night and don't hesitate to put in 15- or 18-hour days.

Rest assured, working so hard didn't kill them. Far from it. Besides, most of the 10 men lived to a ripe old age and worked until just before their deaths. Retirement made no sense to them. What a contrast between them and those whose sole ambition is to retire and who rejoice over 'liberal' policies recommending 'early retirement'. Those people have withdrawn from life and forgotten who they are. They are part of the 'living dead'.

If you want to live a long and happy life, do what you enjoy doing. One of the principle causes of ageing is stress and frustration. To stay eternally young inside, you must respect your heart's desires and do what you enjoy.

Steven Spielberg once said: 'The worst thing this notoriety can bring... is to make me lazy.' He was joking, no doubt. Despite his billion-dollar fortune, he puts in around

100 hours a week when shooting a film. And he creates hit after hit.

Funnily enough, the way the rich and those who love their jobs feel about work is exactly the reverse of how others look at it. Most people unwillingly drag themselves to work on Monday morning and watch the clock until Friday afternoon when they can finally throw off the shackles they have had to endure for five long and painful days. They only really live for two out of seven days, without taking into consideration that Saturday is generally spent winding down and Sunday is already haunted by the gloomy spectre of Monday-morning blues.

This makes no sense at all to people who love their jobs. A day off, a welcome relief for most people, is almost a form of punishment for the others. One thing is certain: it's not something they pine for.

The great French mathematician and philosopher Blaise Pascal once said:

> The past and present are our means; our one and only future, the end. Thus, we never manage to live, but forever hope to live, and since we are constantly planning on being happy one day, it is inevitable that we never are.

Thomas Watson, one of the creators of the formidable corporation, IBM, continually repeated to his salesmen:

> You'll never be successful if you don't convince yourself that selling is the most interesting thing in the world. Make room in your heart for work and put some heart into your work.

The following confession should prove to you that we were not being facetious when we said that depriving a rich man of his work was to punish him. Soichiro Honda himself even used the word 'punishment'.

> 'When people see me working in the lab, some of them snidely remark that the general has donned his battle fatigues. And yet, God knows that I don't go there with a tragic or military feeling. I go for the simple reason that I love working and it's not because

I'm the president that I'm going to deprive myself of
this pleasure. Why should a man, on the pretext that
he is a company president, spend the entire day
twiddling his thumbs behind a desk? Of course there
are other ways to occupy yourself. I don't want to
sound condescending, but I do believe that some
executives prefer busying themselves with facts and
figures or polishing their images instead of coming
down to the workshop. The fact is that it would be
painful for an engineer like me to devote himself to
accounting, especially since I'm lucky enough to have
skilled experts in this field working for me. I've
always supposed that being a president shouldn't be a
punishment.'

Here are a few principles you should reflect on:

● You can do whatever you like, provided you put the
  necessary energy and determination into it

● There is an ideal job or career waiting just for you. You
  must start believing it exists

● Having to do unpleasant things to earn a living is a
  fallacy

● The only way to be happy and make lots of money is
  to do what you really and truly enjoy doing

● You alone can shape your destiny and do what you
  enjoy, regardless of obstacles

● The greatest barrier to success is within yourself. What
  is preventing you from doing what you like is your
  belief that what is valid for others is not valid for you

● Dare to do what you wish. Get rid of your fear and you
  shall succeed

Nowadays our thoughts are frequently divorced from our
emotions. We try to reason everything out. We deny our
feelings and stifle our dreams. We don't believe in putting our hearts into our work. We simply put our heads
into it. Unfortunately, most people forget that human
beings are whole entities. If your heart isn't in what you
are doing, success will always elude your grasp. Or if you

do grab hold of it, it will soon slip away. We have already mentioned that if you want to achieve your dreams, you must constantly feed them. If your heart is not in your work, find a new job. Or try discovering a new dimension or fresh challenges in your work.

Some people slander successful men and women. They often believe that the rich are crass materialists, cold and calculating, and devoid of all human emotion. What they tend to forget is that all of them are ruled by passion and many by their hearts as well. They are, in fact, 'romantics' in the world of business. They carried their dreams, which were often conceived in childhood, in their hearts and did everything they could to achieve them.

The most startling example of this type of romantic is undeniably the brilliant movie director, Steven Spielberg. Nothing seems more outrageous and idealistic than the idea of earning a living in motion pictures. And yet a young man, penniless and without contacts, who was even denied entry into film school, managed to fulfil his dream.

STEVEN SPIELBERG

July 15, 1985. This is the third time that *Time* magazine has dedicated its cover story to Steven Spielberg, the Hollywood megastar. The first major account described the making of *Jaws* back in 1975, while the great white shark was scaring and titillating moviegoers worldwide.

Then in 1982, a second article heralding *ET* and *Poltergeist* was moved off the cover, overshadowed by the war in the Falkland Islands.

In July 1985, an article paid tribute to the talent of Spielberg, who is obsessed with making us delve into the marvellous, yet at the same time nightmarish, world of childhood.

His own childhood is, in fact, the primary focus of attention in his films. *Time* correspondent Denise Worrell explains: 'Reporting on Spielberg's life and work is indeed a process of re-entering the world of youth . . .' This is the secret of his genius, which has not only helped him become the most powerful director in Hollywood, if not the entire world, but has also allowed him to acquire a fortune while doing what he has always most wanted to do.

Steven Spielberg still believes in 'blood brothers' to this very day. Each conversation with him makes people relive secret childhood rituals and rekindles the solemn oaths of eternal friendship.

Spielberg's world is not only goodness and light, however. It is also a world of menace and darkness, peopled with unknown entities and hideous dreams of our own fears. Fear that slowly turns into wonder, the ordinary spinning into the extraordinary, a disturbing trip from darkness to light: this is the journey that forces us to re-experience our haunting fears and rediscover the inexpressible happiness we jealously guard in the depths of our hearts!

Needless to say, Spielberg lives with his head in the clouds. And yet, his feet are also firmly planted on earth, an earth which is middle-class, white, well-off, suburban, and very North American — in appearance, at least! He himself admits: 'I think I'm Peter Pan, I really do.' It's not surprising, then, that he is frequently compared to one of his many idols: Walt Disney. Like Disney, he sees (and films) everything as if we were barely two feet tall. His world is definitely viewed through the eyes of a child!

His movies, however, reflect even more the influence of another one of his mentors: Alfred Hitchcock. Yet they are always imbued with *humour*, since humour is the last bastion of childhood happiness. Moreover, Spielberg's movies always tend to place the most ordinary of characters in the most extraordinary of circumstances. Simply put, what he does is pure *magic!*

The creator of this delightfully magical world was born on December 18, 1947 in Cincinnati, Ohio. His earliest memory is symptomatic of the fantasy world he would later reproduce in his films. This is how it is described in *Time* magazine:

All is darkness — as dark as a minute to midnight on the first day of creation, as dark as a movie house just before the feature starts. Then the movement begins, a tracking shot down the birth canal of a hallway, toward mystery. Suddenly, a light! A bright room filled with old men in beards and black hats: sages, perhaps, from another world. At the far end of the room, on a raised platform, is a blazing red light. The senses are suffused; the mystery deepens.

Curiously enough, this scene resembles many of those found in his films. And yet. . . it is nothing other than a visit he took with his parents to a synagogue in Cincinnati! Spielberg was about six months old at the time!

His attraction to the supernatural has become an integral part of his being.

> I guess I've been interested in strange things since I was a kid growing up in Arizona. We had a lot of starry nights. I remember when my father woke me up one night and took me to a hillside at about 3 a.m. He spread out a blanket and we sat there and watched a fabulous meteor shower. It was... extraordinary! I wanted to know what put those points of light up there.
>
> I was born in the same year [1947] that Kenneth Arnold sighted what he coined the flying saucer. There was [sic] perhaps 10,000 sightings prior to his experience, but he coined the term... So, growing up, I was part of that psychosis — seeing strange lights in the sky, imagining what it would be like to see someone from up there... right here.

Family life was to play a leading role in Spielberg's world. His father, an electrical engineer, was part of the team that built the first computers. In the late 1940s and early 1950s, the computer industry was scattered across the US, causing the Spielbergs to pick up and move quite frequently. In 13 years, Steven moved from Cincinnati, Ohio to Haddonfield, New Jersey, to Scottsdale, Arizona, and finally to Saratoga, a suburb of San José, California. He was just on the brink of getting used to his new environment when they had to move again.

According to Spielberg, his parents had very little in common. They were both passionately fond of classical music and adored their children. But that was it! His father was a fanatic about details, accuracy and punctuality. This led Spielberg to comment that his father spoke only two languages: English and Computerese!

Steven's own interests lay elsewhere and he made his parents understand that the only way he could.

> When I was about 11 my dad came home and gathered us all in the kitchen. He held up a tiny little transistor he had brought home and said, 'This is the future.' I took the transistor from his hand, and I put it in my mouth. And I swallowed it. Dad laughed,

then he didn't laugh; it got very tense... [It was] one of those moments when two worlds from diametrically opposed positions in the universe collide. It was as if I was saying, 'That's your future, but it doesn't have to be mine.'

His mother was a dynamo of energy. The whole family revolved around her. A classical pianist, she often gave recitals at home in the living room with her musician friends. Meanwhile, his father was somewhere else in the house hotly debating how to make a computerized mousetrap with his own friends, who were also in the business. Steven's only refuge was his bedroom. 'My bedroom door remained closed for most of my life,' he later said. He even stuffed towels under the door to block out the sound of the piano and the scientific arguments!

He was first introduced to motion pictures when his mother presented his father with a cine camera for his birthday to 'collect memories on film'. The only problem was that his father didn't have an ounce of movie-making talent. Steven, 12 years old at the time, was utterly fascinated with this 8 mm camera and clearly appalled by his father's lack of knowhow. 'I had to sit, as I'm sure everyone has, through home-movies!'

Either the picture weaved up and down or the subject was so blurry as to be unrecognizable. In short, all the typical errors of an amateur were displayed before the horrified eyes of this budding movie director. One day during one of these picture-taking sessions, he calmly told his father, 'You're not holding the camera steady enough. This doesn't make sense.' His father, just as serene, took the camera and handed it over to him and said, '*You* be the family photographer. *You* take the pictures.' From then on, Spielberg was firmly set on making movies.

It was an escape for me, a great escape

It opened the door to fantasy; it was his royal road to escape, far from reality, from daily routine, from school

with the bullies who scared the daylights out of him, and
from his fears of the dark and especially from his parents,
who seemed to be about to get divorced.

From then on, he had a single goal; to make movies!

But, there is quite a gap between wishing and doing. For
the time being, he had to put up with his parents' endless quarrels. Steven, of course, had a pretty good idea
of what was going on.

> I don't think they were aware of how acutely we
> were aware of their unhappiness — not violence, just
> a pervading unhappiness you could cut with a fork or
> a spoon at dinner every night. For years I thought the
> word 'divorce' was the ugliest in the English
> language. Sound travelled from bedroom to bedroom,
> and the word came seeping through the heating ducts.
> My sisters and I would stay up at night, listening to
> our parents argue, hiding from that word. And when
> it travelled to our room, absolutely abject panic set in.
> My sisters would burst into tears, and we would all
> hold one another.

This, besides his other obsessive fears, was the horrid reality Steven wanted to escape from. When he was a child,
he says, 'I had all the fears most kids have,' meaning
unearthly creatures hiding under his bed, hideous mon-
sters skulking in his closet, and the terrible things that
the ogres he cooked up in his head would do to him. How
many times did Steven see the real evil tree in *Poltergeist*
looming wickedly outside his bedroom window? The pro-
tagonist's nightmares duplicated his own. In short, the evil
and terrorizing world of his films already inhabited his
mind. For him, it was a daily reality.

It was through the magical eye of his camera that Spielberg was finally able to exorcise his demons and make
them his allies, paving the way for his success.

I made my dreams reality

This neatly sums up the key to Spielberg's success. By the age of 36, he had accumulated a monolithic fortune and become one of the most powerful people in film making, the Disney of modern times.

His passion for movies and the 'lights in the sky' soon took concrete shape. His first amateur movie, *Firelight*, was shot in 1964. He was 16 years old at the time and it was his first sci-fi movie. He had already made 15 movies, ever since he had inherited his father's 8 mm camera. And yet, in his eyes, this was his first real 'production'. His initial budget of $300 soon went up to $500 — a habit he would keep throughout his career, much to the dismay of his backers! It was also his first commercial success. His father invited friends, relatives and acquaintances, and managed to collect $600, enough to cover his expenses. A success all around!

Yet, his career had to wait until 1967 to take off. It was sparked by another film and by a chance encounter on a beach in California. He met a man there who wanted to produce movies as much as he himself did. The only substantial difference between the two was that this stranger, Dennis Hoffman, the owner of an optical company, was a millionaire! Hoffman saw some of Spielberg's 8 mm and 16 mm productions and was astounded. He gave him $10,000 to make a short film. It was a fortune in Steven's eyes! There was one condition, however: Hoffman wanted the possessory credits, meaning that the film would say 'Dennis Hoffman's *Amblin*.' Spielberg recounts: 'I said 'Fine.' I took the money and I made the film in 35 mm . . . the big time for me!'

Spielberg also met another camera fanatic — Allen Daviau, a man who was to be a long-term friend, even though they lost touch with each other for several years. Neither of them knew where they were heading but one thing was sure: they were on the road to success. This almost delirious optimism would never leave Spielberg.

Amblin, the story of a teenage boy and girl hitchhiking to California, was so well made that it even impressed the Chief at Universal Television, Sid Sheinberg. Spielberg said:

> Once again, it harkens back to my friend, Chuck
> Silvers. He took this 25-minute short film [which was
> also entered in the 1969 Venice and Atlanta film
> festivals], round to Universal, showed it to Sid
> Sheinberg and I got a call the next day — it's truly a
> Cinderella story — inviting me to his office.

He was already quite familiar with those studios. When he was 17, and visiting cousins, he wanted to see the sound stages; so, when the tram stopped, he sneaked into the studios and wandered around, completely dazzled by it all. Suddenly a man stopped him in his tracks and asked him what he was doing. Steven calmly explained about his passion for the movies, what he did, what his plans were, and so on. This man's name was Chuck Silvers, the man who would later give his career a well deserved boost. Amused by this gangly, audacious youngster (not just anybody would have the guts to walk on to a Universal lot uninvited, especially during a shooting), he talked with Spielberg for over an hour and finally gave him a day pass. The next day, Steven showed him some of his 8 mm films. He was, of course, favourably impressed, which explains his enthusiasm years later upon seeing *Amblin.*

Although this episode was soon forgotten by Silvers, it became an obsession for Spielberg. The following day, dressed in a suit and tie, his hair neatly combed, carrying a briefcase (it was his father's and contained nothing but a sandwich and two candy bars), he strode past the security guard and walked into one of the offices at Universal Pictures. In short, he became a squatter for the entire summer. He found an unused office with a phone and propped his feet up on the desk. He even went so far as to buy some plastic nameplates and register his name in the building directory! Then he started haunting the corridors, watching the thousand and one operations that go into making a movie. He vaguely hoped that providence, perhaps, would appoint someone to give him something to do... but that never happened. Fed up, he left as quietly and as unnoticed as he had entered.

Surprisingly enough, his encounter with the Big Boss, Sid Sheinberg, was going to allow him to become part of Universal Pictures officially... but to do exactly the same thing — *nothing!*

Steven recounts that this period of his life was extremely tedious and boring. He practically camped outside several executives' doors before finally being allowed to do something. The problem was simple, according to him: he was much too young and no one believed in youth there, or anywhere else for that matter.

Spielberg had faith. He believed
in his talent. He knew he was capable
of doing big things even though he
was young. He realized, however, that
it was up to him alone to create
his own lucky break

He pleaded with his boss so convincingly that Sheinberg finally managed to twist someone's arm and get him some work. At last he had what he wanted. He was going to work on the pilot film of a new TV series. Unfortunately, this involved directing one of Hollywood's most 'unmanageable' actresses: Joan Crawford!

Spielberg got through it all quite well, despite his lack of experience. This was just the beginning of the great things to come... or so he thought! He was then asked to do an episode of *Marcus Welby, MD*, then *Dr Kildare*, and then... it all ended.

He had nothing to do for a full year. He begged, cried, threatened, but the fine print of the contract he had signed, and which he had failed to read in his childish delight, clearly stipulated that he had to submit completely to Universal's whims. He couldn't even occupy his spare time making 16 mm amateur films. He was trapped! So when they asked him to direct some TV series, he readily accepted. In fact, he would really have preferred to do nothing at all, but at least he ended up learning his trade, so much so that he was soon able to do just about every job on the set, excluding make-up. He now knew his job from top to bottom!

By the middle of that busy year, 1971, Steven was ready for his 'lucky break'. One day, his secretary unashamedly plopped a copy of *Playboy* on to his desk and suggested he read a story entitled *Duel* by the science fiction writer Richard Matheson. It was about a do-or-die struggle between a mild-mannered salesman and a huge gasoline tanker inexplicably bent on destroying him on some twisting mountain roads.

Spielberg shot *Duel* in 14 meticulously planned days in Soledad Canyon, California. It was presented as an ABC Movie of the Week on November 13, 1971. Two years later it received a special mention from the jury at the 12th Monte Carlo Television Festival. The reception it got from the European public flabbergasted the executives at Universal. They were finally forced to acknowledge that this young director was brimming over with talent.

With a meagre budget of $450,000, Spielberg had managed to make $6 million in profits. This was certainly enough to impress the big shots at Universal in whose minds money always came first.

However, before his true genius was to be fully appreciated, Spielberg had to continue making do with TV movies. It took over two years for the positive reaction to *Duel* to travel from Europe to the ears of Universal chiefs. The box office records finally became known when Spielberg was 25 and still chiefly occupied with TV productions. This time he knew that nothing could hold him back. Now absolutely no one or nothing would stand in his way. He was going to make real movies.

He was then invited to Universal's Black Tower, where he innocently asked: 'Got anything you want to make as a feature?'

Steven had already done the rounds of other film studios, dropping off screenplays he had written during his idle time at Universal. At 20th Century Fox, Richard D. Zanuck and David Brown took a liking to one of his scenarios called *Ace, Eli and Rodger of the Skies*. The film was shot, but Spielberg had virtually nothing to do with it. It turned out to be a flop, earning a paltry $13,400 during its opening week in 16 cinemas in Washington DC and Baltimore. This barely covered the cost of having it filmed.

Zanuck and Brown were nonetheless going to be instrumental in launching Spielberg's directing career. Fired by 20th Century Fox, they eventually ended up at Universal. Both of them loved *The Sugarland Express* script. Meanwhile, Steven was still having problems being accepted as a director, but the Zanuck-Brown duo was about to give him a helping hand up the ladder of success.

The plot was simple: a woman, recently released from jail herself, helps her boyfriend escape from prison. Together they kidnap a police officer on their way to rescuing their baby son, who was to be adopted and lost to them forever. What could have turned into a melodramatic tear-jerker became 'one of the most phenomenal debut films in the history of movies', according to *New York Times* critic Pauline Kael.

Even though it was a financial flop, Zanuck and Brown had had the right intuitive feelings about it. Yet, in Hollywood, the yardstick of success is always money. While *The Sting* brought in a fabulous $68,450,000 in film rentals, *The Sugarland Express* collected only $2,890,000!

Spielberg was learning, though. His first move was to round up allies and close associates. He was beginning to understand a golden rule: put your trust in competent people who are in key positions and who totally espouse your ideals and vision of things.

This is exactly what happened with the cameraman, Vilmos Zsigmond, the Zanuck-Brown duo, and countless others he would meet throughout his career, but especially with the composer John Williams, who wrote the scores for six of Spielberg's most successful films.

Then an amazing thing happened! It was a pure and simple stroke of genius, namely, a movie called *Jaws*.

I pretty much knew what *Jaws* would do to an
audience. It was an experiment in terror. It was a
nightmare to shoot. I didn't have any fun making it.

Universal owned the rights to Peter Benchley's book, but
didn't know what to do with it. Spielberg adored the
scenario, but had no inkling of the nightmarish journey
he was about to embark on. In the end, it took 155 shooting days, instead of the originally scheduled 52. The
budget kept growing and growing. The three giant sharks
weighed about 300 kilos each and cost $150,000 apiece.
Given the complexity of these mechanical beasts, it was
necessary to throw in an additional $3 million to the
already heavy $8 million budget. Around 20 people helped
build this shark, affectionately nicknamed Bruce, and 13
others operated it.

Filming *Jaws* drove everybody crazy. Isolated on the
New England coast, grappling with nasty weather conditions, it reduced brave men to tears and quiet men to make
speeches to the sky, a confession Richard Dreyfuss, one
of the leading actors, was to make later on.

All of the cast and crew, including Spielberg, were so
fed up and discouraged that they had only one idea in
mind: to get out of there! Dreyfuss himself admitted that
Jaws would probably be the 'turkey' of the year.

But it was considered the most horrifying film to come
out that year. The public went crazy over it. On September 5, 1975, 80 days after being released to fewer than
1,000 American and Canadian cinemas and backed by a
$2.5 million advertising budget, *Jaws* had already eclipsed
the box-office records for *The Exorcist, The Sting, Gone
With The Wind,* and *The Sound of Music. Jaws* even
topped *The Godfather,* to become the new number one
movie of all time.

Its success was so phenomenal that the *Washington Post*
correspondent, Ben Bradlee, claimed on his return from
a business trip to Cuba that Castro had released a pirate
copy to Cuban cinemas.

Jaws was a gold mine, to say the least. From the different companies selling *Jaws* products, International Creative Management earned $6 million on its 10-percent
commission!

Universal obviously wanted Spielberg to direct a sequel, but he flatly refused. By 1975, he had other plans very much in mind. All he would say, however, was that Richard Dreyfuss was to be the star of his new film and that it would be 'unique'. The result was *Close Encounters of the Third Kind.*

Given the monolithic nature of his project, Columbia executives thought Spielberg could never do it. But Spielberg believed in it heart and soul.

> This isn't a science fiction film. This isn't a futuristic film. It's about what people *believe* is happening. Sixteen million Americans believe UFOs are visiting us, that we're under some sort of close scrutiny and have been for many, many years.

Spielberg had already memorized his credo by heart: character, first; the rest, second. But in Hollywood, as always, it was money first; movies, second. And the budget, like his film, was going to be colossal. Francois Truffaut, one of the actors and a major French director in his own right, used to a much more intimate work environment when shooting films, was totally amazed by the monumental operation taking place. Those heading the lighting, sets, and sound were all part of the international *crème de la crème*. The extraterrestrial, designed by the grand master Carlo Rambaldi, which came out of the Mother Ship in a quasi-religious finale, cost $3.5 million.

But when the film was released in November 1977, the critics panned it. William Flanagan of the *New York* magazine laconically wrote: 'The picture will be a colossal flop.' Columbia shares plummetted a total of $18 million because of the panic created by the critics' previews.

Close Encounters was nonetheless an instant hit, becoming even bigger than *Jaws*. It made international celebrities of all those who had been involved in it, whether directly or indirectly. After only one month in cinemas, it became the ninth most successful movie in 1977. The following year, it reached third place and was destined to keep on climbing even higher. . . until *ET* arrived!

After his two huge hits, Spielberg experienced his first flop: *I Wanna Hold Your Hand* in 1978. An account of the Beatles' rise to fame and fortune, it had simply come out too late. By then, the band was old news. Then came *1941*, a farce about the panic that grabbed hold of a coastal town in the States after being bombarded by a Japanese submarine. A monumental disaster! Spielberg didn't know the first thing about comedy, and had to face that fact. *1941* was a hard lesson to learn. 'It was a regrettable necessity. Regrettable for the public. A necessity for the director,' were the words of one critic. Spielberg had learned his lesson: from now on, he would stick to what he knew best.

Egged on my his mania for perfection, he directed *Close Encounters of the Third Kind, Special Edition*. A lukewarm success. Then *Used Cars*. Another flop.

But these failures didn't discourage him, especially since in the meantime he had met George Lucas, whose famous *Star Wars* had so enamoured the public. The idea of combining their efforts had taken root in Hawaii when they were on vacation and soon they began shooting a film straight out of adventure comic strips from the 1940s. *Raiders of the Lost Ark* has just been born.

Spielberg had always wanted to direct a 'James Bond' type of film. It was now or never! The project was, however, rejected by every major studio, except Paramount Pictures, which imposed strict conditions on them. Their tendency to overrun their budget was no secret!

Shooting got under way in June 1980 and lasted 73 days instead of the 87 Paramount had scheduled for it. Exteriors were shot in Hawaii and Tunisia; interiors, at Elmstree, California. Miracles were accomplished to cut down costs. Although 2,000 Arabs were originally planned to occupy the dig site, Spielberg managed to make 600 look like 2,000. The dig was meant to be 200 acres, but he made do with 70, thereby saving $750,000, an amount he used to hire 4,500 snakes from a Danish agency. Finally, a whole day was saved by Harrison Ford's brilliant idea of pulling out a gun in the famous whip and scimitar fight.

According to Lucas, *Raiders*, was better than Bond. He was right. When it came out in June 1981, at the same time as *For Your Eyes Only*, it tripled Bond's box office receipts. In Paris, 500 people were turned away at the opening. *Raiders of the Lost Ark* is now the fifth largest commercial success in the annals of movie history with profits of $224 million paid out to Paramount, who had to see it to believe it!

For Spielberg, the most important aspect of shooting this film was that he had inched a little closer to applying the golden rule of delegating power: he used a second team to shoot minor scenes while he devoted himself to major ones with Harrison Ford and the other stars.

Spielberg still had a dream to accomplish: making a movie with and for kids. 'He's marvellous with kids,' Truffaut declared after seeing him work with Carey Duffey in *Close Encounters*. For Spielberg, who kept the sense of wonder and mystery of childhood alive in his heart, this was becoming an obsession.

Before *ET,* he had always been unable to face 'real life': 'I always had to embellish it with tricks and pizzazz.' *ET* was to be his 'resurrection'.

Even though this idea was slowly making its way into his mind and he was working tirelessly on it with his assistants, he was still far from shooting it. He still had another demon to exorcize: *fear!* His fear went all the way back to the time when he imagined nasty little creatures spilling out of the cracks in his bedroom ceiling, or the evil-minded intentions of the weeping willow branches at dusk, or a jack-in-the-box coming to life and attacking a terrified child huddling miserably under his blankets... He had to express that fear somehow, that panic-stricken terror, and get rid of it once and for all.

As a result, *Poltergeist* was created. It was his first horror film.

By shooting this film, Spielberg was merely applying a principle he had learned the hard way:

Do only what you know best and only talk about what you really know!

Spielberg still experienced night terrors, which were

deeply etched in his memory. *Poltergeist* grew out of two old film projects. He decided to present the life of children in suburbia (which he knew so well), but also to show both sides of the coin!

He wrote the script day after day from 8 a.m. to 4 p.m. To direct it, he called upon an expert in the genre, Tobe Hooper, the director of the infamous *Texas Chainsaw Massacre* (1974), an exceedingly controversial film which was banned in many places. When shooting began at MGM on May 11 1981, Spielberg was on the set, hour after hour day after day except for three days during the promotion and premier of *Raiders of the Lost Ark.* His presence caused some tension to surface. In fact, it was actually Spielberg who was directing the movie, not Hooper. Spielberg then learned another invaluable lesson:

> # As far as possible, see to everything yourself

As hard on himself as he was on others, Spielberg asked for miracles in *Poltergeist,* and Mike Wood, the sound effects expert said: '...he'll ask you to do things that are right on the brink of being impossible.'

Poltergeist cost $11 million, but was an instant hit.

Then came Spielberg's next astounding *tour de force — ET.* His greatest film. When he was asked during a press conference how *ET* was made, he gave a simple answer: 'Out of love.'

> I think the movie is one of the better things I've done as a director. It's closer to my heart than any movie...with the possible exception of *Close Encounters*.

With a small budget of $10.5 million (compared to his other productions), Spielberg accomplished the amazing feat of recreating the magical enchantment that only the great Walt Disney had been capable of until then.

Spielberg said:

> I wanted a creature that only a mother could love. I
> didn't want him sublime or beatific... When it comes
> right down to it, ET is the most human of all the
> characters in the movie. First of all, it took 12 hearts
> to make ET's one heart beat. And I'll also say, he's
> half the price of Marlon Brando.

ET was an unprecedented success! It tripled the top box
office receipts that year. It was the greatest all-time success in the history of cinema. The French magazine, *Le
Point,* even said that ET stood for 'Extreme Tenderness'.
That's exactly what his creator thought, too.

In only 44 days, this movie became the fifth leading
movie in history. Spielberg would later say:

> ET will be this generation's Peter Pan. From now on,
> children will stay in NeverNeverland and will never
> grow old. You know...getting old...becoming crusty
> and cynical! Getting...old!

Having recently become a father (he and his companion,
Amy Irving, have a son), Spielberg commutes between his
home in Coldwater Canyon, California, and work, a superb
ultramodern studio called 'Amblin' on the Universal lots
in Hollywood. Curiously, it resembles one of those front-
ier homes designed by Disney.

Here Spielberg meets with his assistants. More than
merely a workplace, it is a place to meet and exchange
ideas. Here is where Spielberg is preparing his next film,
amidst gardens and springs that reproduce a childhood
paradise.

The man who allowed Universal to make more than
$800 million with only two movies, *Jaws* and *ET,* feels
happy surrounded by people who share his ideals and
vision of things. Brandy, his dog, wanders good-naturedly
around the oasis in the Universal business studios. Here,
all is order, beauty, luxury, calm, and sensual delights —
and *love,* might we add.

It is his love for his art that has spurred him to donate
several million dollars to found a film school where aspir-
ing directors can learn their craft.

> ## You have to put back what you take out . . . or the well does run dry

What will he tackle after successes such as the *Twilight Zone, Amazing Stories, The Goonies,* and surprisingly enough, a drama, *The Color Purple*? It will certainly be another challenge and just as successful a movie.

When was it any different for Spielberg, the man with the Midas touch?

WORKING TO BE THE BEST

The story of Steven Spielberg's early career and his meteoric rise shows that money, however important a consideration it may be in the eyes of all businesspeople, is not always the be all and end all. In fact, what goads people like him into action is the need to do things well and to accomplish something that will please many people. Because they are not looking for immediate profit, it seems as though the sums they amass are even greater.

Henry Ford was one of those who shared the same philosophy, which is basically a form of humanitarianism and radically changes the image we have of the rich as ruthless exploiters. Several passages in Ford's autobiography reveal this principle. Here is a good example of it:

> I determined resolutely that never would I join a company in which finance came before the work or in which bankers or financiers had a part. And further, that if there were no way to get started in the kind of business that I thought could be managed in the interest of the public, then I simply would not get started at all, for my own short experience, together with what I saw going on around me, was quite enough proof that business as a mere money-making game was not worth giving much thought to and was distinctly no place for a man who wanted to accomplish anything. Also it did not seem to me to be the way to make money. I have yet to have it demonstrated that it is the way. For the only foundation of real business is service.

Ford's comments demonstrate one of the major principles of wealth. In general, you must start by considering the products or services you have to offer to the public before looking for profits. Money flows in naturally when the product or service is good. Become the best in your field and money will follow. It has been said that anyone who makes the best mouse trap, preaches the best sermon, or writes the best book can build his home in a dense forest; clients will go out of their way to come to him.

DARE TO BE YOURSELF!

People often think that the rich are severe, conformist and attached to traditional values. The study we undertook on the lives of these 10 rich men has shown that just the opposite is true.

Of course being original doesn't mean that they deliberately set themselves apart by concocting some sort of exaggerated character trait or wearing outlandish clothes. What was different was their mentality, as well as the methods they used. They were themselves. Moreover, the fact that they didn't graduate from business schools has perhaps something to do with their originality. School tends to level out the thinking process and to suppress originality, despite its liberal pretensions.

Conformity in thought prevents us from seeing new avenues and different or original solutions. It is possible to doubt the relevance or, in any case, the effectiveness of graduate studies given the track-record achieved by MBAs in business. Furthermore, large firms are increasingly becoming dissatisfied with the rational model of management advocated in the 1960s and are now starting to put more emphasis on on-the-job training. In Japan, business schools simply do not exist. So, how do you account for the 'Japanese miracle' we hear so much about?

Don't misunderstand us. We are not belittling the value of education. Far from it. Technical developments make higher education necessary. Simply put, everything points to the fact that although studying is often necessary, it never seems quite sufficient to guarantee success. Something more is needed — a spark of originality or boldness, which schools fail to teach, indeed, which they often stifle altogether.

Society, schools and education in general all help turn people into clones by eliminating differences and nipping personal aspirations in the bud. This process begins early in life and is often insidious. In fact, people's fears of being different and their need to conform belong to the theory of the subconscious we discussed in Chapter 2.

A tiny inner voice nevertheless survives within each of us. Timid and worried, it whispers to us that our public images are false, that our genuine personalities are hidden and unexpressed. Frustration, sadness, and, in some cases, a feeling of being dead inside are some of the disadvantages we heap upon ourselves.

If you want to succeed, be different from the others. Be yourself. Don't be afraid to assert your true personality. Don't forget that you are unique. As soon as you toe the line, you are denying your true personality.

Repeat the following formulas to yourself:

- Day after day, I'm asserting my true personality more and more

- I'm unique and feel completely free to express my desire to succeed and grow rich

- It's my right and duty to be myself

- The success I achieve will be in keeping with the extent to which I assert myself. I'm asserting myself more and more in all areas of my life

- Every day I'm increasing my self-worth tenfold and becoming more and more successful

One of the richest and undoubtedly the most nonconformist men in the world was Howard Hughes. Naturally his mysterious and eccentric life cannot be used as a role model, but the fact is that he is a spectacular illustration of the principle stating that to succeed you must be true to yourself. The portrait drawn by Max Gunther in his book *The Very, Very Rich and How They Got That Way*, is quite striking:

He conducted his business from public telephone
booths, hotel rooms, wherever he happened to be.
Most of the information he needed to run his
bewilderingly diverse enterprises — information that
the average systematic businessman would store in
file cabinets — he stored in his head. His employees
and even his close associates seldom knew where he
was on any given day. We would dart about among
his far-flung ventures with an apparent lack of plan
and a total lack of formal scheduling that irritated and
confounded the more orderly minded of his
executives.

If you wanted to get in touch with him you called a
phone number and were plugged into a switchboard
that, at various stages of his career, might be in
Hollywood, Las Vegas, or Houston. You gave your
message to a secretary. A few weeks might go by.
Finally, if Hughes felt like talking to you, he would
phone you back, perhaps from a neighbouring city,
perhaps from halfway around the world. The call
might come at 1 a.m. your time. Hughes wouldn't
consider that important. It might be 4 a.m. his time.

Gunther then concludes this portrait of the eccentric
Howard Hughes, whose life was true to Montaigne's
maxim, which says that to succeed you must act like a
wise man, but look like a fool:

The formal structures of the business world meant
nothing to Hughes: its chain of command, its
documents, its timetables. He worked when he
wanted to work, sometimes 36 or more hours at a
stretch. A fit of work might seize him as readily on a
weekend as on a standard business day, as readily
after midnight as between 9 a.m. and 5 p.m. 'He was
the kind of man', says a Hollywood press agent who
knew him in his moviemaking days, 'who broke every
rule taught by the Harvard Business School. Every
rule except the one that says you should make
money.'

The end of this quote contains the key to the behaviour
of successful nonconformists. They disobeyed all the rules
except the one that says you should make money.

Beware of falling into the seemingly harmless trap of

conformity. We all naturally tend to imitate everyone else, a tendency we view to be the principle of making the least effort. Unfortunately, the vast majority of people are not successful and lead mediocre lives.

Ray Kroc said,

> I believe that if two of my executives thought the same way, one of them would have to go.

Make sure you never simply follow blindly. Do just the opposite: ensure that your original viewpoint and personal way of thinking render you indispensable.

The 10 rich men described in this book were all individualists and nonconformists. They were not afraid of straying from the beaten track, of hammering out new methods, or of being creative. Aristotle Onassis, the astronomically rich Greek ship owner, was one of those who revelled in nonconformity.

The harvest he reaped was incalculable. His methods were his own personal ones. He often said, many assumed jokingly, that in his office was his little black address book, which he never left behind on transcontinental journeys intended to make his business flourish. No one really knew if he was serious or not, but this book did exist. Onassis' methods resembled those used by Hughes, even though their personalities were very different. Onassis loved the splendour and shine of high society whereas Hughes finished out his life alone, suffering from acute paranoia (a sad ending for such a brilliant mind). Let us now take a look at the fascinating life of 'the Great Onassis'.

ARISTOTLE ONASSIS

Aristotle Onassis was born on January 20, 1906 in the Greek quarter of Smyrna, on opulent city on the western coast of Turkey. Among the 10 men we have analysed, Onassis definitely stands apart. Like Getty and Rockefeller he possessed a huge fortune, stretching into billions rather than millions. The enormous publicity generated by his turbulent relationships with the famous opera singer Maria Callas, and then with Jacqueline Bouvier Kennedy have also added to his fame. And, as is often the case, numerous exaggerations or half-truths have circulated about him, especially concerning his modest origins. He was supposedly born in a poor family, living in misery. His father was supposedly a door-to-door salesman of knick-knacks made with his own hands, and his mother was a cleaner. Onassis never attempted to set people straight about his past, publicly at least, since these beliefs naturally helped enhance the aura of mystery surrounding him. He was always acutely aware of how important a person's self image is in contributing to success, a point we shall discuss later.

The truth of the matter is that Onassis' father was a prosperous wholesale merchant with considerable clout, since he was also the president of the local bank and hospital. Yet, Onassis is by no means an inheritor, nor does he owe his success to his family fortune. As we shall soon see in detail, he left for South America after a family quarrel when he was only 17 years old, and with only $450 in his pockets, of which only $250 came from his family.

His father agreed to give him this only reluctantly, and at the very last minute, since he strongly disapproved of his son's departure. Father and son were never very close, which was unusual among tight-knit Greek families back then. Raised on a farm, Onassis' father used sheer muscle power to build up his fortune and was a rigidly disciplined man, almost spartan by nature. Although motivated by a keen sense of duty, he was not what you could call a warm and personable man.

Onassis soon rebelled against any form of discipline. He was a turbulent and rowdy child and teenager, a thorn in his father's side. Another fact complicated their relationship. His mother, Penelope, died when he was six years old. Barely 18 months later, his father married a woman called Helen. Viewing his stepmother as an interloper, Onassis was never able to find a place for her in his heart.

As a student, following in the footsteps of many of the rich, he was a first-class dunce and trouble-maker, so much so that he was thrown out of several schools. He was more often than not at the bottom of his class. One of his teachers would later say:

> His classmates adored him, but his teachers and family despaired. When he was young, you could easily see that he would be one of those who would either destroy themselves or succeed brilliantly.

Although Ari's report cards were far from brilliant, his talent for commerce and money-making developed early, as the following anecdotes clearly prove. One of his friends had designed a small windmill, a rudimentary toy consisting of a piece of paper attached to a needle, which was in turn tied to a piece of wood. Proud of his accomplishment, the boy got the brainwave of making several of them and selling them.

'How much do you want for your windmill?' asked Onassis.

'Uh. . . I don't know. How about a needle. . .?'

'You dummy!' Onassis exclaimed. 'You're asking me for a needle when you're already giving me a needle, a sail and a piece of wood, besides the time it took you to make it in the first place!'

Onassis's friend concluded: 'This was my first lesson on the real meaning of profit.' He had no idea then that he had just received a lesson from a future financial wizzard.

Another story illustrates Onassis' precocious business sense. One day, a school supply store caught fire in the town where he was born. Onassis bought a bunch of damaged pencils at a pretty low price. He invested a bit of money in two pencil sharpeners and he and friend got down to cleaning up the damaged sections. He later resold them to his classmates at rock-bottom prices, but which still allowed him to make a handsome profit. This example might seem ordinary, but this is exactly what Onassis was to do later on when salvaging damaged freighters and getting them shipshape again, but on a much grander scale, of course.

As the years went by, Onassis didn't get any better at school. The year 1922 started out poorly. Many of his classmates were now heading off to major European universities. Onassis, however, had failed his exams and his prospects were pretty gloomy. A few days after the graduation ceremony, one of his friends saw him wandering alone in a public garden. He tried to comfort Onassis.

'Don't worry Aristotle, you'll see, everything'll work out OK. You can try again next year. You're sure to pass then.'

'Idiot.' replied Onassis, 'Do you think I'm going to hang around here. The world's a small place. I don't need a diploma. One day you'll be amazed at what I can do.' The future showed that this wasn't pure braggadocio.

In 1922, the Turkish invasion cast a gloomy shadow over Onassis' tempestuous adolescence. Smyrna was occupied and citizens were mowed down without mercy. Onassis' father, a well-known figure, was imprisoned and Ari became the head of the household at the age of 16. This was a difficult period for him, during which time he displayed the true qualities of a diplomat and a survivor. Painful though it was, it was a great character-building experience. A different Ari emerged from the Smyrna catastrophe. The things he had seen never left his memory; they were accompanied by an acute awareness of his ability to survive. He had gambled and been rewarded. Fortune favours the bold and he centered his vision of the world on this knowledge.

Onassis also took advantage of the Turkish occupation to do business. He smuggled liquor to the Turkish army, trying in this way to win favour with the generals to help free his father, who spent almost a year in prison anyway.

Onassis owed much of his success to his incredible charm and skilful public relations abilities. Some of his peers labelled him a genuine chameleon. In fact, he knew how to adapt himself to all the people he met. Generally speaking, if you make things easier for people, you can gain their sympathy, he thought.

Onassis once confided to Winston Churchill, one of his illustrious acquaintances, then a guest on the *Christina*, his personal theory on 'historic necessities', created by hard times. His experience had taught him that when nature provided man with an agreeable climate and abundant food, he had little energy and lacked initiative. On the other hand, those forced to cke out an existence and to fight to survive when times were rough had more chance of being able to adapt to all circumstances, thus allowing them to succeed where others would die through lack of stimulation. Thus, according to Onassis, hardship and misery often spur people to find their own resources, which they never suspected existed until then, enabling them to burst through their personal limitations. Onassis' life story is an excellent illustration of this principle.

Once released from prison, Socrates, Onassis' father, refused to recognize the providential role his son had played during enemy occupation and was unwilling to allow him to continue sharing the family responsibilities. Onassis resented this attitude and confessed to having experienced bouts of impotent rage for many months afterwards. His father's ingratitude and his own vivid impression of being rejected from the family motivated his decision to try his luck in South America. At first, he had naturally thought of going to the US, but getting a visa wasn't easy. Onassis turned towards Argentina: rumour had it that many Greeks had already struck it rich there.

Onassis disembarked in Buenos Aires on September 21, 1923, carrying an old suitcase and $450. But he carried an even more valuable cargo inside him: the fierce desire to prove to his father that he could get rich without him. This self-confidence would stay with him throughout his life.

Without a diploma, a profession, money, and influential contacts, Onassis was forced to take up menial jobs. He was a mason's assistant, carried bricks on a construction site, worked as a dishwasher in a restaurant, and ended up as an electrician's apprentice at the River Plate United Telephone Co. For a man with a healthy ego, as he had, this was no accomplishment!

A few months after beginning this job, Onassis asked to be transferred to the night shift, using the excuse that he had other things to do during the day. Being fiercely ambitious, Onassis had no intention of spending much time soldering wires.

In those days Greek tobacco was reputed to be quite good, even passing as some of the world's finest in the eyes of many connoisseurs. However, import and supply problems made it a rare commodity. Onassis wrote to his father asking him to make the necessary arrangements to have it delivered to him. Socrates agreed and shipped off the first samples. Initially, results were disappointing. He left tobacco samples at various manufacturers, hoping they would contact him.

Weeks went by without a word. He then understood that instead of wasting his time with small dealers he would have to go to other bigger fish, in this case, Juan Gaona, the chairman of one of the largest tobacco firms in Argentina. For 15 days in a row, Onassis could be seen leaning against the Gaona building, watching the boss's comings and goings. Intrigued by this singular young man, Gaona invited him up to his office for a chat. Onassis gave him his best sales pitch and outlined his proposal. Favourably impressed, Gaona referred him to his supply manager whom Onassis managed to con by judiciously dropping Gaona's name, a ploy which led to his first contract: $10,000 worth of tobacco with the usual five per cent commission. Later on, Onassis would insist that his first $500 was the cornerstone of his vast fortune. Instead of blowing this money, he prudently put it in the bank for a rainy day. Both thrifty and wise, Onassis lived on his salary from the telephone company and hoarded the rest away, which helped launch him into business without having to borrow a penny.

Onassis was sometimes forced to take out loans while waiting for his clients to pay up. But he rarely borrowed more than $3,000 and always paid his debts back as soon as he could. Later on, of course, after having discovered the virtues of Other People's Money (OPM), a point we shall examine later, Onassis would contract debts worth several million dollars, scheduled to be reimbursed over a number of years. However, one of the major principles when starting up a business is to pay back what you owe as quickly as you can. Onassis built up a sound credit rating at several banks: something he would greatly need in the years to come!

After spending a year on the night shift, Onassis quit United Telephone, simply stating that he had an idea he wanted to pursue. His new dream was to manufacture his own cigarettes. He financed this operation with the $25,000 he had patiently saved, and by borrowing an equivalent amount. His impeccable credit rating was already bearing fruit. His small company soon employed 30 people, unemployed Greek immigrants for the most part. Despite rapid expansion, his business regularly showed losses, and Onassis soon put an end to this venture. His first private enterprise was a failure. Onassis wasn't discouraged, though. On the contrary, this initial setback was to increase his determination. Meanwhile, his tobacco importing business remained quite profitable.

During the summer of 1929, the Greek government voted on a substantial tax increase, putting his tobacco business on the line. Onassis decided to use this opportunity to go back to Greece to plead his case with government authorities. At first, though, the Minister who had agreed to see him appeared more interested in manicuring his nails than in listening to the young merchant's grievances. He finally cut Onassis off and abruptly sent him on his way.

Onassis was annoyed. He replied:

Thank you. If we ever get a chance to meet again I hope you will show more interest in my proposal. I thought you had a lot of work to do, but your nails seem to be keeping you quite busy. Your hands are obviously more important than our country's exports.

His words hit the Minister hard. Visibly impressed, he started talking seriously with Onassis. Later on, negotiations between Greece and Argentina were re-opened.

Ari Onassis took advantage of his stay in Greece to make amends with his father. Now that he had proved himself, his family had much more respect for him. He still went back to Argentina, however, not only to continue importing tobacco, but to develop an idea he had in mind about the shipping business, which was destined to ensure him his fortune.

Onassis bought his first ship in Montevideo, Uruguay. 'Ship' was hardly the right word to describe it, though, since the rusty crate he had bought looked more like a ship*wreck*! His plan was to overhaul it first and then refloat it. All his friends tried to dissuade him by arguing that this venture would bankrupt him.

All the rich have heard this same old song time and again. Yet, what distinguishes successful people from the rest is their ability to see possibilities where others are blind. In this case, those who nagged Onassis to drop his crazy scheme were right and wrong. Refloated at great expense, the 25-year-old ship, anchored off shore, sank when a cyclone came sweeping into the Port of Montevideo. Bad luck seemed to dog Ari's steps. In spite of this, his advisers were wrong, because Onassis' colossal fortune ended up being built on ships. This setback taught him to be more careful, however. Fortunately, his tobacco importing business was still bringing in money and easily soaked these losses up.

The end of 1932 marked a time for great decisions in Onassis' life. His first flop as a ship owner didn't discourage him from reinvesting in that sector. Ships obsessed him. He was egged on by the inner certainty that they and nothing else would be the catalyst for his success. So, he collected his fortune, which was already considerable at that time, and left for London. He was only 26 years old. He had already acquired a reputation as an astute businessman, which was further enhanced by his appointment as the Greek Consul General in Buenos Aires. This diplomatic function did not occupy much of his time, however.

The market, badly affected by the 1929 Wall Street Crash, greatly favoured investors. Ships were cheap, going for much less than their original worth. The best thing to do was to buy 10-year-old vessels. Initially costing $1,000,000, nine-ton ships could now be negotiated down to a ridiculous $20,000, the same price as a Rolls Royce. What Onassis had done as child with his burnt pencils, he was now about to repeat with freighters.

Although he was now doing brisk business in London, Onassis went to Montreal to buy his first two ships, paying $20,000 apiece for them. These were the *Miller* and the *Spinner*, which he quickly rebaptized the *Onassis Socrates* and the *Onassis Penelope*, in honour of his parents. To make money in the shipping business, it was vital to pay close attention to fluctuating freight charges and to make the right decisions. Onassis was able to do both.

Furthermore, he was an incurable optimist. Adventurous and bold, he soon stood out from the other Greek ship owners established in London because, unlike them, he had no conception of the economic crisis. So, he wasn't afraid of investing.

Onassis' natural tact and diplomacy swiftly opened the doors to high society for him. It should be mentioned that his rise up the social ladder was greatly facilitated by one of his first mistresses, the gorgeous Norwegian, Ingeborg Dedichen, whose father had been a famous ship owner.

Another character trait that helped Onassis succeed was his ability to listen to people. True, glibness and eloquence play a major role in persuading people and selling both your ideas and yourself. But there are few people who really know how to listen to others. Most of the rich learned this invaluable lesson, which allows you to pick up not only on what people know, but to tune into who they are as well. Consequently, to be able to influence people and guarantee that they will help you on the uphill climb to success, you must start by knowing who you are up against. Onassis was a master in the art of listening.

Perhaps because he didn't practise this art himself, Lord Moran failed to make note of Onassis' ability to listen in his book, *The Great Onassis*. All those who came into contact with him were struck by it. When they were in his presence, he gave them the impression that they were the most important people in the world.

Because of this skill, Onassis could have been an outstanding politician. He pushed this talent of his to the limit, as witnessed in his Norwegian mistress's memoirs:

> This charming young man who could play every note
> so well, imitated the person he was speaking with
> perfectly.

Some will interpret this as wiliness; others, as hypocrisy, denouncing it as pure mimicry. But we believe it to be special kind of empathy and sincere interest in people and in the entire world as well. Incidentally, throughout his life Onassis had an unquenchable thirst for knowledge, combined with an astounding memory. His incredible recall meant that his powers of concentration were highly developed.

The ability to listen to people is one of the vital characteristics of any good salesman. It was thus not surprising that Onassis was an extraordinary salesman. Walter Saunders, who was far from being naïve since he was a tax adviser to the prestigious Metropolitan Life when he met Onassis, describes the impression this Greek ship owner made on him:

> I had the feeling that this sprightly fellow could sell
> refrigerators to Eskimos. But I also had the feeling
> that every detail was exquisitely worked out
> beforehand.

Most of those who met Onassis felt the impact of his powers of persuasion and had the feeling that Onassis was not improvising, but knew everything in his files down to the last detail.

Paul Getty, a close friend and associate of Ari's, retained a clear impression of his talents as a bargainer:

> He was a very good friend, and it was always a
> fascinating experience to see him operate. I discussed
> business with him many times. Very often, I had a

retinue of assistants, executives, attorneys and engineers with me. Ari would come to such meetings alone. Yet he easily held his own on all points that were discussed. Every enterprise he owned or controlled was his *personal* business; *he* was the business, and the business was Aristotle Onassis and no one else.

Christian Cafarakis, who was the *Maître d'hôtel* on the luxury liner *Christina* (named after Onassis' daughter), revealed the secrets of Onassis' intricate preparations on the eve of major negotiations:

> One night, I was on the bridge and discovered a great secret of his — perhaps the key to his success: before going to an important business appointment, Mr Onassis asked himself aloud all the questions he might have to answer. The night I'm referring to he tirelessly questioned himself for over two hours. He answered exactly as if he were facing an audience. Sometimes he would wait and think before answering; other times he would answer right away or pretend to be angry. I understood then and there that Onassis was just like an actor rehearsing his script and trying to foresee what his co-actors would say.

Onassis started building his fortune by buying ships at bargain prices. After the Second World War, he did the same, but on a larger scale. The United States put several *Liberty* ships up for sale. After getting around a few administrative snags, Onassis bought 13 of them, worth $1.5 million each, and which the Navy was selling for $550,000. These ships later became a major source of income, allowing Onassis to build his huge fortune. The war also favoured him in the sense that none of his tankers had been damaged, unlike many of his less fortunate competitors.

That same year, 1946, Onassis, who had broken off completely with his Norwegian girlfriend, decided to marry Athina Livanos on December 29. To all appearances, this was a love match. Onassis was 47; Tina, 17. Her youth was not her only charm, however. Her father was none other than Stavros Livanos, considered the richest Greek ship owner in New York. This marriage bond didn't harm his interests and Onassis was able to cultivate friends, especially among his business associates.

Towards the end of 1947, Onassis crossed another threshold in his brilliant career. For the very first time, he was going to systematically apply the principle known as OPM (Other People's Money), by convincing the Metropolitan Life Insurance Company to lend him $40 million to build new ships. The trick he used was to have an oil company act as collateral. Onassis did their shipping and had a contract with them that lasted as long as the term of his loan. Since the reputation of oil companies was impeccable at that time, financing this deal was easy. In a certain sense, the financial institution was lending money to the oil firm rather than to Onassis. Onassis recalled this crucial period in his career not without a touch of boastfulness, explaining that the wealthy and powerful oil companies were in relation to his ships what a tenant was with respect to the house he occupied and for which he paid the rent. If the tenant were Rockefeller, it didn't matter whether the roof had holes or was gold-plated. If Rockefeller agreed to pay the rent, that was good enough for anyone lending money on the house. It was the same with ships.

This principle is now quite commonplace, being the very foundation of all real estate investments. When someone borrows money for a business property, the bank is really lending money to the tenants. They are the ones who will reimburse it, except that the building belongs to the investor! This principle was in fact quite revolutionary then and Onassis's originality was that much greater since the majority of Greek ship owners of the time adhered to the principle: 'To get ships, pay hard cash.'

Although he was an innovator insofar as he shunned his rivals' methods, he did not invent OPM, regardless of his claims. This concept was originated by Daniel Ludwig, a prosperous American businessman, who started out investing in ships (his flotilla, by the way, was far superior to Onassis's) and then continued into real estate. It was in the mid-1930s that Ludwig developed what later became common practice. The idea blossomed in his mind after a bank had refused to lend him the money he needed to buy and convert an oil tanker. He then had the idea of offering the rental contract he had with the oil company, using his ships as a guarantee. The rental fees were to be paid directly to the bank. The bank accepted without delay. OPM had just seen the light of day. Even though Onassis didn't invent this theory, his sense of opportunism and nonconformity allowed him to make full use of it when it was falling into discredit.

Onassis' fortune never ceased growing in the years to follow. In 1953, partly to diversify and partly to embellish his social status, Onassis purchased a controlling interest in the *Société des Bains de Mer* and the Winter Sporting Club. This in itself means little to those unaware that the *Société des Bains de Mer* also owned the famous Monte Carlo Casino, the Hotel de Paris, and several other businesses. Onassis became an instant celebrity, both to the man in the street and to those in the know in financial circles. He became known as 'The Man Who Bought the Bank at Monte Carlo.' Later on, his jet-set existence became partly responsible for his divorce, his wife preferring a more orderly life.

In 1956, Onassis estimated his fortune to be worth $300 million. But although Onassis knew how to have fun and spend money, he never stopped travelling around the world looking to increase his fortune, and making headlines, particularly because of his turbulent romance with Maria Callas and controversial marriage to Jackie Kennedy.

Towards the end of his life, Onassis asked one of his accountants if he could find out how much he was worth, rounded up to the nearest ten dollars. His accountant assured him that this was indeed possible if all of his accountants and secretaries spent all of their days for the next two years calculating what he had stashed away in the bank, the value of his companies, the money he was owed, and his debts.

'And people say I'm rich!' answered Onassis, who was nevertheless a billionaire several times over.

When he died on March 15, 1975, it was still impossible to figure out how much Onassis' estate really amounted to. As a result, he was a perfect illustration of Paul Getty's theory that being truly rich means it is impossible to calculate your fortune.

Onassis, unlike many others, never succumbed to the temptation of relating his life story or writing down his success principles. However, he did give a reporter the following advice:

- Take care of your body. Be as good as possible. Don't worry about minor problems. Look at me. I'm no Apollo, but I haven't wasted my time crying about my looks. Remember, you are never as ugly as you think you are

- Eat moderately; when you have urgent work to do, avoid rich foods and wine. Spending hours at the dinner table, when work is also encroaching on your time, is still the best way of shortening your life

- Wait for the evening to come and don't feast until your cogitations are over. Then have a good meal in the company of your friends and never talk business at the table

- Do the exercise you require and stay fit. Basic yoga is advisable as much for your body as for your mind. If you can do judo one or two hours a week, this sport will get rid of all your complexes

- Stay tanned even if you need a sunlamp to do it. For most people, a winter tan means you have just arrived from sunny spots and for everybody, sun means money

- Once you have taken care of your physical appearance, choose a fancy lifestyle. Reside in a beautiful house even if you have to live in the attic; you will frequent rich people in the halls and elevator. Go to elegant cafés even if you have to sip one drink all night long. You will soon learn that solitude haunts those who manage to earn a lot of money

- If you are short of money, borrow some. Never ask for a small amount. Ask for large ones and always pay them back as soon as possible if you can

- Never confide your problems in anyone and always pretend you are having a good time

● Don't sleep too much; upon waking up, you might tell yourself that you have failed. Three hours less sleep at night during a year will give you an extra month and a half to succeed.

BECOME AN EXPERT IN YOUR FIELD

I HAVEN'T A CLUE WHAT I'D LIKE TO DO. . .

This is unquestionably a common complaint in modern times. Our society seems to be overwhelmed with confusion, a feeling few can escape from. This is largely due to the breakdown in the traditional roles. Times have changed radically, however. Women have joined the workforce and have met with rapid success. As for men, they no longer automatically do what their fathers did. Furthermore, today's career profiles resemble yesterday's very little. People make rapid and often drastic career switches. Choices are no longer as clear as they used to be, both for women, newcomers on the work market, and for men. Alvin Toffler describes this phenomenon well in *Future Shock*, saying that we are now living in a society that offers us an infinite array of choices. Countless new avenues have opened up to people of all ages, traditional roles having gradually lost their hold over us.

This choice has led to greater freedom. But it can also mean we no longer know where to turn.

Rapid and profound change is part of the problem of people who can't seem to put their finger on the type of professional activity that would help them get going. But that is not the only thing. The fact that people constantly moan about not knowing what they want to do with their lives is due to their having spent years stifling their aspirations and ignoring their inner selves. By wishing so desperately to conform, they have forgotten who they are, thus sowing their own seeds of confusion.

This uncertainty is all the more serious insofar as anyone who doesn't really know what he wants to do and doesn't establish clear-cut goals for himself will never be able to succeed. The opposite is also true. When you know perfectly well what you want to do in life, when your desire is crystal clear, the conditions enabling you to achieve it soon show up. Often, extremely precise desires come true almost immediately.

And yet, such a thing as a perfectly straightforward desire, that is, devoid of hesitation, ambiguity and contradiction, is very rare indeed. It's not so difficult to find, however. You only need the means to do so. Vague, confused ambitions programme your subconscious to be just as muddled. Since your aspirations are foggy, your results will be likewise. A metamorphosis must take place within yourself — you must get a clear picture of your ambitions and desires. You must shape them, truly sculpt them so that they become blindingly clear and precise.

Don't make the mistake of underestimating the importance of this inner change. Until you are sure what you want, you will not get it.

All the rich had unmistakeable ambitions. Many of them used the expression, 'I knew'. Their career choices were spawned by a deep sense of intuition which left no room for doubt.

One of the keys to success is knowing exactly what you want to do

---

Many people go through periods of hesitation and uncertainty. They are at a dead end, not knowing how to overcome this state of confusion. The most important thing to do is to actively decide to change this character trait.

It can easily be done. Many have done so already. Self-suggestion is the road to this transformation.

Relax and withdraw into yourself. Drop your guard and usual barriers. Let your thoughts and imagination flow freely. Recall the old dreams you abandoned along the way; they often contain the seeds of your true vocation in life.

Submit your dream to your subconscious and repeat formulas such as:

- My subconscious will infallibly help me discover how I can be a complete success in life and make all the money I need

- I'm worthy of a job that pleases me 100 per cent and allows me to grow rich beyond all my wildest dreams

- I'm successful

- My life is a triumph

- I do what truly pleases me, so I excel in my job and my income is constantly increasing

- I'm unique. My self-worth is growing every day and allows me to do a job that I like and that pays me well.

Issue the following command to your subconscious:

Subconscious, help me discover what I really like

Fall asleep knowing perfectly well that the answer already lies within you and that you have already obtained what you asked for. The formidable power of your subconscious will work continuously for you day and night, as long as you have steered it in the right direction.

Besides making use of these powerful techniques, you can also consult specialists in career counselling, your friends, newspapers, and magazines. Each decade has its own particular trends. Nowadays, computers are the state of the art. The author of the bestseller *Megatrends* states that since 1985, 75 per cent of all jobs are linked directly or indirectly to computers and computer science. This trend will surely not disappear any time soon. By the year 2000, all jobs will probably be affected by computers. This could be a clue for you. Even if computers don't interest you as such, they will probably be useful to you.

Needless to say, our intention is not to push you into one field rather than another. This would be a foolish thing to do, since it's not enough for something to be fashionable for you to be interested in it. Instead of blindly following trends, stick to your inner feelings. Keep a close watch on whatever is currently popular, but place more importance on your personal inclinations.

DO FOR YOURSELF WHAT YOU ALREADY DO FOR OTHERS

One of the most profitable things you could do is to set up your own business in a field you have already worked in. Experience has shown that this is one of the surest avenues to success because you probably already know this field well. In fact, one of the fundamentals of success is having an in-depth knowledge, also called a 'specialization' of the area you are about to embark in. A lack of knowledge is one of the major causes of failure. Both these points shall be examined in detail in the rest of this chapter.

THE SECRET OF A TRUE EDUCATION

Earlier on we spoke about education and its role in success. We showed that several of the 10 men whose lives we have analysed did not go to university. The same goes for countless other millionaires, and this has led many analysts to wonder whether education actually hinders success. We, however, wouldn't go that far. Besides, all it would take to refute this argument would be to cite the case of Paul Getty, who graduated from Oxford University.

Formal education is not detrimental in itself, especially in our society, where science and technology have become so advanced. However, several people, including millionaires, have mentioned that there could be certain disadvantages, one being the length of study courses, which inevitably delay going out into the world to make millions. Many long and perhaps important years are lost in this way. Those setting out to become rich at the ages of 18 or 20 are generally five or six years ahead of university graduates.

In his book *The Very, Very Rich*, Max Gunther comments on how remarkable it is that so few fabulously wealthy men even bothered to finish college or even school for that matter and includes some of their academic records to illustrate his point. For example, Clement Stone dropped out of high school believing that it had nothing to do with the goal he had set for himself. Howard Hughes 'had money and leisure to attend college but refused.' William Lear was a 'school dropout.'

During the Second World War, Henry Ford was treated as an ignorant pacifist by a *Chicago Tribune* reporter. Ford, insulted by this slanderous remark, decided to sue, charging the newspaper with libel. This is how Napoleon Hill relates this enlightening story in his book *Grow Rich With Peace of Mind:*

When the attorneys for the *Tribune* had Mr Ford on the witness stand they cross-examined him in an attempt to prove their statement was true. One question they asked him was: 'How many soldiers did the British send over to subdue the rebellion in the colonies in 1776?' With a grin, Ford replied: 'I don't know just how many, but I have heard it was a lot more than ever went back.' There was laughter from the court, the jury, the spectators, and even from the frustrated lawyer who had asked the question. Ford kept calm through an hour or more of similar questioning on 'schoolbook' topics. At length, in reply to a question which was particularly obnoxious to him, the industrialist let off some steam. He observed that he had a row of electric push-buttons hanging over his desk, and that when he wanted a question answered, he placed his finger on the right button and

called in the right man to answer that question. He
wanted to know why he should burden his mind with
a lot of useless details when he had able men around
him who could supply him with all the information he
needed.

Long-term studies are also liable to dampen a person's
boldness, sense of initiative, or risk-taking ability, since
logical reasoning and analysis are often given priority over
action.

In his book *The Rich and Super-Rich*, Ferdinand Lundberg states the following:

> Educators, trying in desperation to rally popular
> support for education, and mulling over statistics, like
> to point out to philistines that on average educated
> people earn more than the meagrely educated. And
> this is true when it comes to offering marketable skills
> for modest salaries in an existing establishment that
> requires ever-increasing skilled personnel for its
> complex operations. But it has never been true where
> really big money is concerned. An education can be a
> severe handicap when it comes to making money

He goes on to say:

> The reason for this is that in the process of being
> educated there is always the danger that the
> individual will acquire scruples, a fact dimly sensed by
> some of the neo-conservatives who rail against the
> school system as 'Communistic'. These scruples, unless
> they are [diluted], are a distinct handicap to the fully-
> fledged money-maker, who must in every situation be
> opportunistic. But a person who has had it deeply
> impressed upon him that he must make *exact* reports
> of *careful* laboratory experiments, must conduct *exact*
> computations in mathematics and logic, must produce
> *exact* translations and echoes of foreign languages,
> must write *faithful* reports of *correct* readings and
> must be at least imaginatively aware of the world in
> its diversity, and who has learned these lessons well,
> must invariably discover that some element of
> scrupulousness — even if he hasn't been subject to
> moral indoctrination — has been impressed on his

psyche. If he enters upon money-making in a world
bazaar where approximate truths, vague deceptions,
sneak manoeuvres, half promises and even bald
falsehoods are the widely admired and heavily
regarded order of the day he must [adjust] his
standards. The very process of laboriously making the
adjustment, even if he succeeds, puts him at a
disadvantage *vis-a-vis* the unschooled, who need
waste no energy on such adjustments, who pick up
anything lying around loose as easily as they breathe.

We must nonetheless admit that education does contain
positive elements. In our society, a diploma opens up many
doors. Of course, this does not necessarily guarantee you
success, but often gives you your first opportunity.
General knowledge can also be valuable. Since success is
always linked to other people and nobody ever gets rich
completely on his own, some knowledge of psychology,
sociology, and history, to name a few fields, allows us to
broaden our vision and fine-tune our judgement. This
knowledge is, of course, valid only if you know how to
put it to good use.

The most important point concerning the relationship
between education and success is this: *even if many of
the rich did not attend school for very long, all of them,
without exception, became experts in their fields.*

All of them made sure that they learned as much as possible about their areas of business. Refusing to bend to
this necessity inevitably leads to failure and condemns us
to mediocrity.

The spectacular rise of computers, along with the growing numbers of researchers in all domains, has caused a
rapid evolution in the facts we assume to be true. We live
in a world that is in a perpetual state of motion but which
is relatively constant at the same time. Those who long
for success must keep learning more and more about their
fields throughout their lives. What you discover today
could very well be obsolete tomorrow. To keep up to date
with the rapid evolution of society, you must stay on your
toes and live in a state of wonder and curiosity to sustain
your desire to learn.

Knowing as much as possible about your discipline and

becoming the best in it are absolute musts. This is the educational style of the rich. Besides, unlike some academically-trained entrepreneurs, others on the road to success are not afraid to roll up their sleeves and get their hands dirty.

In many cases, their desire to know everything in their speciality areas appeared excessive, even a manic obsession. Yet, their determination to do things carefully and to take note of the tiniest details was most often responsible for their success.

Ray Kroc became almost lyrical when he spoke about the hamburger bun, confirming the principle we have just stated:

> Consider, for example, the hamburger bun. It requires a certain kind of mind to see beauty in a hamburger bun. Yet, is it any more unusual to find grace in the texture and softly curved silhouette of a bun than to reflect lovingly on the hackles of a favourite fishing fly? Or the arrangement of the textures and colours in a butterfly's wings? Not if you are a McDonald's man. Not if you view the bun as an essential material in the art of serving a great many meals fast. Then this plump yeasty mass becomes an object worthy of sober study.

The way Kroc talks about French fries is no less surprising, at least for those in the know. His search to discover the marvellous taste of the McDonald brothers' fries before he had bought the company was like the tireless work of a detective hunting for clues in a murder mystery novel. Later on he continued to perfect them until he had them just right. His efforts produced results since one part of McDonalds' popularity is due to the taste of its French fries.

Spielberg is also a movie 'maniac' in the sense that he gets involved in every aspect of production: the screenplay, of course, but also casting, music, editing and special effects. He leaves nothing to chance and watches over each production stage.

Honda, never hesitated to throw on overalls and lend a hand in the workshop either, even after he had become a company president. A simple-hearted man despite his prestige, he never stopped wanting to learn, as you are about to discover.

SOICHIRO HONDA

Soichiro Honda was born in 1906 in a small village in Japan. Even when he was very young, motors fascinated him. In fact, it is rare that someone's true calling manifests itself so early in life. In his memoirs, Honda states that, even at the age of two or three, he was vividly impressed by the sight, but especially the sound, of a rice-husking machine on a neighbourhood farm.

> This was my first music. From the veranda of our wooden house, I could see the faint wisps of blue smoke it was giving off. One day I asked my grandfather to take me there. It became a habit . . . I loved the smell of fuel oil that stank up the air, the firecracker-like noises, the smoke belching out, and I would spend hours crouched down low watching the machine while my grandfather impatiently beckoned me to hurry up and get going on our walk.

Honda inherited his precocious affinity for machines from his father. While other village families devoted themselves exclusively to farming, Honda's father was intrigued by the new technologies which were emerging at the turn of the century. He had a workshop where he repaired farming machinery and later on opened up a bicycle repair shop. He was in a sense paving the way for his son by initiating him into the world of machinery at an early age. Because of activities such as these, Honda Sr was soon viewed as an outsider by the peaceful villagers and they predicted that his family would go bankrupt and meet its ruin. Soichiro Honda himself was often to hear the same old prophesies of gloom and doom. Each time, however, he showed that these pessimistic voices could not undermine his faith.

Honda was a poor student at school. Thanks to a devious stratagem he concocted, he always managed to grab a seat out of the teacher's range of vision. Here he was able to daydream or cook up ingenious inventions.

> I got poor grades in school. It didn't upset me very much. My universe revolved elsewhere, around engines, motors and bicycles. . .

That he didn't like school can also be attributed to his weak, awkward physique. The inferiority complex he developed because of this contributed to his fierce desire to distinguish himself, come what may, through altogether different means. His case, along with Spielberg's, is a further example of the astonishing value of personal frustration.

As a boy, Honda suffered miserably from humiliation. He always came last in village sports competitions or races. At school, he usually managed to come down with some illness or other just to avoid PE classes. The only way he could compensate for this was to use machines as the natural extension of his feeble body. This is how he was going to get his revenge. The confession he makes on this subject is disarmingly candid:

> I got into car and motorcycle racing because I could win and I loved to win. I was getting back at the others, at my weak, poorly developed body by making use of other talents, of my head and of my hands. So, I fell in love with machines, which helped my body win and turn me into a winner.

One day, Honda wanted to learn how to swim. At school, most of the older children already knew how. So, he asked one of them to tell him what the secret was.

'Oh! There's nothing to it,' one of the bigger boys said. 'All you have to do is swallow a medaka and you'll be able to swim just like it does in the river.' A medaka, by the way, is a tiny, black and rather unappetizing fish, which resembles a tadpole. Honda innocently went to the river, caught a medaka and swallowed it, blindly following the strange instructions. He had already taken the precaution of drinking lots of water to make the little fish's death easier — a touching gesture! Now relatively confident, Honda plunged into the water and... sank! Fortunately he had not jumped into deep water. After several attempts, and after having swallowed what seemed like gallons of water, he had to face facts: the miracle had not yet happened! Had the other boy left out a vital step? Maybe nature had never intended him to be able to swim like all the other boys his age because of his puny body and weak constitution. Thwarted, but not yet resigned, he went back to the older boy to set his mind at ease.

'I guess you're already too big,' the boy told him. 'Go back to the river and swallow a bigger one. This time it's bound to work.'

This piece of advice, besides being pronounced with utter confidence, appeared to have a rational, scientific basis to it. Honda went back to the river, but his second try was no successful than his first. Nevertheless, Honda was still not resigned to the fact that he could never swim like all the other boys of his age. He started running alongside the river, swallowed a fish and jumped right back in. In the end, he learned how to swim.

> Several years later I learned that the miracle lay in my willpower and repeated attempts, and that by swallowing all that river water I had learned how to swim... Believing deeply in something allows all of us to find tremendous inner strength and to surpass our limitations.

The reason we recount this rather lengthy anecdote is because it is a rather pleasant illustration of a fundamental success principle: the absolute need for faith.

My dream was to become the Napoleon of mechanics!

An illustrious character was going to greatly inspire and influence Honda: Napoleon. He learned about him from his father, but didn't know any details of his life.

> I pictured him as a man whose physical size and strength equalled his power and fame. When I found out later in history books that he was short and squat, I wasn't disappointed. I'm not very tall myself and obviously believed that a man shouldn't be measured by his height, but by his actions and the imprint he leaves on the history of mankind.
>
> I also learned that Napoleon came from a humble background and that his family was probably quite poor... I concluded that it wasn't necessary to be born rich or noble to succeed in life. Other qualities also entitle you to success: courage, perseverance, and... ambitions.

To reinforce his son's admiration, thus programming him in a positive way, Mr Honda would say: 'When you grow up, you must become famous and powerful ... like Napoleon.' It didn't take Honda long to find points that he shared in common with his hero. Like him, the general was short, came from a poor family, was born on an island, and managed to conquer a continent.

> What I retained most from this man was the moral or philosophical lesson that guided his future tendencies: a poor, young student manages to thumb his nose at kings, to clamour for revolution, and to dominate the entire Western world, and one day, I, too, would become a Napoleon, short and famous... Napoleon, my dear Napoleon, my childhood idol because both of us were entitled to keep our crazy dreams.

Not much of an intellectual by nature, Honda restricted his reading to a technical magazine called *The World of Wheels*. One day while leafing through it, he saw an advertisement seeking to hire a garage apprentice for the Hart Shokai Company in Tokyo. He applied for the job. A few days later, he got a positive response. His father begrudgingly allowed him to quit school and head for Tokyo. He was 15 years old.

The job he was given did not quite live up to his ambitious expectations. Instead of being a garage apprentice, he was assigned to baby-sit the boss's youngest child. To all intents and purposes, he was much too young to be given a motor to repair on his own.

> How humiliating! I was so close to my goal, but unable to reach it. Nevertheless this experience strengthened my determination. It would have been downright stupid to drop the kid there and go home defeated, destroying my chances of becoming a mechanic. It is said that every man bears a tiny trace of God's brain. I believe I owe it to the bit I got that I found the patience to stay in Tokyo, to bide my time, and to grab the next opportunity that came my way.

Honda managed to take advantage of this experience even so. While taking care of his boss' child who he carried around on his back, he was completely free to wander around the repair shop and to examine in detail the operations taking place. He was therefore able to get a general feel for mechanics, something that would not have happened had he been assigned to one specific task.

Business was booming; so Mr Saka Kibara, his boss, finally decided that it was perhaps time to give this young man a chance. The day he got his first pair of dungarees was indeed a great one in Honda's eyes: at last he was making a start in the fascinating world of mechanics. The young apprentice soon showed great promise as a mechanic. No suspicious noise, no oil leak escaped his attention. He spent six years learning his trade. When he was 20, his boss called him into the office and asked him if he wanted to go back to his village. At first, Honda thought that this was a polite way of getting rid of him. But it was nothing of the sort. His boss, foreseeing a brilliant career ahead of him, was proposing that he start up a branch in Hamamatsu, seeing that this town had a vast market which he could tap. Needless to say, Honda enthusiastically accepted this challenge, especially since it would allow him to return to his family from whom he had been separated for years.

> I finally became an independent adult, a real man, the master of my arms, legs, brain, destiny, timetable, and the risks facing me.

This tremendous sense of freedom is experienced only by those starting up their own businesses. The study we carried out has shown that this feeling largely compensates for the anxiety that comes from burning your bridges. However, it appears necessary to have a special kind of character ready to 'take the plunge' without being paralysed by material insecurity at the beginning.

During Honda's long years away from home, many things had changed in his native village. For one thing, two or three garages had opened up. Honda thought at first that his would be the only one in town. Now he would somehow have to find a way to deal with his competitors and to do more and better than they. He soon discovered that he had two ways of doing this: first of all, he would have to accept tricky repair jobs that discouraged the other mechanics; and secondly, he would have to work as fast as possible so owners wouldn't be deprived of their vehicles for too long. Honda quickly carved out a solid reputation for himself. Of course he sometimes had to work all night long to return his customers' cars the following day, but that was the price he was willing to pay. His creative ingenuity became evident then. Back then, the spokes in car wheels were made of wood and were not very shock-absorbent. Honda had the idea of replacing them with metal.

When he was 30 years old, Honda signed his first patent. His metal spokes were an instant hit and were exported all over the world.

This invention had opened my eyes to the patience needed to operate in our cottage-like industry. A garage or store is run like a train. It stops at every village and picks up locals, but is unable to go greater distances. Sure, you can be happy chugging up and down this milk-run, but as for myself, I dreamed of operating bigger, faster trains.

Little by little he got the idea of breaking ties with his boss and setting up his own operation. What could he specialize in? Piston rings seemed to offer him good possibilities. But his associates, much more conservative than he was, did not share his enthusiasm. He eventually brought them round, however. He invested all of his savings in 'Tokai Seiki', a piston ring production factory. His first tests were not very successful. The first rings he manufactured were not flexible enough and were simply not marketable. Honda remembers his friends' reactions regarding his failure.

> My friends came in great numbers to tell me that I
> should have stayed in my garage, expanded it
> gradually and let my business prosper instead of
> jumping into shaky ventures. I had invested all of my
> savings in this scheme. I felt responsible for those I
> had dragged into this affair and told myself that I was
> 30 years old and had possibly destroyed all of my
> chances by selling off my garage.

Crushed by the weight of his failure and responsibility, Honda became seriously ill. But, after convalescing for two months, he came back to head his operation, determined to overcome his problems.

The local foundries obviously refused to disclose their secrets. He was on his own. He worked day and night to find the solution, but could see none. The pistons he made were always as hard as rock. Even with all the determination in the world, Honda was forced to face facts: he lacked the technical know-how to go any further.

Needless to say, many others in his shoes would have given up at this point, but Honda, swallowing his pride, agreed to go back to school. He enrolled in university courses to complete his engineering training. Every morning he would go to university and as soon as classes were over would race to his workshop and try to put what he had learned into practice. He stayed there for two years and was finally thrown out. The problem was that Honda, as stubborn as ever, skipped all of his classes except those dealing with manufacturing parts.

> I was like a person dying of hunger receiving a long,
> drawn-out explanation of the general laws of dietetics
> and their effects instead of being given something to
> eat.

Honda tried in vain to explain to the director that he

wasn't attending school for a diploma but for knowledge. This was a slap in the director's face!

Honda returned to his factory, armed with new facts, and began producing better pistons. He had won. Tokai Seiki gradually strengthened its market position and began enjoying a reputation for excellence. The Second World War abruptly put a stop to all of this. In June 1945, American bombs destroyed his factories.

After the war ended, Honda decided to take a year off to develop several inventions and to do some thinking. Still optimistic, despite the gloominess that had settled over the country, he set up his own technical research laboratory, firmly intending to safeguard his independence. He had an idea at the back of his mind. The country's economic situation appeared desperate in the eyes of most industrialists. But Honda's diagnosis was just the opposite. Public transport had been virtually wiped out by the bombings. There were no more than a few trains and buses left. Cars and petrol were both rare and expensive. The Japanese had naturally fallen back on bicycles, which soon became the most popular means of transport. Honda's idea was simple, but brilliant, and, more importantly, corresponded to the needs of the public. Honda fixed a motor to a bicycle, thus producing a cheap motorized bike.

At first, Honda simply converted the motors he bought from the army at cut-rate prices. His motorcycles were an instant hit! Faced with a growing demand and the army's depleted reserves, Honda had to develop his own motor: the Honda Model A. His invention began to be called a 'motorbike'. The success of these bikes was partly due to the fact that Honda had ingeniously found a way to reduce petrol consumption by mixing resin and fuel and by creating a suitable carburettor.

Spurred on by the rebirth of his business, Honda opened a motorcycle assembly plant in February 1948. But he couldn't stop there — he had to do better — he had to make motorcycles. His plan seemed mad. Since Japan's defeat, there was hardly a single motorcycle in the country. But, on September 24, 1948, Honda set up the Honda Motor Company. His first tests were rather disappointing, since the cycle body was too flimsy to withstand the

weight of the motor. But in August 1949, the first prototype was born. It was called 'Dream'. The new motor had
a capacity of only 98 cc and 3 horsepower.

Despite Honda's first success, he now faced heavy financial problems. The market was unstable and limited, and
many distributors were going bankrupt. Honda soon
experienced losses which put him on the verge of
bankruptcy, too. He even made the startling confession
that he was basically an inventor and not an administrator. He had the foresight to recognize his own weaknesses.
He would even say, 'If I had had to manage my company
on my own, I would have gone bankrupt in no time.'

One of his old friends introduced him to Takeo Fujisawa,
a gifted administrator, who helped save Honda's budding
company. This association between the two, one a
dreamer, the other a manager, is a good example of the
principle that nobody forges his success completely on his
own. Referring to the human factor, Honda says:

> When I take temporary stock of my life, I measure
> how important contacts are, how this is worth more
> than all machine inventions because meeting people
> allows us to expand our vision of things and get
> thousands of different experiences that we would
> never have had otherwise.

Far from letting 'Dream' discourage him, Honda developed a new revolutionary model that was faster and
quieter than its predecessor. Almost 10 years later, this
same model would be copied by producers worldwide.
Honda said:

> I never basically regretted the public's first reactions.
> They forced me to push my talents to the limit and
> create a motor that was way ahead of its time.

This is living proof that each failure, however disastrous
it may be, can be of value to those who refuse to be beaten
down by adversity.

This motorcycle met with unprecedented success and
soon 900 of them were rolling off the assembly line every
month. Honda was then faced with the need to increase

production, modernize his factory and even set up new plants. To do this, he needed capital, and lots of it. For someone not part of the establishment, a self-made man in the full sense of the word, convincing the bank to lend him the necessary money was not going to be easy! But Honda was very persuasive and the banks agreed. He modernized his plant and started manufacturing 25,000 bikes a month, sold in 13,000 Honda distributorships. The five factories he owned made him a millionaire.

Honda now faced another challenge: he had to prove to the world that Japan could build motorcycles as fast and reliable as those made in Europe. 'I started out with the simple conviction that if others could build fast engines, so could we,' he said.

Honda went to Europe and bought the best bikes on the market. He brought them home, took them apart, studied them carefully, and created his own racing bikes. They were then entered in races and were hugely successful. Within a few short years, Honda's reputation for excellence spread everywhere and his various models, from scooters to racers, flooded the market. In fact, over the years, Honda subsidiaries sprang up in countries across the world, including the United States, Germany, France, England, Switzerland, Belgium, Australia, Canada, Brazil, Mexico, Peru and Thailand.

> The time had now come to take the plunge and realize another one of my dreams. Attempting to win in Formula One was like trying the impossible. But I had made up my mind once and for all. I would again put in the necessary time, but nothing could stop me from winning sooner or later.

What he had accomplished with motorcycles, he now hoped to do with cars. In 1962, the Honda Motor Company officially declared that it was entering the field of car manufacturing. Honda did not have an easy task, because it meant that he was now facing competition from the United States, which dominated the world market.

Once again, Honda chose to rely on competition to pierce this market, and so he entered his cars in the prestigious Formula One races. Despite the problems he at first encountered, Honda's dream came true on October 24, 1965. One of his entries came first in a major competition, beating world-famous cars such as Ferrari and Lotus, the products of firms who had years of experience in racing and research.

Encouraged by these wins, Honda decided to produce cars for the general public in 1967 and, again trying to produce low-consumption vehicles, he decided to stick to small cars. This proved to be the right decision, since the oil crisis in the 1970s, unforeseeable at that time, was about to put Japanese cars miles ahead of their competitors, who were still concentrating on building larger, less economical cars. Because of the impact of this crisis, manufacturers were forced to redesign their cars to reduce petrol consumption. The American industry was to take 10 years to regain its position in the market.

While his competitors were being indecisive, Honda was flooding the market with a small car that consumers loved: the Honda Civic. Moreover, Honda was one of the first to install anti-pollution devices. So, when many governments were legislating, the Honda Motor Company was ready to respond to the new standards, while its rivals had to scramble to adapt their cars to fit the new regulations. Another major factor accounting for his success was the early use of robotics in his factories.

Honda's outstanding success story is especially enlightening since it illustrates the principle that it is possible to succeed not only when starting from scratch, but under very difficult circumstances as well. During the post-war period, Japan lay in ruins. The average salary was about £600 a year. The so-called 'Japanese miracle' is undoubtedly due to individuals such as Honda. Remember his example when you complain that the economic situation is preventing you from growing rich.

Over the years, Honda took care to write down in his memoirs the major principles of his success. To conclude his story, here is his recipe for success summed up in five points:

● Always be ambitious and youthful

● Respect sound theories, find new ideas and devote time to improving production

- Take pleasure in your work and try to make working conditions as pleasant as possible

- Constantly look for a smooth, harmonious working rhythm

- Always keep in mind the value of research and hard work.

THE MAGIC OF GOALS

Once you have discovered the field in which you wish to excel and grow rich — and you now have the means to do so — you can concentrate on carrying out your plan. You will realize by now that some of the best plans are actually quite simple. Every large company started out small, and was generally the brainchild of one individual alone whose values, enthusiasm, and dreams took concrete shape. Let us hear what Thomas Peters and Robert Waterman have to say about the paradox of simplicity in *In Search of Excellence*:

We will conclude with one strange contradiction that may really hold. We call it the smart-dumb rule. Many of today's managers — MBA-trained and the like — may be a little bit too smart for their own good. The smart ones are the ones who shift direction all the time, based upon the latest output from the expected value equation. The ones who juggle hundred-variable models with facility; the ones who design complicated incentive systems; the ones who wire up matrix structures; the ones who have 200-page strategic plans and 500-page market requirement documents that are but step one in product development exercises.

Our 'dumber' friends are different. They just don't understand why every customer can't have personalized service, even in the potato chip business. They are personally affronted . . . when a bottle of beer goes sour. They can't understand why a regular flow of new products isn't possible, or why a worker

can't contribute a suggestion every couple of weeks.
Simple-minded fellows, really; simplistic even. Yes,
simplistic has a negative connotation. But the people
who lead the excellent companies *are* a bit simplistic.

This conclusion should come as a surprise only to those
not 'simplistic' enough and who have not really succeeded, or at least not past a certain limit. To believe that
you can become a millionaire or make as much money as
you want, to believe in your dream, to disregard other
people's snide comments, you need a good measure of
'naïvety' and 'simplicity'. People who are too rational,
too 'intelligent' can succeed, but their 'intelligence' often
limits the degree of their success.

In order to understand and believe in the rule we are
about to state, you need simplicity. Many of those we
spoke to raised their eyebrows or even laughed at it out-
right. On the other hand, several people we met while
writing this book confessed to us that they only really
started making money as soon as they put this rule into
practice. Many of them, all working in different fields,
became millionaires several times over. The 10 rich men
we have chosen to analyse never lost sight of this rule,
which is the following:

You must set yourself a precise target, an amount and a deadline to make it

---

Some of you are probably beginning to wonder why we
are wasting your time. Yet, what has probably kept you
from succeeding up to now is the fact that you have not
obeyed this rule, or that you haven't set yourself a goal
because you have limited yourself subconsciously.

Remember, people who fail never have precise goals.
Or perhaps, at a more secret and subtle level and for all
sorts of subconscious reasons, they set themselves
unrealistically low objectives. In other words, they succeed in being failures.

This reminds us of a story often told in books. It's the one about an insurance salesman who could never sell more than £5,000 worth of premiums a month. When assigned to a territory where sales were well below this amount, he always managed to reach this £5,000 target. However, when he was sent to a larger territory where other salesmen were performing much better than this, he was never able to top his £5,000 average. The dilemma facing him was clearly based on goals and self-image (we will discuss their close interrelationship shortly). He didn't believe that he could sell more (or less) than £5,000 and his subconscious target was set accordingly. This is proof of the power of the subconscious and the fact that it can be either easy or difficult for our subconscious to help us reach any objective.

Consider your own experiences. Haven't they always been directly linked to your objective? Anyone with a vague, uncertain target or none at all will get results that match this. On the other hand, anyone who has a specific goal and puts a specific plan of action into motion always achieves it.

Why is this? The theory of the subconscious provides the solution. A target is the most simple and effective way of programming your subconscious. It's a kind of secret password, and it is indispensable in gaining access to the world of success. You won't necessarily have to work harder to achieve this goal and you might even have to work less, especially if you are among those who feel that they don't reap the benefits of their efforts.

Don't get us wrong. You normally have to work very hard to succeed. But it is possible to work less and get better results. You can work the same number of hours as usual and increase your results. Once again, the secret lies in your goal.

One thing is sure, even among those who are hard-working and have success-orientated qualities: most people do not have a specific objective in mind. Most people are satisfied with a slight improvement in their lives without ever considering or daring to set themselves a clear-cut figure.

What about you? What is your goal for next year? How much do you want to earn? £20,000? £30,000? £50,000?

£100,000? Half a million? A million?

If you are already earning a salary, you know that your career is following its normal course, and that if you do nothing special to change it, you will be entitled to a pre-set raise, generally a meagre one. If this satisfies you, so much the better. But if you want your lifestyle to improve substantially — a perfectly legitimate desire — ask yourself what goal you have set for yourself. Many salaried workers, who complain about the pittance they make, state that their situations are hopeless and that even if they established a goal for themselves, they wouldn't have time to find the means to achieve it. This is simply an excuse.

If your job promises no forseeable raise or promotion, and thwarts your objective, make sure that as soon as you leave work, and despite your family obligations, you spend at least an hour or two searching for new opportunities. It's the only way to get out of your current situation, and it's not as hard as it sounds. If, on the other hand, you ease up at the end of your work day and indulge only in leisure activities, it is most unlikely, impossible even, that you will ever better your situation.

If you want a brighter future for yourself, discover your goals and work out how much time and energy you are willing to channel into reaching them. If all you can do is dream of getting a promotion or a fantastic job offer, but haven't fixed a specific objective, the 'miracle' you are expecting will never happen. Your self-worth is exactly what you think it is.

Let's start with a simple little test. Take a piece of paper and write down how much you'd like to earn next year. Finished? Good. Now read what follows very carefully.

When you created your goal, you automatically based it on your self-image

---

If your current salary is £12,000 a year, you perhaps started to write down that you would like to earn £25,000.

But you immediately stopped yourself and put £20,000 instead or, if you were feeling optimistic, £22,000. The reason you subconsciously checked yourself was because you believe you are not really worth £25,000 a year, and that you have neither the qualities nor the potential to qualify you for such a generous reward, or perhaps, that your circumstances would never in a million years enable you to reach such a salary. In other words, although this might surprise you, you are worth exactly what you think you are worth. But the reasons you mentally conjured up to limit or reduce your objective appeared reasonable and logical. They are neither. They are purely and simply the products of your self-image.

AIM HIGH!

Remember the important principle we indicated earlier. The greatest limitations people can impose on themselves are the ones created in their own minds. We have established that a person's worth is what he believes it to be. As a rule, most people underestimate themselves, even if they appear self-confident. Those who think deep down that they are truly valuable are few and far between. Everyone has an inferiority complex to some degree, and it causes them to believe that they are not worthy of success, of other people's esteem or of much money.

The best way to increase your worth is to build up your self-esteem. We have already seen the techniques you could use to bring about this fundamental change. One of the best ways of accomplishing this is to work with a monetary objective.

Do the following exercise. A few moments ago, you set yourself a goal. Double it right away. Now, assess your reaction. Let's say you wrote down £25,000 a year. Why didn't you put £50,000? How do you feel about this target? Do you think it's completely far-fetched? Do you think that £50,000 is a lot? You're right in a way, since only a small percentage of people can hope for such an income. And yet, each year, thousands of people around the world become millionaires. And thousands of people have yearly incomes far in excess of £100,000.

All rich people, men and women alike, started out with the self-image of a millionaire before becoming one. To increase your self-worth, aim high. Don't be afraid of doing so. For the first year, however, don't set yourself an amount that will appear totally unrealistic to you. Do it step by step, but make it ambitious enough. If you aim high and almost make it, you will still have achieved a satisfying result. But if your target is low and you barely make it, you will be disappointed and will have made very little progress.

Setting yourself an exact objective is truly magical. What usually happens the first time you set yourself a monetary goal is that you keep a measure of scepticism that limits your ambitions. But as soon as you achieve your first goal, you can and must set yourself even higher goals. And what generally surprises those who set themselves a target for the first time is that they reach it! Not only this, they often go beyond it. Why don't you do the same? Challenge yourself to reach your goal. It's an exciting game that normally brings surprising dividends. Perhaps you will reach your goal in six months instead of the year you had initially given yourself. You will be the first to benefit from this.

You are worth much more than you believe

You are worth infinitely more than you believe. The only problem is that no one has ever told you this before. People have probably done their utmost to persuade you that the opposite is true. Keep this point well in mind: intelligence, work, motivation, imagination, discipline, and experience are of course important ingredients for success, but how many people do you know who have these qualities and who still do not succeed at all or live up to their full potential? Perhaps the same is true for you. Despite your obvious talents and efforts, success seems to inexplicably escape you. Conversely, you have met people at work or in rival firms who do not appear to be gifted with special qualities — and who are not, in fact — but they get the raise in salary that you deserve or present a year-end balance-sheet that makes their associates or stockholders swell with pride.

The real reason is not due to luck or coincidence. These people have different self-images and have set themselves precise goals. They sincerely believe that they deserve substantial incomes. They harbour no doubts about this at all. As for you, it is probable that deep down, without knowing it, you do not believe that you deserve a high income.

Get rid of your mental limitations and increase your self-worth by aiming as high as possible. And remember that it is no harder for your subconscious to help you reach a higher objective than a lower one. And one thing is sure, it will be so much more enjoyable, for this is the start of your journey towards success!

WRITE YOUR GOAL DOWN

> ...the discipline of writing something down is the first step towards making it happen. In conversation, you can get away with all kinds of vagueness and nonsense, often without even realizing it. But there's something about putting your thoughts on paper that forces you to get down to specifics. That way, it's harder to deceive yourself — or anybody else.

These sharp-minded and psychologically astute words were written by Lee Iacocca.

Take the time to re-read this quote, written by a man who, over the years, displayed the exceptional qualities of a leader of men and of a creator.

'The discipline of writing something down is the first step toward making it happen.' This is by no means a trivial statement. It is very meaningful. The act of writing down your goal makes it concrete. Writing it down is equivalent to going ahead with your first action; it is the first step towards achieving it. And since you must take the first step, you can imagine how important this action is.

The second advantage of Iacocca's method is that you can no longer deceive yourself. Don't be afraid to announce your objective, or at least open up about it to your family and close friends. Naturally, you're running the risk of being the butt of jokes and of sarcasm. But rest assured: all successful people have had to put up with this too. They would never laugh at you. They might smile a bit, but theirs is the smile of an ally who understands that you too have found the secret and will soon be joining them in the circle of winners. As for the rest, ignore their mockery and snide remarks. Soon it will be your turn to laugh. You know a truth that they are unaware of and do not wish to share:

A precise goal is the springboard
for any accomplishment

A MAGNIFICENT OBSESSION

Make your goal your magnificent obsession. Write it down in several places. Keep it well in sight. Above all, keep it constantly in mind. A major principle ruling the mind is that *energy goes wherever your thoughts go*. By constantly thinking of your goal and making it become a fixed idea, all your energy will channel itself into helping you be successful. Better still, thanks to the mysterious work of your subconscious, circumstances and people will help you reach your goal in a new and surprising way. A goal is like a magnifying glass. It focuses your energy on your target.

This fixed idea, called 'monoideism' by some writers, not only allows you to increase your energy and success coefficient but prevents a very serious mistake — that of scattering your energy. All rich people had a fixed idea and this goal led them to success.

Another advantage of singlemindedness is that it enables you to direct your professional and overall life more

precisely. How does it do this? Very simply. Everything
that helps you come closer to your goal must be
encouraged. Everything that distances you from it must
be rejected. How can you know if something brings you
nearer to or farther from your goal? A well-programmed
subconscious will tell you in its usual way. You will have
a feeling of intuition or you will be influenced by a book
you might have read, or by a friend's or a partner's advice.

One of the rich men who achieved success throughout
his life through singlemindedness was Walt Disney.

WALT DISNEY

Who among us, young or old, hasn't watched *The Wonderful World of Disney* and seen that man with a good-natured expression on his face, seated at his desk, speaking to us about animals or, book in hand, inviting us to visit the fabulous world of his cartoon characters? This image of Walt Disney is that of a man who has succeeded in reaching all his goals.

Walt Disney's life can be summed up by a golden rule that has been shared by all rich people.

> To succeed, work hard, never give up, and above all cherish a magnificent obsession

Walter Elias Disney was born in Chicago on December 5, 1901. His mother, Flora Call, was of German descent, whereas his father, Elias Disney, was an Irish-Canadian. In 1901, Theodore Roosevelt became the President of the United States. His inauguration marked the beginning of a period in which success was synonymous with work and audacity. Regardless of origin, wealth seemed accessible to anyone willing to put in the effort and take charge of his destiny.

The Disney family moved from city to city, since Elias Disney, although fascinated by business, had no particular aptitude for it and had frequent financial setbacks. He was the sort of man ready to move mountains for a prosperous business. Unfortunately, his dream never came true. For his son, however, it would be an altogether different story.

In 1906, the Disney family settled down in Marceline, Missouri, where Disney Snr had just bought a farm. Country life and direct contact with nature sparked Walt's passion for animals, the stars in the animated films he was going to produce. He always remembered the little creatures that inhabited this farm much more clearly than the people he met while he lived there.

On the other hand, one character who remained permanently etched on his memory was his Uncle Ed. Uncle Ed was not bright, and because he was unable to earn a living, he received free room and board from the different family members. This strange character soon won over the young boy's heart. In Walt's eyes, Ed was totally different from all the other adults he knew; he was free to do what he liked and seemed completely happy. Disney once said that his Uncle Ed was kindness itself. He was, perhaps, a bit of a simpleton, but he enjoyed life fully in his own way. He knew the names of all the animals and plants and could recognize birds from the tunes they whistled. Going for walks with him was Walt's greatest joy. Uncle Ed was the happiest, gentlest person he had ever met. He represented *joie de vivre* in its simplest, purest form.

Walt was going to draw a great lesson from this strange man, a lesson he would apply throughout his life:

> ## To really succeed and be happy, you have to do what you enjoy

For the moment, Walt was enjoying himself. His Aunt Margaret had given him a colouring book and crayons, and he spent hours and hours in the woods watching animals that he would later immortalize on his drawing board.

Following a series of poor harvests, the Disney family's situation took a turn for the worse. In 1910, the farm was put up for sale and the family set off for Kansas City. The profits Disney Snr made from this sale allowed him to purchase a newspaper-selling business. Walt's happy days were over. Facing him were the city's harsh realities and . . . work. With his older brother Roy, Walt, who was not even 10 at the time, had to get up at 3.30 a.m. to watch for the arrival of the delivery truck. This was followed by a long trek across town, where Walt could sometimes be seen wet and shivering from the cold and almost doubled over from the weight of a bag much too big for his size. Sometimes, the cold was so bad that he would huddle near the front doors of houses just to warm up and rest a little.

Elias Disney personally saw to it that the boys carried out their work well. Walt had to put up with his father's outbursts on a number of occasions because a disgruntled customer had complained that his paper had arrived a few minutes late, and soggy as well. For the rest of his life, Disney would wake up with a start in the middle of the night, soaked in sweat, dreaming that he had forgotten to deliver a customer's newspaper and that he had to face his father's fury.

To make ends meet, Walt's mother often helped her husband, who also worked as a salesman for a local dairy farmer. Often, after delivering his papers, Walt would give her a helping hand. The sight of her pushing a huge cart was something he could never get used to and it raised a lot of questions in his mind. Was working like a slave and getting only a miserable salary in return all you could expect from life? Wasn't there a way of getting out of this vicious circle?

There had to be a way, judging from the huge houses Walt had seen when delivering his papers, and from the expensive toys carelessly scattered all over their front lawns and porches. While doing his early morning paper round, he couldn't resist playing a little with a toy train or car left lying there. Then, a few minutes later, he would put the toy back where he had got it and start working again.

Events such as these probably helped him understand that people were divided into two categories: those who succeed and those who don't.

He secretly swore that he would be successful one day

Another thing irritated the young boy. Ever since his brother Ray had left home, Elias Disney had hired other boys to do the work. What was particularly frustrating was that these boys did the same work as he did but were paid in return! Despite his insistence, his father had closed the debate once and for all, saying, 'I dress and feed you, so don't bother me with your demands!'

During the six years he delivered newspapers, he never got a single penny. He was forced to find some other way of getting some pocket money. For example, behind his father's back, he had the ingenious idea of delivering papers to new clients he had recruited in other neighbourhoods. In addition, he also worked as a messenger boy for a sweet shop owner. He made sure that he was financially independent. For the rest of his life he would always have a single goal: to be his own lord and master!

After the First World War, things went sour and Elias Disney had to sell his newspaper business. The family moved to Chicago, where he had just bought shares in a small jam-making company. Walt worked there for a while, but crushing fruit and stacking cans all day long was boring to this 16-year-old who dreamed only of adventure. In spite of the art courses he was taking at the Chicago School of Fine Arts, the temptation to join the army got the better of him. He enlisted as a volunteer Red Cross ambulance driver by lying about his age. His training had not yet ended, however, when Armistice was declared. But by a combination of circumstances, the special unit he belonged to was shipped to France to assist in repatriating American soldiers injured on the front.

It didn't take long for his commanding officers to discover that he had a special talent for drawing. Besides driving ambulances, Walt drew his first posters, which were designed to direct the soldiers to the various medical services. With a friend, he also used his talent for less commendable purposes. To make a little money, one of his friends had the idea of taking German helmets left on the battlefields in order to sell them to American soldiers at home as war trophies!

Aware of Disney's artistic talents, his friend asked him if it would be possible to add a realistic touch to these precious 'souvenirs'. He got the brilliant idea of applying poor-quality paints (which chipped almost as soon as they were applied) to give them a battle-scarred look. Once this was done, he shot a hole into each of them and glued a piece of hair inside them. And there it was, a war trophy bound to be a showpiece for its proud owner and to spark many memories of bravery.

Disney's stay in France changed him from a gentle teenage dreamer into a mature and determined man. He would later recount that the 11 months he spent in France were what really taught him about life and self-reliance.

I learned to be totally self-reliant

When he returned home, he discovered that his father had already mapped out his future for him: he would work in his jam-making company in order to take it over one day. Walt, however, already had a clear vision of his own future. Above all, he wanted to do what he really enjoyed doing — drawing! Despite bitter opposition from his father, who believed that it was silly to try to earn a living by dabbling in art, Walt refused to back down. He put a halt to the dispute — he simply left home, and headed for Kansas where Roy was then living.

As soon as he arrived in Kansas City, Disney sped off to the *Star,* one of the town's biggest newspapers. Unfortunately, the manager told him that he had no work for a cartoonist and that he had better try his luck in another field. Despite this, he didn't lose hope. A few days later, he went back to the same newspaper to meet the personnel manager instead. This time he put on his army uniform to give him more prestige and credibility. Shortly after the usual conversation, the manager said: 'Sorry, but you're too old.'

'But, I'm barely seventeen.'

'Anyway, the type of job you want doesn't pay very well.'

'I don't care. I really want to work as a cartoonist.'

'What kind of experience do you have?'

'Well. . . I did a bit of drawing in the army and I drove ambulances.'

'In that case, you should go to the Department of Transport.'

The manager obviously had no idea that the young man he had just turned away was soon going to be one of the greatest cartoon animators ever, the man who would feed the imaginations of thousands of children the world over.

By a strange coincidence, Roy Disney, then working in a bank, knew two clients who ran the Gray Advertising Company and were looking for a junior commercial artist. Walt must have looked very determined, because he was given the job on the spot. It was during the few months that Disney worked for this agency that he really learned his craft, mastering the techniques and special effects used in film advertising.

Nevertheless an idea kept niggling at his brain — working for himself — especially since he had found out that part of the staff was going to be made redundant at the end of the busy season. This prospect appealed to him for two reasons. First of all, he wanted to be independent, secondly, he was yearning to do something new and original, not content just to satisfy the requirements of his boss and of the firm's clients.

Disney, along with a friend of his, Ube Iwerks, set up his first commercial art agency. Their first client was a restaurant chain. Disney and his partner were able to make arrangements to set up their workshop and office in a room in the same building as the new restaurant without paying anything. In exchange, they had to make advertising posters for this company.

Besides working on this contract, they were completely free to do other projects. To attract clients, Walt devised a special plan. He would go to a store or company and find out if they had an art department. The person in charge might reply that they didn't, usually adding that they had absolutely no need for one. This is when Walt would offer his services on a freelance basis. If the company had no work to give him, that was fine, but if ever they needed this kind of work done, he and his associate would be ready to take full charge of the project. Within no time at all, this little strategy allowed both of them to save much more money than they would ever have earned if they had been working for someone else.

This business seemed highly promising, but one day Walt happened to spot a newspaper ad looking for a cartoonist for the Kansas City Film Ad Company. It presented him with dilemma. Should he keep his business with Ube going or attempt to fulfil his lifelong dream of doing cartoon animation? Once he had mastered new skills, nothing would prevent him from starting up his own company again. This argument tipped the scales in favour of his taking the job. In 1920, Disney finally entered the world of cartoon animation. He would soon create a name for himself in this field, and his characters would become popular all over the world.

KC Film Ad Company was responsible for all aspects of film advertising and before long took notice of this young cartoonist. In fact, not long after he started, Walt was given a poster to do of a man dressed in a fashionable hat. He drew the poster, but in place of the man's nose he drew a lightbulb! When the poster was shown on a screen, the boss exclaimed: 'Finally something new in this place. I'm fed up with these pretty faces!'

Walt's originality and vision of things annoyed some of his superiors and colleagues. They were jealous of him and thought he was a trouble-maker. So they refused to allow him to try out a new technique for perfecting his cartoons. He had had the brilliant idea of making several drawings on celluloid, photographing them, superimposing them and finally filming them. Walt's bosses didn't want to hear anything about this. They felt that their way of doing things had produced good enough results until then. They didn't see any reason to change their techniques, since all of their clients seemed perfectly satisfied. Walt Disney knew he was right.

After months of pleading with his boss, Walt finally got permission to bring one of the company cameras home to do a few tests. From that day on, Disney never looked back.

In an empty garage converted into a studio, he started making short animated films using the technique he had devised. He then showed them to a top cinema director, who was thrilled with his results. Walt's sketches and film technique were very different from traditional ones. His first cartoon films were soon released to cinemas.

At first they were meant to replace commercials to keep the public amused during intermissions. Walt called them 'Laugh-O-Grams'. They delighted the public and from then on in Kansas City Walt Disney was no longer viewed as 'that eccentric young man' but was considered with respect. He even got a raise. Disney quickly became a celebrity in his adopted city.

He returned the camera he had borrowed and bought his own with the money he had saved. Since the cartoons were rapidly growing in popularity, Walt rented more office space to found his small company, Laugh-O-Grams Corporation, with an initial $15,000 capital investment. He hired a few apprentices and a salesman to promote Laugh-O-Grams in New York City. His dreams of independence were coming true when he was barely 20 years old!

He then decided to leave KC Film to work entirely for himself. Success was not automatic, however. Production costs were high and Disney's perfectionism (which led him to reinvest all his earnings to improve his product), as well as the limited market he was working in, soon led to bankruptcy.

This was a very bleak period in his life; he had naturally assumed that bad times were finally over. He was penniless and was forced to live in his workshop, eating and sleeping on a small couch, the only piece of furniture he·

owned. Worse still, once a week he had to go to the train station to take a shower.

He finally managed to dig up a small animated cartoon contract to teach children the importance of brushing their teeth. One night, the dentist who had commissioned this film called, asking him to come to his office and discuss the project. 'Impossible,' Disney was obliged to answer. 'How come?' asked the dentist. 'Because I don't have any shoes. The only pair I have are at the shoemaker's and I can't pay to get them out!'

Despite adversity, Walt Disney wasn't the type to get easily discouraged. He had an idea in mind. One night in July 1923, stuffing his money into his pockets, this skinny young man dressed in an old grey oilskin suit, boarded the train for Hollywood. He was firmly determined to become a somebody in the world of motion pictures.

When Disney arrived in Hollywood, he was just another unknown hoping to make his dream come true. His brother Roy had been living in California for a little while and was glad to offer him a roof over his head. Walt then began to visit each film studio one by one. He was ready to accept anything at all, provided the job was related to the movies.

> To get ahead in a speciality
> area you must get your foot
> in the door no matter what it
> costs

Disney quickly realized how difficult it was to get into Hollywood film studios. Many others before him had knocked at the door and received the same reception.

He refused to let this dampen his spirits, however, If others had managed to get their feet in the door, why should it be any different for him? In his eyes, there were two categories of people:

> ## Those who feel lost and forsaken when they can't find a job and those who manage to earn their living any way they can in times of trouble

Disney had always done his best to belong to the second category.

Experience had taught him that you have to be totally self-reliant. He went back to the drawing board, determined to find a place for himself. He drew comic strips with the intention of selling them to cinemas. This was a matter of re-using the experience he had acquired in Kansas City with his Laugh-O-Grams. This concept enchanted one cinema owner, who bought a whole series of comic strips and ordered a sequel to *Alice in Wonderland,* which Disney had begun to shoot in Kansas. He was offered $1,500. This was much more than he had expected. The series ran for three years, enabling Disney to buy himself a house and even to set up his own movie studio.

After the *Alice in Wonderland* films, Walt wanted to create something new and completely original. This resulted in the birth of that clever little creature called 'Mickey Mouse', a name thought up by Disney's wife, Lillian Bounds. Mickey Mouse quickly became an international celebrity, and was even more popular than many Hollywood stars! Producers nevertheless greeted Mickey with reserve.

At about the same time, talking pictures appeared and the public began to 'boycott' silent films. It didn't take long for Disney to react. With a team of assistants, he introduced a new method for synchronizing sound with animation.

Constantly searching for new techniques to improve his art, Walt applied the new 'technicolour' process, which freed him from having to rely on a two-colour combination. In the movie *Bambi,* he used up to 46 different shades of green for the forest. His first colour cartoon, *Silly Symphony*, delighted movie buffs. Disney increasingly realized that if he wanted to continue on a larger scale he would have to set up a mastermind group, that is, surround himself with the collective brain power of competent assistants able to offer a quality product.

> To establish ourselves, we knew that we would have to train our assistants ourselves

Disney felt that the cartoonists working for him were using worn-out tricks of the trade much too often. He knew that the only way to change this would be to set up training courses for them.

> His goal was simple: to improve the quality of the drawings and animation techniques

As his company kept expanding, he decided in 1930 to create his own school, where he would teach future cartoonists all the techniques of cartoon animation. The school soon began to look like a zoo. In fact, to make his cartoon heroes more realistic, Disney had converted his classrooms into real-life biology laboratories where the students spent long hours observing different animals asleep, awake, eating, and so on. These studies were also going to help him make future documentaries on the wonders of nature.

In 1938, Disney introduced his first feature-length animated film, *Snow White*. It had required two years of hard work. This film was one of his masterpieces.

A little while later he had modern film studios built in

Burbank, California, where he would eventually have up to 1,500 employees working for him. By then it seemed as though he had achieved his goal.

He was gradually becoming the man he had sworn he was going to be: the head of a complex operation demanding patience, persistence, and professionalism.

> I only work well when I have obstacles to overcome. I worry when things are working too well, fearing a sudden change in this situation

During the Second World War, Roy and Walt Disney received several army contracts to produce documentaries and war posters. Once the war was over, business became even brisker for the Disney Studios and Walt devoted himself to his art more than ever. He would often work late at night. One story has it that he would often sift through wastepaper baskets to see what they contained. The following day, he would get his assistants to go over what he had found, claiming that these bits sometimes held great ideas! It was during this time that Walt created most of his great films, including *Cinderella*, *Peter Pan*, and *Bambi*.

In the 1950s Walt's phantasmagorical dream — Disneyland —developed. At the time, all of his friends, and especially his bankers, claimed that the project was insane. Once again, Disney was going to show that man's dreams can come true.

The idea of creating Disneyland came to him during his walks in the park with his two daughters, Sharon and Diana. He pictured a gigantic amusement park where children could meet with their favourite cartoon characters. When Disney finally made up his mind to execute this project, nothing and no one could change his mind.

Disneyland finally opened in Anaheim, California, in

1955. It was a great day for Disney, who said:

> If I listened to myself, my park would never be
> finished. Here is something, finally, that I can perfect
> forever and ever.

In 1985, Disneyland greeted its 250 millionth visitor.

When Walt Disney died in 1966, the cinema lost one of its greatest creators. Two major principles had motivated his entire life: doing what he enjoyed and believing in his ideas.

Without these principles, he never would have been the man he was: the recipient of 900 citations, 32 Oscars, five Emmies, and five honorary doctorates, a pioneer in the history of animation and one of the richest men in the world. He had realized his dreams far beyond his wildest expectations!

A PLAN OF ACTION

What is surprising when we set a goal for ourselves that is the least bit ambitious is that it normally creates a sudden, compelling insight for us. This realization is usually something like this:

It is obvious that I won't earn £5,000, £10,000, or £100,000 more this year, or land a new job, or get a promotion if I do nothing about it. If things stay the way they are, I'm going to find myself in basically the same position at the end of the year as I'm in now. I must therefore do something about this. I need a plan of action to reach my goal.

This reasoning is right. Often, you must do something totally different. It's good to become aware of this. Some jobs will unfortunately never make you rich. For example, no civil servant has ever become a millionaire. Some senior government officials are relatively well paid, but they are the exceptions. This is just one example among many. A grocery clerk or a shoe salesperson can become a millionaire — there are many examples of this — but certainly not in this minimum-wage type of job. So, if you are burning with ambition, choose to work in a field full of potential. May we remind you that you must come to grips with the fact that your financial condition will not improve if you do nothing about it.

DEVELOPING YOUR PLAN OF ACTION

If you are looking for your first job, type up your curriculum vitae, make telephone calls, and line up some interviews. If you are looking for a good opportunity in which to invest some money — for example, in real estate — stay on the look-out. Talk to people you know who work in this field, read specialist magazines, go hunting for opportunities. If you want a raise, analyse your situation well. Find the person in the best position to help you get it. Try to formulate the best arguments to describe to your boss how he will benefit from giving you a raise. If you are an entrepreneur, do your best to discover new markets, to capitalize on current markets, or to reduce your costs.

We are aware that these suggestions are overgeneralized. This is inevitable. Each situation is special and we don't have the space here to describe how to write up a CV, shine in an interview, or find out about the profitability of a real estate deal. We recommend that you do some serious reading on these topics, especially if you are inexperienced in these areas.

The most vital step is to prepare a step by step plan of action so that your intentions become possible. You must also stick to your original plan, despite the problems and obstacles that may arise. However, it is also essential to know how to make adjustments when necessary and to adopt a better plan when one comes to mind. You must also be able to ditch a plan when failure is looming on the horizon. Some products never catch the public's eye or become popular. Certain jobs in some companies will never be within your reach. But console yourself with the idea that you might find a better one elsewhere. This *will* happen if your subconscious is programmed positively.

No human being is infallible, not even the most experienced businessperson. Only those who do nothing never make mistakes. The law of averages, which we mentioned previously, as well as a positive mental attitude, will come to your rescue. What counts is that, even if you undergo temporary setbacks, you will still achieve your goals, if your subconscious is properly programmed.

The only difference is that it will take a slightly different and sometimes unexpected path. This is the secret power of a precise monetary goal and a deadline. All roads lead to Rome, so the saying goes. The subconscious seems to have appropriated this adage. These roads are sometimes mysterious, but one thing definitely isn't — your goal.

When making up your plan, be both rigid and flexible, remembering that too much of either one or other can cause you problems. But remember this as well: most people fail because they give up too quickly after their first failure or setback. So, if you are faced with a choice to make, stick to your original plan. All the rich and successful did precisely this.

To apply your plan of action, you will probably be forced to take certain risks, which are sure to make you feel insecure, especially if it's the first time you have set a goal for yourself and hammered out a plan of action. Any change generates a measure of anxiety and insecurity. Don't be afraid to forge ahead. In his memoirs, Lee Iacocca commented on this:

> A certain amount of risk-taking is essential. I realize it's not for everybody. There are some people who won't leave home in the morning without an umbrella, even if the sun is shining. Unfortunately, the world doesn't always wait for you while you try to anticipate your losses. Sometimes you just have to take a chance — and correct your mistakes as you go along.

If you count yourself among those who never leave home without an umbrella, even when the sun is shining, it is highly unlikely that you will have seen fit to set yourself a new objective and establish a plan of action to reach it.

A goal doesn't involve only money. You could set your sights on becoming the best lawyer, the best novelist, the best accountant, the best real estate investor, the best insurance broker or the best shoe manufacturer within a given period of time. This is perfectly legitimate. Besides, it's one of the best ways to achieve success. Remember the true definition of wealth: it is the reward you receive in exchange for services you have rendered to people. If you give the best service, then you can expect your reward to be in keeping with that. The same rules apply for any other kind of goal. In fact, ideally, it's best to combine the two: the desire to become the best in a given field and to receive a specific income within a set time. This combination is particularly effective.

NO MORE THAN TWO GOALS AT A TIME

Be careful not to set yourself too many goals at the same time. This rarely, if ever, leads to success. However, wishing to become the best in your field and to make a specific income does not constitute two goals, it is a double aim, since both desires are intimately linked.

WHAT DO YOU WANT TO DO WITH YOUR LIFE?

Limiting yourself to two objectives a year such as becoming an expert in your field, reaching a set income, or getting a new job, doesn't mean that you shouldn't set yourself long-term goals. It wouldn't be a bad idea to establish a five-year goal that would naturally overlap with your one-year goal. Many rich people go so far as to set goals for their whole lives. You might well have noticed that several of the men we have met up with knew what they wanted to do with their lives even when they were very young. The expression 'I knew that my whole life would be devoted to such and such an activity,' is a common one.

Why not follow their example? Put your book down for a minute and ask yourself what you want to do with your life, what you want to be. Don't limit yourself. Let your imagination run riot. You are alone. No one is there to criticize you or to sneer at you. What kind of person would you like to be in 5, 10, or 25 years from now? What kind of life are you dreaming of? What job would you like to have? Disregard your present situation, previous failures, and past life, Forget about your age, as well. Remember Ray Kroc, who believed at the age of 52 that the best was yet to come. You can make your life rich and full at any age. And often the dreams you nourish come true much more easily than you realize, and come true regardless of your age or current situation.

The advantage of knowing what you would like to do for the rest of your life and to picture yourself in the distant future is that it gives meaning to your short-term goals. Take a piece of paper and write down what you would like to do with your life. Add as many details as possible. What kind of work would you like to be doing? How much money would you like to be earning? In 5 years? In 10 years? In 25 years from now? What kind of house would you like to live in? What kind of friends would you like to have? Will travelling be part of your life? What about vacations? Your family life?

Write all of this down in as much detail as possible. Picturing your life in this way can literally shape your future. In fact, by dreaming like this you are programming your subconscious. You are flooding it with images that are likely to come true in your life. The advantage is that you hold the reins of command. You become the architect of your own life.

As of now, you can become the architect of your life

This long-term objective will become your ideal in life and will simplify many of the choices facing you which would otherwise have been difficult to make, or worse still, would have appeared arbitrary, or even absurd, to you. When you don't know what you want to do with your life, it is difficult to justify the most insignificant day-to-day decisions. They don't seem to be part of a greater plan that gives meaning to your actions and even thoughts. Those who don't know what they want in life or can't picture their future, cannot shape it to suit their desires

and rarely, if ever, achieve success. They are like rud-
derless ships floating on the sea.

Making up a life plan is very stimulating and motivating, and it contributes to success in all areas of life.
However, always keep in mind the need to remain flexible regarding the future, since life involves constant
adaptation. What you will be doing in five or ten years
from now won't necessarily be what you had expected.
This doesn't mean that whatever happens to you can't
be even better than you had dreamed possible. When our
minds are well programmed, the situations which develop
are always better. As you develop your potential and
become more and more positive, the plans you dream up
will be bolder, more ambitious, and you will, most likely,
drop some of your initial ones. Don't worry. This is what
often happens in life. What counts is your constant pro-
gression towards greater self-fulfillment and total personal
enrichment.

IDENTIFY NEXT YEAR'S OBJECTIVE

Once you have your goal clearly in mind for the year to
come, divide it up. Put in order the things you must
accomplish. Don't forget to write all of this down. Set a
date for each of the stages, and respect your new deadlines. Try to see whether your monthly income equals a
twelfth of the amount you intend to earn as outlined in
your new goal. If you get paid on a regular basis and
there's no way you will be earning a twelfth of your goal
in one month, you must clearly do something else. This
does not necessarily mean quitting your job, but it may
mean doing something extra to reach your objective.

Of course, some incomes can't be divided in such a clear-
cut way. But there is certainly one thing that you can and
must plan out as carefully as possible, while still remaining
flexible enough to respond if a once-in-a-lifetime opportunity arises, and that is the work and effort you must put in
to reach your goal. Divide your yearly goal into months, and
then into weeks. Sound planning prevents a lot of worry.

DISCIPLINE YOURSELF!

It's all well and good to set yourself an objective, and it is necessary for anyone wishing to grow rich, but to try to work towards it day by day, you need discipline. And the best discipline is the one that you, and no one else, impose on yourself. The Greek philosopher, Heraclitus, said: 'Character equals destiny.' Think about this simple, but profound, equation. Look at the people around you. Think of those you know. There are no exceptions to this rule. All successful men and women have strong characters and temperaments: they are highly disciplined. Consider the people you know. You will see that no one succeeds without strength of character. Everyone has a master. To become your own master and take your destiny in hand, you need discipline. Incidentally, the 10 rich men in this book were all rigidly disciplined. This disproves the popular notion that the rich are idle and lazy. True, some inheritors are the proverbial idle rich, but this because they simply didn't need strength of character and self-discipline to earn their money; it was handed to them on a silver platter. The opposite is true for the self-made men in this book.

> Character equals destiny

You mustn't believe that when we say discipline we mean behaviour that leaves no room for fantasy and relaxation. Disciplining yourself also means putting time aside for leisure activities, relaxation and physical exercise. The mistake many people who are setting out to build a fortune make is to lose sight of the fact that they need to take breaks to function well. Overworking is never productive. You have to devote time to recharging your batteries. You need to find an equilibrium.

Many people are overworked but never accomplish much. Complaining of overwork is fashionable these days. And yet, the vast majority of people don't use a tenth of their potential.

Those who manage to work so hard are not really different from the rest of us. They are not more energetic, either. However, they do know how to use their energy better. Whereas it lies dormant in most people, they have awakened it. You now know how to do it, too. Furthermore, these highly disciplined men and women have developed sound working habits. For most people, the problem is that they have picked up bad habits. Through discipline and positive mental programming, you will be able to develop the habit of success.

Success is a habit

Become a slave to the habits of success in the same way as you have, until now, been the slave to habits leading you to failure. By replacing one with the other, you will create a new habit, and a new second nature to yourself. Success will then be irresistibly attracted to you.

One man who, in his youth, cultivated the habit of success and self-discipline was the famous billionaire John D. Rockefeller. Let us now look at the story of his life.

JOHN DAVISON ROCKEFELLER

The man the multimillionaire steel king, Andrew Carnegie, first nicknamed 'Reckafellow' and then later 'my co-millionaire' was born in 1839 in a small farm house near Moravia, in the state of New York. His father, William Avery Rockefeller, was neither a faithful husband, nor an exemplary father. He was a tall man, and was built like a bull. Always well dressed, he reputedly distrusted banks so much that he always carried around a 'modest' $1,000 in his pockets.

Mystery surrounded William Rockefeller. He would disappear for long stretches of time, leaving his wife the job of raising their children. When he returned, his pockets were usually stuffed with money and gifts which he would dole out to his family. It was many years later that John Rockefeller found out that his father was a confidence trickster. In fact, William Rockefeller visited Indian reserves pretending he was deaf and dumb and sold them all sorts of knick-knacks.

Later on, however, he discovered a much more profitable source of revenue — pharmaceutical drugs. From then on he followed itinerant preachers and introduced himself as a cancer specialist! He handed out this card:

Dr William A. Rockefeller,
the celebrated cancer specialist
Here for one day only!
All cases of cancer cured unless
too far gone and then they can
be greatly benefited!

This 'miraculous' elixir (probably a mixture of the same oil that was going to make his son's fortune) sold very well and he gave many consultations.

John Rockefeller was much closer to his mother, Eliza. John had a long, almost expressionless face, veiled, impassive eyes, a thin mouth and was a quiet boy. Frederick Gates, who would later become his chaplain and financial adviser, described him as a 'very reserved man' who revealed 'little or nothing of his own innermost thoughts.'

Eliza didn't just hand down physical traits to her son, she also inculcated him with her Calvanist morals as well Eliza was extremely pious and strict and often repeated maxims such as 'Waste not, want not'. These words shaped his mind and guided his conduct throughout his entire life.

In 1853, the Rockefeller family moved to Cleveland, Ohio, then a booming port on Lake Erie. For John Rockefeller, this move was a revelation. It stirred up his interest in finance even more. He had a talent for making money almost from infancy. As a child, he earned pocket money by selling small painted rocks to his friends. Instead of spending the pennies he made, he accumulated them in a blue earthenware bowl stashed away at the top of a chest of drawers in the family sitting-room. According to him, it was his first 'strong box'. As a result of these 'financial operations', he had soon saved $50.

These $50 were going to determine the boy's future. A neighbouring farmer needed this amount to settle an urgent debt. John Rockefeller willingly lent it to him... but charged him seven per cent interest! The farmer agreed. One year later, Rockefeller received $3.50 in interest, besides the capital he had lent out. He would later write that from that day on:

I was determined to make money work for me

He had just learned that money makes money. Henceforth, all of his profits were carefully registered in a small book which he called 'Ledger A'. Some people even said that towards the end of his life John Rockefeller still kept the book containing the treasures of his youth. Ledger A is, to some extent, Rockefeller's autobiography, since in his eyes the figures listed there were more eloquent than words. He declared:

> Learn to make figures talk!
> They will tell you harsh
> truths and will reveal
> the future

His aptitude for finance was stimulated in Cleveland. After school, Rockefeller paced up and down the docks, watching the bustle in the shipyards, granaries, and coal companies.

When he graduated from school in 1855, Rockefeller decided to enter the world that fascinated him so much.

> I tried the railroads, banks, wholesalers, ignoring all insignificant establishments. I was looking for an important enterprise!

On September 26, 1855, he got his first job at Hewitt & Tuttle, a brokerage company handling grain and vegetables. This was a decisive moment in his life. Every year until his death in 1937, a flag was raised on the mast towering over his estate, Pocantico, on the shores of the Hudson River, to commemorate this anniversary.

He began work at 6.30 a.m. every morning. He was so efficient that his bosses congratulated themselves for having appointed such a talented employee. John Rockefeller made business his religion. In bed at night, he would mull over the day's financial operations, trying to discover how he could have made them more profitable!

He always told himself: 'This is a good opportunity. But he careful. False pride is a trap. Don't be hasty, don't make blunders. Your future depends on every passing day.' Henceforth, his philosophy would be:

> # Discipline, order, and a
> # faithful account of all debits
> # and credits

In 1858 he was earning $600 a year, but, aware of his value to the firm, he asked for a $200 raise. His bosses refused. It was then that he decided to set up his own company with an acquaintance of his, Maurice Clark, an Englishman 12 years his senior who was working for a brokerage house. Rockefeller had saved $800, but needed $1,000 to start up his commission and forwarding business. He determined to ask his father for a loan. His father agreed, but charged 10 per cent interest every year until he had paid off the loan. He was then 18 years old!

At the beginning of his career, Rockefeller was often forced to rely on his father, and each time had to pay the same yearly interest rate. About this he later wrote:

> This discipline should have done me some good.
> Perhaps it did, but in truth, although I carefully hid it
> from him, I did not really appreciate my father's
> policy of pulling a fast one on me just to see if my
> financial acumen was equal to his tricks.

Clark and Rockefeller's company made $4,000 in profits during the first year. The second year was even more profitable, and the profits rose to $17,000.

In 1861, the Civil War broke out. Although a source of misery for the vast majority of people, it was the key to their fortune! It was all a matter of organization, method, attention to detail, and ruthless contracts — all areas in which Rockefeller excelled. From that time on, their success was guaranteed.

Rockefeller brought to his business an inborn seriousness of purpose. He was pious until the day he died, and regularly went to a small Baptist church in Cleveland while he lived there. In fact, he always gave part of his profits to the church, even when he was a multimillionaire.

This seriousness would be manifested in all aspects of his life. Years later, when one of his partners was asked about Rockefeller's age, he replied: 'In my opinion, he must be 140, since he was surely 100 when he was born!'

At this time a revolution was taking place. In 1859, two years before the American Civil War, Edwin Drake had struck oil in Titusville, Pennsylvania. Until then oil had been viewed only as a source of medication and as lighting fuel. Drake's discovery sparked a great oil rush. For many in business, it was a unique investment opportunity, but it didn't impress Rockefeller. Astute as ever, he realized that if there was any money to be made it would be in transportation and refining, not in drilling. Since the transport system was in chaos and refining methods practically nonexistent, John Rockefeller chose to wait for a better time.

Four years later, the Atlantic & West Railroad Company built a new line to Cleveland, joining it with New York and passing right through the oil region. The time was now ripe!

At this time, Rockefeller had met Samuel Andrews, one of Clark's acquaintances, at the Baptist Church. It didn't take Clark and Andrews long to infect Rockefeller with their enthusiasm for black gold. Rockefeller, who was still only 23 years old, invested $4,000 in the new Clark, Andrews and Company.

In March 1864, he became engaged to Laura Spelman and married her on September 8 of that same year. Laconic as ever, he duly noted the following in his Ledger:

> At 2 p.m., married Miss L. C. Spelman, celebrated by
> the Reverend D. Wolcott, assisted by Reverend Paige
> in the young girl's home.

Once married, he went back to his business affairs. Refineries were mushrooming in Cleveland, which was becoming one of the most important oil centres. Rockefeller slowly began to show more interest in the oil business, abandoning the grain commissioning business. His strict discipline brought him commercial dividends. In a town full of wily dealers, he was considered to be one of the shrewdest, best informed traders.

For one who had been so reluctant at first, Rockefeller was now the most enthusiastic of all the partners. Even with net assets of $100,000, Clark was afraid of the expansion recommended by Rockefeller, who believed that:

The Golden rule of success is expansion

Clark obstinately refused to follow this course. They had reached an impasse. There was one solution and that was to auction the company. This took place on February 2, 1865.

The bidding rose until Clark stopped at $72,000. Rockefeller snapped: $72,500. Clark, defeated, said: 'All right, John, it's yours.'

The company, now called Rockefeller and Andrews, became the largest refinery in Cleveland, with a capacity of 500 barrels a day and an annual revenue of one million dollars. Rockefeller's mind was totally free of doubt; he had absolute faith in the future. He was going to bend fate to his will!

He also knew how to attract valuable employees, such as Henry M. Flagler, who had won and lost fortunes, but was now rich again after a profitable marriage. He was only one of the many bold directors Rockefeller placed at the helm of his company.

The ability to handle people is a commodity that can be bought like sugar and coffee, and I'm willing to pay more for it than for any other commodity in the world

---

What he meant was that success is built on several ingredients and one of the most important is knowing how to choose associates who are honest, loyal, and totally devoted to the leader's ideals. Rockefeller, with his proverbial mania for detail, was supremely successful in this. Flagler's business acumen was so sharp, that he managed to negotiate better freight charges with the railway companies just by extolling the strength of the Rockefeller & Andrews Company. The big problem facing railway companies was the regularity of orders. Rockefeller & Andrews, alone, could guarantee regular business. The companies had no choice but to accommodate Flagler's requirements. Of course, when news of this leaked out, there was a public outcry, but it was too late. Rockefeller was already much too powerful.

This arrangement became another weapon in Rockefeller's arsenal. On January 10, 1870, he added another one to it: he founded a new company with a capital stock of $1,000,000 — Standard Oil!

At this time, Standard Oil was one of the largest oil refineries in this region of the United States. But Rockefeller had the idea of including other smaller refineries in the gigantic business he was creating. So, in 1872, he repeated what Flagler had done a few years earlier, but on a much greater scale. He met two of the most important refiners in Pittsburg and Philadelphia. They signed an agreement that would permit them to dictate their terms to the railway companies. Whereas transport normally cost $2.50, they received a preferential rate of $1.25. Better still, the extra $1.25 that their rivals were paying went directly into their pockets.

It was a stroke of genius. The poorer his competitors got, the richer Rockefeller became. Barely three months later, Rockefeller bought out 22 of the 23 refineries in Cleveland. Standard Oil was now refining a quarter of all American oil!

When he had started his company, Rockefeller had 15 competitors in New York, 12 in Philadelphia, 22 in Pittsburg, and 27 in the rest of the country. In the end, there was only one oil company — Standard Oil!

In April 1878, Flagler mentioned in a study presented to the Board of Directors, that the total refining capacity in the United States was 36 million barrels a day. Standard Oil alone refined 33 million!

In 1880, 95 per cent of the total refining capacity was fulfilled by Standard Oil. Through sheer obstinacy, discipline, constant work, and unwavering faith in his destiny, Rockefeller had become what he had always wanted to be: the Emperor of capitalism!

But Rockefeller's strength did not lie in innovation (which he distrusted, especially because of its financial implications), but in the organization and deployment of power. His principle was:

Method and organization

In 1882, Rockefeller set up a trust. The law forbade companies to do business in states other than their own, so Rockefeller got around this law through his trust. From then on, there would be Standard Oil of New York, Standard Oil of New Jersey, Standard Oil of Pennsylvania, and so on.

Rockefeller created one of the most powerful financial empires that had ever existed. The team comprised the most astute financiers in the United States. And all were millionaires! During an inquiry into Standard Oil's affairs, William Vanderbilt declared to the Senate:

> I have never met a group of men as informed and able as they in business... I do not believe it is possible to make them put down their banner by legislative decree or any other way, neither in this State nor in any other. Nothing can be done about them. They will always have the upper hand.

By the end of the century, industrial technology had created dozens of oil by-products. Standard's revenues were astronomical! Standard Oil seemed to be everywhere.

In 1903, Standard offered its gas and lubricating oil to

the Wright brothers. In 1904, its representatives opened up a service station to the participants of the first international car race from New York to Paris, Texas.

Shortly afterwards, the South Improvement Company, an organization uniting refiners and railway companies to protect their respective interests, caused a scandal, and Rockefeller became the victim of virulent attacks and slanderous remarks, both in the Press and in political circles. He defended himself by saying:

> It was my right. My conscience
> · told me it was my right.
> Everything was clear between
> the lord and myself

Rockefeller remained silent at the time, but later commented:

> Look at that earthworm over there on the ground. If I
> step on it, I am attracting attention to it. If I ignore it,
> it disappears.

Unfortunately, far from disappearing, the scandal grew more intense. Rockefeller became, in a sense, the symbol of the malaise of those times. He received death threats. When he went to church, people would gather to insult him. The minister of the church had to hire private detectives to circulate among the crowd outside and in the church to watch over Rockefeller. Rockefeller himself always kept a loaded revolver next to his bed.

But nothing could put a halt to Standard's expansion. Standard Oil's best world agents (since the United States had become too small a market for the company) were the members of the American Diplomatic Corps! To detect new markets and outsell its competitors, especially the Russians, whose oil was beginning to sell all over Europe, Standard Oil gained access to secret reports. These were sent to Rockefeller by ambassadors. Many of them received payment for their 'services', from Standard's secret funds.

Rockefeller's personal fortune in 1897 had reached $200 million. The irony was that it was during his retirement that he earned most, since the internal combustion engine, marketed in 1913, quadrupled his earnings. From $200 million it spiralled to over $1 billion!

Determined to clear his name and secretly persuaded that his fortune was a gift from God rewarding him for services rendered to humanity, he launched himself into philanthropy!

Rockefeller sincerely believed that God had given him money and that this was the one and only secret of his phenomenal success. To the surprised reporter to whom he had just made this declaration, he explained:

> I believe that the power of making money is a gift from God . . . to be developed and used the best we can for the good of humanity. Having received a share of this gift, I believe it is my duty to make money, more and more money, and to use this money for the good of my fellow man by listening to the voice of my conscience.

In the early 1880s, in order to accomplish his new destiny and calling better, he hired a young Baptist clergyman called Frederick T. Gates, who gave him spiritual as well as financial advice.

Rockefeller's problems were not over, however. The hatred for this self-made man was astonishing. The Government was bent on dissolving the trust. A detailed study was undertaken and the true extent of Rockefeller's power became known. In 21 volumes, including 14,485 detailed testimonies, it was discovered that the young broker's initial $4,000 investment now produced 35,000 barrels of refined petrol and oil a day and included a pipeline stretching over 150,000 km and 100 tankers to transport his products abroad! In fact, the trust was worth $660 million!

The Government finally brought Standard Oil to its knees. The company was split up into 39 smaller companies, supposedly independent of one another. But once again, Rockefeller recovered from defeat.

However, he converted this 'failure' into a success. The

shares of the newly founded companies quadrupled, and so Rockefeller's wealth multiplied three or four times.

From then on, Rockefeller had one preoccupation: *to give*. And Gates, his new right-hand man, was well suited for this job. In 1901, the Rockefeller Institute for Medical Research was founded, the first of its kind in America. Then in 1903, the General Education Board was created to oversee education for black people. Later, Rockefeller saw to it that this institute served to promote a better national system of higher education. After this came the Sanitation Commission.

This Commission finally brought public opinion back on to Rockefeller's side. The Rockefeller Foundation, incidentally, is still the largest philanthropic organization in the world.

Some people claim that Rockefeller began these charities only after he had made his fortune. Yet, his Ledger A clearly indicates that he set aside part of his very first earnings to give to his church. He continued to do this all his life. In later years his annual donations rose to over one million dollars.

Reconciled with the public, to whom he believed himself responsible, Rockefeller retired to his mansion at Pocantico Hills. He called it 'Kikjuit', the Dutch term for 'look-out', and here he could enjoy a well-deserved rest. Despite his old age, he did not lose the sense of humour that most people were unaware of.

During a massage session, upon hearing his bones crack, he said, with a touch of irony: 'They say I control all the oil in the country and I haven't enough even to oil my own joints.' To the sculptor making his bust, he asked whether it would be possible to make his sketch while he was playing golf. 'I can't carry my clay with me!' he protested. Rockefeller laconically replies: 'Why not? I carry mine with me all the time!'

John Davison Rockefeller died in 1937, faithful to his great principle,

---

Time is money

He kept an eye on his interests, especially his works of charity, until the last day of his life. Both in this sphere and in business, Rockefeller was able to make good use of his organizational talents, gifts from God which he had managed to make bear fruit beyond his greatest expectations.

LEARNING TO WORK EFFECTIVELY

HOW TO MAKE EACH YEAR HAVE 13 MONTHS

If you are not used to working hard, start little by little. Gradually increase your rhythm. At the beginning, try working one hour extra each day. By the end of the week, you will have put five extra hours towards success. By the end of the year, you will have contributed 250 additional hours to success. A normal work week contains 40 hours. These 250 extra hours will have earned you 6 extra weeks. Your new year will comprise 58 weeks instead of 52. As such, you will have worked more than 13 months that year. This could give you a considerable edge over your colleagues. Now picture working two extra hours a day. You will have made 500 extra hours in a single year, yet all these added hours will not make you any more tired. It's simply a matter of habit.

SUCCESS MUST BECOME YOUR ONLY HABIT!

Stay alert to your success habits. Never hesitate to put yourself into question on a regular basis and to review your plan of action. This is one of the keys to success. Always try to improve your skills and aptitudes. Never believe that you are infallible. Reconsider your methods. Perfect them constantly!

FINISH IN ONE HOUR WHAT YOU USUALLY DO IN THREE

Working one or two extra hours a day is a constructive thing to do, but more profitable still is increasing your effectiveness by finishing in one hour what you normally take several to do. The secrets of enhancing your efficiency are these: first, you must establish different deadlines, meaning shorter ones, and secondly, you must improve your concentration.

Let's start with the first point. Scientific studies carried out by psychologists have shown that the time needed to accomplish a task can be reduced considerably (up to a reasonable limit) without the quality of the work being sacrificed. It has even been proven that in some cases the quality has actually risen. Furthermore, some people cannot function without very short deadlines.

Studies conducted on a large number of subjects demonstrate the following rule: *The average individual tends to need all the time he is allowed to do a certain task even when he could finish the same task more quickly if an emergency arose.*

Reducing the time needed to do a task is once again related to the subconscious. What people do when they set themselves or are given a deadline is to programme their subconscious. We have already seen that it is not any more difficult for the subconscious to programme itself for failure than for success, since it is a power that is blind, so to speak, or neutral at least. Similarly, it is not any harder for your subconscious to help you accomplish a task in less time, so long as it is actually feasible, of course. The subconscious is much more powerful than you believe it to be — and faster. In fact, it can provide you with an endless amount of creative energy.

Being aware of the two laws regarding time and productivity can have dramatic practical consequences. The time needed to do a job is much more flexible than people generally believe. So, if you want to do in an hour what you usually do in three, pretend you only have an hour in which to do it in.

In other words, invent an urgency. In so doing, you are issuing an order to your subconscious. Try it. The results will surprise you. This doesn't mean to say that you have to activate yourself with black coffee as the French writer, Balzac, used to do. He, incidentally, provides us with an astonishing example of how well you can work when you have a strict deadline. In order to put himself under pressure, and in a state of peak creativity, he would promise to submit his manuscripts to his editors in what seemed like unrealistically short periods of time. It was in this way that he managed to write 300-page masterpieces in two weeks. Of course, this great writer had his share of talent and skill, but never make the mistake of underestimating yourself. You have probably been doing so for much too long already. You, too, are talented. You, too, can work fast and well. . . and without causing yourself extra stress. You can do it as soon as you believe you can. . . and as soon as you try it.

Set yourself tighter deadlines; you will accomplish more without sacrificing quality

---

Let's consider the second point now: concentration. It is one of the fundamental keys to success in every single field. Closely related to this is the fact that anyone who cannot concentrate seriously on what he is doing will never be able to succeed. It is absolutely impossible. All rich people are and were superb concentrators. Howard Hughes left the impression that he was simply an extravagant millionaire, an impression confirmed by those who knew him intimately. But those people overlooked his exceptional ability to concentrate. In his book *The Very, Very Rich*, Max Gunther writes:

Hughes worked on his film personally, constantly changing hats as he flitted from scriptwriting to directing to set designing to editing. He often worked more than 24 hours at a stretch without even pausing for a nap. 'I never saw a man who could concentrate that hard or for that long,' said Jean Harlow, who seemed to be [attracted to] Hughes but who never received [any attention] in return.

Honda was also a remarkable example of deep concentration. When he was a novice inventor, so he recounts, he was always completely absorbed in his work. No one could have broken his concentration, not even his closest friends with whom he loved to go out and have fun. At dinnertime, his mother would call the family to come in and eat, but his mind was elsewhere.

Paul Getty was also so wrapped up in his work during the early stages of his career that he would often stay up all night.

The author of *The Practice of Meditation* recounts the following anecdote:

One day a man of note invited Isaac Newton to dinner. Newton arrived and sat down in the living room. But his host, who had forgotten about his guest, ate his dinner and went back to his business affairs. Meanwhile, Newton, completely engrossed in important scientific matters, didn't budge an inch. He forgot about the dinner and sat on the sofa as motionless as a statue. The next morning, his host spotted him still sitting there in his living room and remembered his invitation. He was naturally upset by his *faux-pas* and apologized profusely.

All these stories are fine, you say, but the truth of the matter is, *you* simply can't concentrate. You complain about this regularly since you are aware that it does you a lot of harm. Don't worry. There are a number of easy exercises that can help you to increase your concentration. The first one is to repeat, preferably at night, during your daily self-suggestion session, the following formula, or any other that you might have adopted.

My concentration is getting
better every day. I can now do
all of my tasks more quickly
and efficiently

The second exercise is extremely powerful and has been used for centuries. It can produce miracles in your life, and will increase your powers of concentration.

CONCENTRATION EXERCISE

Draw a black dot about a quarter of an inch in diameter on a cardboard sheet and stick it to the wall or put it on the floor in front of you. Sit down comfortably, breathing slowly, and stare at this dot, trying not to blink. After a while, your eyes will begin to itch. Close your eyes and open them again. Start over. Don't worry, this exercise will not harm your eyes. On the contrary, it strengthens the optical nerve and can even help some eye disorders.

Start by spending two or three minutes on this exercise, gradually increasing the time. By the end of the first week, you should have reached five minutes. When you have reached approximately 20 minutes, your concentration will be excellent. To occupy your thoughts during this exercise and to maximize its effects, why not repeat some of your favourite auto-suggestion formulas?

You will discover a noticeable improvement in your powers of concentration even by the first day if you have spent a few minutes on it. The results will speak for themselves. You will be able to concentrate longer and better. Problems that appear complex to you will seem simple. Your thoughts will speed up. You will easily do in one hour what you normally did in three. And you will do it better, more precisely and neatly. This exercise also enhances your memory, the source of all logical reasoning. Another consequence is more acute presence of mind. This, in fact, is normal, since when you are concentrating you are sharply aware of the moment passing and of the situation in hand. The right answer, the one that always used to come to you too late, will appear more naturally at the right moment. You will be better able to seize opportunities instead of letting them slip by.

In addition, this exercise also helps develop your sense of intuition. This is especially useful in business. Some people will claim that they don't have 20 minutes to spend on this exercise each day. (Daily practice is, in fact, recommended, especially every morning shortly after waking up to 'warm up' the 'muscles' of your mind.) The busier you are during the day, the more you will feel the need to do this exercise. To a certain extent, it is when you don't have 'a minute to yourself' that it becomes imperative for you to take a few minutes out to do this concentration exercise. As soon as you can see the results of this exercise, it will become part of your daily routine.

You probably know that the amount of concentration you put into an activity is directly proportional to the pleasure you get out of it. Take an interesting book or movie, for example, or even a love affair. In all of these situations, your level of concentration is very high; you are so engrossed in it that you sometimes feel hypnotized. What is the reason for this? These activities please you, fascinate you. If concentration is the key to success and our level of concentration relies on the pleasure we get from an activity, then in order to succeed, we must do what we enjoy. We have again reached the same conclusion we discussed earlier, but this time a different logic has led us there.

ONCE YOU HAVE SET YOURSELF A GOAL, KEEP AT IT UNTIL YOU SUCCEED

You must cultivate persistence and the habit of believing that every failure is just a temporary setback. Failure is a step that will lead you to success, provided you don't give up along the way. Many people failed because they couldn't see that success was just a stone's throw away. All it would have taken was one more step, or what is called 'the extra mile'.

Most rich men and women could have admitted in retrospect that if they had thrown in the towel when the temptation was the greatest they would have missed out on success.

In the inspiring book *The Greatest Salesman in the World*, there is a passage that clearly illustrates the virtue of persistence, and the fact that it doesn't pay to be too impatient since success often likes to keep people waiting. But victory always comes to those who refuse to give up:

> Life's rewards appear at the end and not the beginning of the journey; there's no way I can foresee how many steps it will take me to reach my goal. I will perhaps meet failure at the thousandth step, and yet success will be there, hidden behind the last bend in the road. I will never know just how close I am to it if I don't [turn the corner]. I will always take one more step. If this doesn't work, I will take another, and then another... one step at a time is not so very difficult. I will persevere till I succeed.

Remember this: 'The longest journey begins with the first step'. Success is sometimes found on the thousandth step and you are perhaps just a few feet away. Don't make the mistake of stopping at the 999th step, the one before success.

SUCCESS OFTEN FOLLOWS A SERIES OF FAILURES

The lives of the rich show for the most part that they met up with numerous, sometimes spectacular, failures along the way. The same goes for many artists who became famous after having struggled for years. This is what happened to Picasso. Some time before being introduced to the public by Gertrude Stein, he went through such a bleak period that he threw out some of his paintings. He couldn't get any dealer to take them. But if Picasso had given up just before meeting Stein and had decided to pursue another career, he would never have experienced the fame he did and would never have become the multimillionaire he was. This poor, unknown artist became the richest artist in history.

On his death, his fortune was worth an estimated £500 million. But a more detailed study came to a rather different conclusion: Picasso was worth over one billion pounds. And since three-fifths of his fortune included his personal art collection, made up of his own work and those of other masters, this figure continues to grow. These paintings were valued at between £50,000 and £150,000, and that is without considering masterpieces such as the *Nude Woman*, painted in 1910, which was not long ago sold for over one million pounds. Picasso had almost inexhaustible energy, and sometimes finished three paintings a day. Persistence paid off for him in the end. It was the same for many other artists and actors. Most great film stars began as obscure unknowns forced to take on the most menial jobs or to accept roles in third-rate films.

There is something mysterious about success, or so it seems at first. It comes quickly and often completely unexpectedly. Many people have said that they were taken by surprise, especially since they had just recovered from a defeat. Yet, if you take a closer look, their success, albeit unexpected, was not unforseeable. It was inevitable. Their efforts, their dreams, their investments of time, energy and courage were the seeds that they sowed.

Failures and obstacles build character. In this sense, they are profitable. The stronger your character is, the more you will be able to shape your own destiny. People who allow an initial setback to defeat them are not worthy of success. Their weak characters will make them fail. Obstacles are inevitable in any undertaking and success is rarely, if ever, achieved without having to overcome some difficulties. This is precisely what makes life a challenge.

THE RIGHT KIND OF PRIDE

People often give up because they are too proud to tolerate failure. This is the wrong kind of pride to have. This is really cowardice, and lack of self-confidence. Genuine pride is a quality shown by all these 10 wealthy men. It is the ability to persevere despite failure. Men and women who are already rich or destined to be so never doubt that success will be theirs in the end. They know that it is only a matter of time before they reap the benefits of their efforts. They know that time is inevitably on their side.

People who have the mentality of the rich never accept 'no' for a final answer. They know the value of patience. They understand that persistence and determination influence people. These qualities leave a deep impression on others. Someone working for Andrew Carnegie recounts that when he asked for his first promotion, Carnegie answered:

> If you want what you are asking for with all of your heart, there is nothing I can do to prevent you from getting it.

People who want someone with all of their hearts never accept 'no' for an answer because by doing so they would be wrecking their dreams. And that, they can never accept.

Never accept 'no' for an answer

One of the 10 rich men whose life is a model of persistence is Thomas Watson, one of the 'fathers' of IBM. Here is his life story.

THOMAS WATSON

The history of IBM, one of the most prestigious companies in the world, is intimately linked with Thomas Watson. This man, who started out in life as a small-time sewing-machine salesman, was one of the founders of IBM.

Thomas Watson was born in 1874 on a small farm in the state of New York. He never seemed attracted to the manual labour required by the timber business his father had set up. He nevertheless took his first step into the business world by helping his father manage his affairs. His father was disappointed when his son refused to become a lawyer. Instead he took up teaching in a village school, but soon tired of this often thankless work. Some time later, Watson, who was 18 at the time, got a job as a bookkeeper in a meat market. For a man about to become the father of one of the largest multinationals, a future as a simple bookkeeper did not seem very attractive. In fact, Watson hated his boss as much as he hated his work. Many people spend their lives in a similar situation and complain about it, but never dare to take the decisive step. Thomas Watson was made of different mettle, though. And like many other young men of his time, he was attracted to a career in sales. He dreamed of making a fortune and believed that becoming a travelling salesman would allow him to do just that.

In any event, this lifestyle seemed more exciting and romantic than his monotonous work as a bookkeeper. He would get to see places and sleep in hotels. So, it didn't take him long to make up his mind when a man called George Cornwell, peddling pianos and organs, asked him to be his assistant. It was in this optimistic frame of mind in the summer of 1892 that Thomas Watson gave up his job and took to the road. It was still better than lining up figures all day long, he thought.

However, the fairy story he had conjured up in his mind wasn't quite the same as the harsh realities of his new-found job. True, he was earning $10 a week, exactly double his previous salary, but Cornwell had probably forgotten to tell him that his territory lay right in the heart of a poor, rural area. In fact, Cornwell and his young assistant had to try to convince penniless farmers that they needed pianos and sewing machines. It was a far cry from the sumptuous restaurants and luxury hotels that had filled Watson's dreams. Despite all of this, Watson was able to grow familiar with sales techniques and acquire experience which was going to be useful to him later on.

Of the roads that lead to fame and fortune, selling, without being the easiest, is definitely the most accessible to many people and has allowed many men and women to acquire their first millions. When Watson had become really successful, a reporter wrote this about him:

> Let him discourse on the manifest destiny of IBM, and you are ready to join the company for life. Let him retail plain homilies on the value of vision, and a complex and terrifying world becomes transparent and simple. Let him expound on the necessity for giving religion the preference over everything else, and you could not help falling to your knees.

Watson's talent for selling, which he began to develop very early in his life, unquestionably enabled him to scale the ladder of success quickly.

When Cornwell decided to give up his job as a travelling salesman, Watson stayed on alone. He was then earning $12 a week. He was satisfied with his earnings for about a year, until he found out that other salesmen were being paid by commission. He understood then and there that he had been cheated. His pride was wounded and he resigned on the spot. He took the first train to Buffalo, in New York state, in search of a new job as a salesman, but this time making sure that he would be put on commission.

Unemployment was high at the time and job opportunities were rare in Buffalo. Two full months went by since he had arrived and still he didn't have a job. He was a little disheartened, and was on the verge of writing to his parents to ask them to send him the money to go back home when he had a stroke of luck. He finally got a job at Wheeler & Wilcox as a sewing-machine salesman. His stay at this company was brief, but it allowed him to meet a man who was going to have a profound effect on him: C.B. Barron.

Barron was a born salesman, besides being good at making friends. He impressed his clients with his polite manner and slightly flowery language. In addition, he liked to dress well and took great pains with his image. In short, he possessed all the qualities needed to succeed in sales and was, in fact, breaking all of his company's records. Watson modelled himself on his friend, considering him to be the ideal of what he wanted to become. Watson didn't hesitate when his mentor invited him to become his partner in a new business. Barron had approached the Building and Loan Association and convinced its board of directors that he could sell their stock. He believed that Watson would be the ideal person to serve as his partner. Watson had guts and his craving for success was impressive.

Through Barron, he learned a great deal about the subtle art of selling. What is encouraging about Watson's case is that it exemplifies the principle that good salesmen are not born that way, but can be made if their desire is strong enough and if they are ready to make all the necessary sacrifices. Watson by now was so deeply impressed by Barron that he imitated him, adopting his manner and repeating, word for word, the key phrases Barron used when closing a deal. Robert Sobel sketched a portrait of Watson in his book:

> As was and is the case with almost all successful salesmen, he paid great attention to appearances, trying to present a proper face to all, potential clients in particular. Underneath this was the shrewd

tactician, continuously assessing the impacts of statements and movements, trying to read subtle signs sent out by the client, always with the goal of nailing down the sale. Watson appreciated that his middle-class customers prized sincerity, dedication, earnestness, and other such public virtues and that most even believed in and applied them to one degree or another. So did he. They would be impressed by a well-informed and properly groomed representative, which Watson had become. He knew the value of being able to listen to a story and then to laugh with conviction at the proper moment, for the right amount of time. Guile was necessary to sell machines, and so was flattery; but the successful salesman could not be obvious in their use. He had to accept all this but at the same time not become cynical about it.

Watson, a man who used moderation in everything, had learned his lesson well. He was soon pocketing more money than he had ever earned before.

They say money isn't everything. It isn't everything, but [it] is a great big something when you are trying to get started in the world and haven't anything. I speak feelingly.

Watson's self-confidence clearly shows that you can't have any hang-ups about money if you want to succeed in life. One of the first things he did upon cashing his first pay cheque was to buy a new wardrobe. Barron had suggested he do so to look good in front of clients and to cover up his country background. Watson would later say:

Clothes don't make a man but they go a long way towards making a businessman.

At this time chain stores were beginning to become popular in the United States. Watson became interested in this new trend right away, seeing a unique opportunity to make a fortune. Feeling capable of doing battle on two fronts at the same time, he got the rest of his savings together and, without quitting his job in sales, opened up a butcher's shop in Buffalo. His plan was to set up

branches all over the state if all went well. In a few years'
time, he hoped to be the 'Meat King' of Buffalo. He em-
loyed qualified personnel and bought a cash register, in
order to be able to control things while he was away.

In the beginning, things looked promising and Watson
believed that he had finally devised a scheme that would
lead to wealth. Unfortunately, there was trouble ahead.
One morning, Barron disappeared with all of his money.
Watson tried in vain to find him. For the second time in
his life, he had been cheated and he swore that it would
be the last.

A short time after this, Watson lost his job at the Buffalo
Building and Loans Association. Bad luck seemed to be
dogging his steps. Short of cash, he was soon forced to
close up his butcher's shop, which was proving to be much
less profitable than he had hoped it would be. His dream
of becoming the Meat King of Buffalo had come tumbling
down around him.

And yet, despite this bad luck, Watson's confidence was
still not shaken. He was young. He had his beautiful
clothes, and above all, even though he had been tricked
by his partner and had lost every cent he had in his
butcher's shop, he possessed another form of capital that
is invaluable on the road to success: the selling skills Barron had taught him. It was 1895. The country was eco-
nomically depressed and unemployment was high. Watson
had to find himself a job quickly.

Watson had learned a valuable lesson from his 'distress-
ing' experience. He was going to devote himself body and
soul to selling. His self-confidence was intact. The hesitation and the trial and error you go through in the beginning must not discourage you either: you will always
benefit from them!

Watson sold everything in his butcher's shop, except
for the cash register he had leased. While taking it back
to the National Cash Register (NCR), he took the opportunity to offer his services as a salesman. John Range, the
regional manager, was not terribly impressed with him
and refused to employ him. But Watson wanted to work
for this company. He refused to lose hope or to take 'no'
for an answer. Undaunted, he showed up at Range's office
again and again until the day when Range, impressed by

his tenacity, decided to hire him on a trial basis.

Watson had just applied one of the key principles in sales: never take 'no' for a final answer. If he had been able to change the mind of a man as determined as Range, then he could certainly do as much, and more easily, with thousands of future clients. Think about this principle. Everyone, even the most strong-willed person, can be influenced to some extent, and a categorical 'no' one day can change into a wholehearted 'yes' the next.

But the battle wasn't won yet by a long chalk. In actual fact, in spite of his previous experience, something didn't click and Watson came back empty-handed after ten hectic days on the road. Range decided to give him a demonstration and to go along with him for a few days.

The problem was that he didn't know what to do when a potential customer told him he didn't want to buy a cash register. Range demonstrated the correct way to do this. He would put on a smile, get the customer's confidence, and then say:

> I know you don't. That's why I came to see you. I knew if you wanted one, you would have come down to the office and picked one out. What I've come for is to find out why you don't want one.

Years later, Watson confessed that:

> It was Range who taught me to use that important word 'why' in selling.

Armed with this new information, Watson swiftly became a phenomenal salesman. Several years later, he confided to a reporter that John Range's advice had had the greatest impact on his life. If was as follows:

> Pack your todays with effort — extra effort! Your tomorrows will take care of themselves. They will also take good care of you and your money.

Barely three years after having begun working for NCR, Thomas Watson broke all the company sales records. In one week alone, he managed to earn $1,255 in commissions, a phenomenal amount, given that he received only 15 per cent on each cash register he sold. Compared to the other salesmen, who were earning $100 or $200 a week, Watson was a wonder-worker!

A tried and tested salesman, Watson was now ready to face new challenges. In 1899, he was promoted to general manager, in an area which was not considered to be a very promising territory. Watson worked hard, and took up the challenge. Sales revenues climbed soon after. Mr Patterson, then the company's chief executive officer, seeing Watson's amazing performance and motivation, soon appointed him manager of the second-hand division. Three years later, Watson became the general sales manager. Never before had anyone climbed the corporate ladder as quickly as he had and Watson's reputation was becoming widely known.

When he was 36 years old, Thomas Watson had an excellent position with NCR, thanks to his indefatigable work and boundless enthusiasm. And yet, a troubled period was about to begin. American Cash Register filed complaints against NCR, charging them with violating the American Antitrust Act. The matter was brought before the courts and NCR was found guilty. Watson and Patterson were given a $5,000 fine and sentenced to one year in jail. They appealed the decision, however, and the judgement was overturned. Watson was saved, but was no longer in Patterson's good books.

During the trial, the two had quarrelled, so, in April 1914, Thomas Watson was fired. Even if Watson hadn't fallen out with Patterson during the trial, he probably would have been fired later, since Patterson, who was jealous of his power, could no longer tolerate one of his employees threatening his authority.

The day Watson left NCR, he made this declaration to a friend:

Now I am going out to build a business bigger than John H. Patterson has built.

This is a perfect example of what is known as creative frustration. This turning point in Watson's career is also a classic illustration of the principle known as *spin-off*.

The future was going to prove Watson right. From that day on, he was going to participate in the creation of one of the most prestigious firms in the world, International Business Machines, better known as IBM.

Watson was unemployed for a while and reflected on his future. The business world knew what he was worth. Watson received offers to manage companies in the car, boat and retail industries, but rejected them all. Instead he chose to accept an offer from Computer-Tabulating-Recording Corporation to act as general manager. The other jobs would have obliged him to work in the shadow of a boss. He would have had to content himself with executing orders, and Watson had grown much too ambitious by this time and was no longer willing to put himself in a situation which would require him to ignore his own personal objectives. Watson knew what he was worth only too well. Besides, he had accounts to settle. He had not forgotten his promise to get even with Patterson. He *had* to work for a rival company. The choice he had was clear. This was a field in which he had already acquired substantial expertise. It would have been unthinkable to start over again from scratch. His major asset was his years of experience.

Watson was able to set his own conditions: a decent salary with a share of the year-end profits, plus the option to buy company stock. He was finally offered $25,000 a year.

The company was the amalgamation of several relatively different firms: first, International Time Recording, a manufacturing company, then Computing Scale, specializing in the manufacture of knives and commercial scales, and finally, Tabulating Machine. The truth is that for Charles Flint, the chairman of CTR, and his partners, this company was really a tax shelter, devised to hide the revenue coming in from other enterprises. This attitude did not hold much promise for the company's future. Watson never shared this philosophy. He intended to make this company prosperous.

Because of his experience in a similar field, Watson showed much more interest in the activities of Tabulating Machine. He was convinced that the market for typewriters and calculators lay wide open. If Patterson had succeeded so well with NCR, why couldn't he do the same?

Watson began by changing the structure of Tabulating Machine and by assembling a team of talented salesmen, who would shortly outsell those at NCR. Watson remembered that NCR's strength lay in its sales team, trained according to Patterson's method. This is the territory in which he wanted to make a name for his company, knowing that, among products of comparable price and quality, the one presented by the best salesman always sold best. In addition, Watson set up an experimental laboratory to perfect and invent new devices. This initiative was going to prove exceptionally profitable, putting the company miles ahead of its closest competitors.

Watson's efforts did not go unnoticed. Flint was so impressed by Watson's determination and daring that barely a year after he had joined CTR he was made president. Many years later, Flint told a reporter that Watson was:

> The most creative businessman he had ever worked with and one of the true giants of American corporate management.

During this time, Watson's goals were clear and precise: to create a company similar to NCR and to outsell it by manufacturing superior products and by selling those products better!

Watson was a superlative administrator, and was recognized as being extremely skilful in motivating people. Gaining inspiration from his personal experience as a travelling salesman, he had developed a genuine sales philosophy at CTR. In regular weekly meetings with his sales personnel, he gave speeches transmitting to them the principles that had guided him throughout his life.

Watson loved slogans and made liberal use of them during these motivation-building meetings. Here are some of them. They might appear trite, but they nevertheless allowed Watson to become one of the greatest managers of his time: 'Sales and service'. 'Aim high!'. 'Time lost is time gone forever'. 'Teaching is of no value unless somebody learns what is being taught'. 'Never feel satisfied'

'We forgive thoughtful mistakes'. 'There is no such thing as standing still'. 'We sell service above all'.

One of Watson's favourite slogans was: 'Read-Listen-Discuss-Observe-Think'. This notion is clearly centred on thinking, but Watson was quick to add that thinking is nothing without action. Ultimately, the importance IBM accorded to people was the determining factor in its phenomenal success. The same goes for Honda Motor Company and for Walt Disney Enterprises, for example. This attitude is basically a subtle form of humanism.

In one of his most important speeches, which became part of IBM's history and which he called *The Man Proposition*, Thomas Watson declared:

> We have different ideas, and different work, but when you come right down to it, there is just one thing we have to deal with throughout the whole organization — that is the *man*.

Getty's formula describing all business activity was:

> Management is the art of directing human activities.

Last but not least, one of Watson's most popular slogans, emblazoned everywhere on the company walls, was the word 'THINK!'

When he had been at NCR, Watson had learned all the subtle techniques of selling. One of these was always to have the right answer prepared in advance so that one could skilfully put down the most common objections such as: 'I don't have any money'; 'I don't need it'; 'The system I have works well enough for me'.

The most delicate moment in any transaction is undoubtedly the time for closing the deal, that is, getting the client to sign the contract and put in an order. Watson had learned how to do this very well. Instead of abruptly proposing that the client sign the contract, which often frightened customers off, Watson had learned to ask the client what colour he wanted his machine to be or what day he would like it to be delivered as if the client had already agreed to make the purchase. He enthusiastically taught his salesmen these techniques. The results were phenomenal.

By the end of the First World War, Tabulating Machine had managed to break all sales records. Watson believed strongly in the machines. They saved hours of work, particularly for census-taking and compiling data in long reports.

In 1919, CTR's experimental laboratory began to direct its activities towards research and development. It designed a printer capable of reproducing copies of the data fed into it. The age of computers was getting nearer and nearer.

In 1924, Thomas Watson, who was 50 years old at the time, was elected chief executive officer and chief operating officer at CTR. At last he had total control. This was also the year that Watson changed CTR's name to International Business Machines (IBM) to indicate the new direction he intended to have his company pursue. Watson set aside the typewriter and calculator market to plunge into the new data processing machines, which were soon going to change the face of Western society, and were to herald the beginning of the computer revolution.

Under Watson's wing, IBM grew rapidly. Scientific sales methods were used. So, in 1949, revenues topped $33 million and the company had 12,000 employees. When Watson passed the reins of command over to his son, Thomas Watson Jr in 1956, one month before his death, IBM had 888 offices and six factories across the United States. Furthermore, IBM's World Trade division had 227 offices and 17 factories in 80 countries. In 1975, IBM was the second most prosperous company in the US. In 1980, IBM had 340,000 employees and had net revenues of about $24 billion.

Needless to say, Watson also profited from IBM's meteoric rise, since he had a large stock portfolio. He had become a billionaire. His secret, as we have seen, lay in his great skill in motivating people. He considered his employees as individuals in their own right, and so was a unique employer in those times.

Watson's life story is exemplary. He had been a small-time sewing-machine and piano salesman, and he became the president of one of the world's largest multinationals. Watson's story proves that selling can lead to many profitable things, provided you stick to it.

As we have just seen, Watson's life is the perfect illustration of the power of persistence. Here is his advice, from his autobiography, *Press On*:

> Nothing in the world can take the place of persistence. Talent will not: nothing is more common than unsuccessful men with talent. Genius will not: unrewarded genius is almost a proverb. Education will not: the world is full of educated derelicts.
> Persistence and determination alone are omnipotent.

Each stage brings success that much closer. Each adversity harbours within it the seeds of great benefit and better luck.

GOING THAT EXTRA MILE

Earlier on we mentioned the idea of going that extra mile. We explained that many people (most, we should say) fail because they give up too soon. Countless success stories come about when people are going that extra mile.

The extra mile principle has another more subtle meaning. It includes one of the less well-known rules of success. To get ahead in your work, to get a raise or promotion, to win public favour or to satisfy a client, you must constantly force yourself to give more than you are being paid for. This is precisely the reason that a salaried employee who does strictly what his job requires and nothing more simply does not deserve a raise.

This law is simple. It is the law of returns. You get what you give.

Those who give little, get little in return, whether at work or elsewhere. These 10 wealthy men all gave a great deal. They devoted themselves entirely to their work.

The principle of going the extra mile is related to the idea of wealth as the recognition of an individual's social contribution.

Those who go the extra mile will be rewarded sooner or later. This reward can come in an unexpected and surprising form. The most common, of course, is a raise or promotion. But this inevitable reward can also come from someone other than an employer. Often those who are not rewarded for their extra efforts will be offered another job at a higher salary. The extra mile principle has been applied, albeit indirectly. This principle has manifested itself again and again in the lives of the 10 men we have studied, particularly early on in their careers. Often an employee who feels resentful that his work is not acknowledged will start up his own company. This person will then profit from his earlier efforts.

This principle is, in essence, the financial equivalent of the Law of Conservation formulated by the famous chemist, Lavoisier:

Nothing is lost. Nothing is created. Everything changes.

Remember this law and never lessen your efforts. Even if they are not rewarded immediately, they are like money in the bank, and this money is working for you all the time.

All your efforts are like money in the bank

This philosophy shouldn't lead you to believe that you have to work non-stop to make a fortune. Some of the work you put in will have no direct effect, but you can still learn something from it. Ideally, you should try to learn as much as possible and to steer your efforts in the right direction. In this sense, expertise is work that has been transformed. Knowledge is power. The more experience you acquire, the harder you will be able to work. The sharper and deeper your thoughts are, the more productive they will be. If you want to get rich, don't be content with working intelligently. Work hard *and* intelligently.

THE PSYCHOLOGY OF SUCCESS

SUCCESS IS A TEAM EFFORT

No man is an island. This saying is particularly true in business. No one can hope to get rich without the help of people around him. In other words, success is always a team effort. Sadly enough, most people seem to forget this and they neglect to cultivate their professional contacts. They isolate themselves and spend too little time developing friendships. Every one of the 10 wealthy men we analysed spoke of the vital role their partners and associates played in their success. Remember Honda, who openly confessed that had he not met a brilliant manager he would have faced bankruptcy. Onassis, as well, was assisted by a highly talented financial administrator.

> The ability to handle people is a commodity that can be bought like sugar and coffee, and I'm willing to pay more for it than for any other.

This was what Rockefeller, who was skilful in surrounding himself with key people, declared. Think about the last part of this statement: 'I'm willing to pay more for it than for any other.' In fact, the further you advance along the road to success, the more you will notice that what counts is not so much cash, ideas, or enthusiasm, but *people*. Contacts, money, ideas, and enthusiasm, although they are important and necessary, are not enough if you can't count on people.

Learn to like people. Those who can't get along with people and who are persuaded that everybody else is always wrong will never succeed. They forget that everybody prefers working with likeable people. This may seem a platitude, but most people ignore this principle every day. They also forget that they are not the only ones who count in the world and that they are not the only ones with needs and priorities. Those who take this law into account, who are not blinded by their own egos can go far. They can have a considerable impact on the people around them and they can work together towards success.

Success depends much more on this psychological quality than on intelligence or pure expertise. Lee Iacocca had this to say:

> Look at my own career. I've seen a lot of guys who are smarter than I am and a lot who know more about cars. And yet I've lost them in the smoke. Why? Because I'm tough? No. You don't succeed for very long by kicking people around. You've got to know how to talk to them, plain and simple. Now, there's one phrase that I hate to see on any executive's evaluation, no matter how talented he may be, and that's the line: 'He has trouble getting along with other people.' To me, that's the kiss of death. 'You've just destroyed the guy', I always think. 'He can't get along with people? Then he's got a real problem, because that's all we've got around here. No dogs, no apes — only people. And if he can't get along with his peers, what good is he to the company? As an executive, his whole function is to motivate other people. If he can't do that, he's in the wrong place.

These same words could have been uttered by one of the greatest American businessmen of all times. During his lifetime, he displayed acute awareness and understanding of the human factor and of the notion of service. This man was Conrad Hilton.

CONRAD NICHOLSON HILTON

I believe in God and I believe that through prayer we can obtain God's love.

I believe in my country. I believe that its destiny is great and noble.

I believe in truth. I believe that any man who purposely tells a lie is purposely mutilating himself. But, above all, I believe in courage, in enthusiasm, for without them people hinder their strongest desires.

These four magnificent statements neatly sum up the philosophy of the man destined to revolutionize the hotel industry and to become one of the greatest hotel magnates in the world.

In the preface to the biography written by one of his friends, Whitney Bolton, Conrad Hilton declared:

It is impossible for a man to start out in life without knowing which direction he wants to go in. As far as I can remember... I have been branded with the mark of enthusiasm. With enthusiasm to propel me and prayer to shield me, I can say that I like what I have done with my life. Inevitably, with such assets, it would be difficult not to lead a life that is active, rich, and above all, happy. Give a man ambition to spur him, faith to guide him, and good health to allow him to realize his full potential, and he inevitably has to reach success in one way or another.

Obviously the success Hilton mentions here began very

early in his life. His rise to fame and fortune was due not to the administrative talents needed to run a luxury hotel, but to his business acumen. He mastered the art of finance and became an excellent negotiator, extraordinarily prudent in all his transactions. Furthermore, he had a highly refined sixth sense which gave him a perfect sense of timing, and he also had a keen eye for recognizing good investment opportunities. Besides, Hilton respected this fundamental law:

> Choose competent people,
> place them in key positions
> and trust their judgement
> implicitly

Hilton headed 185 hotels in the United States and 75 overseas when he died at the age of 91 in January 1979. Before making major decisions, Hilton spent days and days observing and pondering all the implications.

He studied everything.

When Hilton couldn't buy a hotel, he rented one. When he couldn't rent one, he built one. This tall, imposing man, bubbling over with vim and vigour, ate and slept hotels; he dreamed about them at night.

Hilton was born on Christmas Day 1887 in San Antonio, New Mexico. He was the second of eight children, and the first son. His father, Augustus Holver Hilton, fondly called 'Gus' had been born in Oslo in 1854 and had emigrated to the United States during the 1860s. For a while, Gus Hilton lived in Fort Dodge, Iowa, where his wife, Mary Laufersweiler, who was of German descent, had been born. He was fascinated by the vast opportunities in the West and so he settled down in Sorocco, New Mexico and later in San Antonio. He understood the needs of the coalminers and of those travelling back and forth across the Mexican border, and this encouraged him to establish a general store.

Gus was an energetic man, full of vitality, a trait he was to share with his eldest son, Conrad. Besides running his store, he acted as the postmaster, he sold cattle, opened up a pharmacy, managed a horse stable, and owned a petrol station.

Conrad and his brothers and sisters mastered Spanish at an early age, since they were growing up among Mexican immigrants. As his father was much too busy to help raise his large family, Hilton was most influenced by his mother. She was the one who instilled in him faith, respect for honesty and love of truth, values which would guide him throughout his life. He once admitted that he delighted in the company of frank and honest men and was instinctively horrified by dishonesty, adding that he could not conceive of ever rejoicing for one moment in having earned a single dollar through cupidity or trickery.

Since Hilton had seemed much more interested in business than in religion, his mother began to worry a little about him. The education he was being given in San Antonio did not come up to the standards of Hilton's deeply pious mother. He could speak both English and Spanish when he was only nine years old, but his level of education left a lot to be desired. His mother did her utmost to get him to study more, but the environment they were living in confounded all her efforts. So she decided to send him to the Goss Military Academy in Albuquerque, in New Mexico.

Unfortunately, soon after, the Academy was razed to the ground in a fire. Mary Hilton, however, was not yet beaten. After thinking the matter over for two weeks, she sent her son to St Michael's College in Santa Fe, a parish school which satisfied two of her requirements. First of all, it was a Catholic school, and secondly, the teachers didn't spare the rod.

During his summer vacations, Hilton worked in his father's shop. His father paid him $5 a month, which was a generous sum back then. Gus told him that if he showed interest he would double his salary.

By accepting his father's offer, Hilton was subconsciously obeying the golden rule of hard work, the basis for fortunes built the world over.

His father was thrilled at Conrad's passion for business

Connie, as he was called, ingeniously contrived to increase his income by selling the vegetables he grew himself in his own garden. His success earned him his family's admiration.

That summer, Hilton managed to earn well over $50. His father was always eager for school holidays to begin because he recognized that Conrad was gifted with a rare business talent and would probably carve out an extraordinary place for himself in the future.

Hilton was now studying at the New Mexico Military Institute, but his business successes made him think about leaving school. Gus understood his son's passion for business and urged him in this direction by raising his salary to $25 a month. This was in 1904, and business was booming for the Hilton family, by now quite comfortable indeed. Gus had earned $135,000 by selling a coal mine he had bought several years earlier at an incredibly low price. To celebrate this event, he took his family on a luxury holiday to Chicago. This vacation was a turning point for Connie. For the rest of his life, he would always have a preference for first-class travel, good hotels, and fast cars.

The family's happiness did not last long, however, Mary Hilton became seriously ill. Gus decided to move to Long Beach, California. Then, disaster struck — the economic crisis of 1907. Prices plummeted and Gus rapidly lost his money. Of course the shop was stocked with orders he had just filled at low cost, but prices had fallen lower than that and money was so short that all his sales were carried out at a loss.

He came up with an idea of going into the hotel business. Gus had explained to his family that they were bankrupt, but that this had happened before and was nothing to be afraid of. He reminded them that their mother was in good health again, and that this was nothing to be afraid of. He reminded them that their mother was in good health again, and that this was the most important thing of all. But they had to survive somehow, and he wondered if they had any ideas.

Hilton's career was launched as he replied calmly:

Why not use five or six of the rooms in our house and turn them into bedrooms, like a hotel. This town needs a hotel. We might not have clients at the

beginning but the news will travel and then it'll run
on its own steam. The girls and Mother can take care
of the kitchen and I'll look after the luggage. We can
easily put up several guests in each room. At $2.50 a
day, I think we can manage quite well.

Clearly, the major problem was to attract clients. This
marked the start of a period of extremely hard work for
Hilton. His mother and sisters took care of the hotel itself
while he and his father continued working in the store.
But as soon as the store closed at 6 p.m., Hilton had a light
supper and went straight to bed. At midnight he would
get up to meet the people getting off the 1 a.m. train. He
saw to their luggage, got them registered, checked to see
whether they had everything they needed, such as
blankets, soap, and towels, jotted down what they wanted
for breakfast in the morning and at what time they wished
to be woken up. He then posted these notes up for his
mother and sisters to see and returned to the train station to do the same thing over again for the 3 a.m. train.
When the last traveller had settled in for the night, Hilton could finally get some sleep, at least until 7 a.m., when
he would get up, take care of the guests, and then open
the store up at 8 a.m.

It took only six weeks for the news to spread throughout the area, and even as far east as Chicago. 'If you're
forced to make a stopover', people would say, 'make sure
you do it in San Antonio and get a room at the Hiltons.'

The lesson Conrad Hilton learned was an important one.
He was always willing to work long and hard to succeed.
Until his death, he would say that he wouldn't take a million dollars in exchange for all the things he learned during this time.

The success of his first 'hotel' allowed him to study at
the New Mexico School of Mines in 1907. This period
marked a turning point in his life. Within two years, Gus
was back on his feet again. He began to dabble in real
estate in Hot Springs, New Mexico, even dreaming of
openening up a bank, and he had bought land to build a
house. This land was located in Sorocco, where the School
of Mines was. Hilton hated that town. His father gave him
the option of staying in San Antonio and taking care of

the store, while the rest of the family would move to Sorocco. Hilton knew that his sisters would stand a better chance in this town, so he agreed. This was the beginning of his apprenticeship in the world of business.

He later said that this period taught him everything he needed to know: to do business honestly, to rely on common sense, and above all, never to be afraid of being bold when necessary.

> I learned that you will never get anywhere if you park yourself comfortably in an easy chair

Hilton's life was not a case of one success story after another, however, Once an old prospector had tempted him with promises of huge profits to be made from a silver mine he had discovered. Hilton financed the affair, bought a licence, and left with the prospector. Unfortunately, the man died soon after and Hilton lost his investment.

It was shortly after this that he left school and got involved briefly in politics. In 1912, New Mexico Territory was about to obtain statehood. Hilton was taken by surprise when he found himself elected a member of the legislature at the age of 23. This lasted only two years, however, since Hilton quickly got fed up with the hypocrisy he saw around him in the world of politics.

Instead, something else had attracted his attention — banks. He had the dream of opening a bank in San Antonio. This venture turned out to be extremely successful, and at the age of 27 he became the vice-president of a bank. However, the double-dealings of jealous businessmen destroyed the business. While Hilton was in the army during the First World War, the Bank of Sorocco took over his bank. From this experience, Hilton learned an invaluable lesson:

> ## If you work with steadfast determination long enough, you will make your dream come true

Hilton was assigned to the Quartermaster Corps because of his business background. Then, in March 1918, He was shipped to France. Several months later, he received a telegram from his mother telling him that his father had been killed in a car crash on New Year's Day. He was discharged from the army in 1919, and returned to the States to take care of the ailing family business. Again he dreamed of opening a chain of banks.

To put his hands on the capital he needed, he went to Texas, where oil was helping to build many entrepreneurs' fortunes. He was unable to buy a bank in San Francisco, but happened to spot the bustling Mobley Hotel. From then on, he was to be a hotel man.

He bought the Mobley Hotel for $40,000. During the next few months he worked non-stop. He slept on a sofa in his office, since all the rooms were occupied. This is where he learned a rule that would serve him well throughout his career and would generate his colossal fortune: Not a single square inch must be wasted in a hotel. He also discovered his famous principle, which he called 'Minimax'.

> ## Minimum price, maximum service

He began to make radical changes in the hotel. Since the restaurant was not generating any profits, he converted it into bedroom space. The reception desk was cut down to half its size to open up a little boutique. Three sofas and a canopy were removed from the foyer to make room for a stall. When he redesigned the first floor of the New York Plaza Hotel he included the 'Oak Room Bar' which increased the profits from this floor from $5,000 a year to over $20,000!

Hilton believed that any businessman who wanted to succeed would have to apply the following rule religiously:

> ## Abhor wasted space, wasted efforts, and wasted money, in other words, convert everything into gold and constantly search for that gold mine

What he had learned during the war he repeated in his hotel business. The Mobley had only 40 rooms but with his new associate, Major Jay C. Powers, who he had met in the army, he purchased the Melba Hotel in Fort Worth, Texas. This one had 68 rooms. The furniture was a mess; the kitchen buried under mounds of grease, the carpets worn out, but in Hilton's eyes, it possessed one great virtue: he could buy it for only $25,000! He did buy it, and enthusiastically set about renovating it.

For Hilton, it was essential for each of his hotels to have its own personality.

> ## I buy tradition and do everything to get the maximum benefit from it

The Melba was an unprecedented financial success!

The third hotel in Hilton's empire was his first 'Waldorf' hotel in Dallas, Texas. He had become a sharpminded negotiator. Talks continued over 10 days before an agreement was reached, but Hilton got what he wanted: the initial price of $100,000 was brought down to $71,000. Hilton and his two partners, Drown and Powers, invested $40,000 and borrowed the rest, a debt which they paid off in only 21 months.

The Wall Street Crash of 1929 and the recession which followed it dealt a serious blow to the hotel business. During the 1920s, Hilton and his associates had bought, rented or built hotels in many places. The depression forced Hilton to close four of his establishments and to reduce costs drastically. Rooms and even entire floors were shut. He took out loans, using his life insurance policy as a guarantee, and even worked part-time for Affiliated National Hotels. At least 80 per cent of the hotel industry was on the verge of bankruptcy. Finally in 1935, revenues from oil investments allowed him to pay off some of his most pressing debts and to breathe a little.

His long uphill struggle was now almost over. In Los Angeles, Hilton bought the Sir Francis Drake Hotel, but sold it again almost immediately. Then he purchased the Town House Hotel in 1942, which cost him over $1 million. Because of his efficient organization and sound principles, this hotel made $201,000 in profits after its first year of operation.

His next acquisitions were the Roosevelt Hotel and then the Plaza Hotel in New York in 1943. He was spending more and more cash to buy his hotels, despite his talent for negotiating lower prices. He paid $19,385,000 for the Palmer House Hotel and $7,500,000 for the Stevens Hotel, both located in Chicago.

The Stevens Hotel, which had been built for $30 million, was renamed the Conrad Hilton Hotel, and, with its 2,800 rooms, was to remain the largest hotel in the world for many years to come.

During his rise in the hotel business, several shrewd businessmen backed Hilton. In 1946, the Hilton Hotels Corporation was founded, with Hilton named as chairman. His company reached its peak when, on October 12, 1949, Hilton announced that he had just purchased the Waldorf-Astoria Hotel, With its 1,900 rooms, this hotel was the most luxurious of American hotels. This was a moment

Conrad Hilton had been dreaming of for years. Negotiations had lasted several months. His associates and advisers came out of these meetings completely worn out. Besides the meetings, they had to continue doing their normal day-to-day work. Hilton also made sure that they all got up at 6.15 a.m. and led them to church for a half hour of prayer. They all obediently followed him, even those who were not Catholics.

One of his associates later said:

> When Conrad prays for
> something, he gets it, perhaps
> because he never forgets to
> give thanks to the one he
> prayed to

When the wheeling and dealing for the Waldorf-Astoria finally came to an end, his partners crawled into bed, figuring that they could at least sleep in the next day. This was underestimating Hilton! At 6.15 the next morning, their phones rang as usual. When they were all assembled, one of them grumbled: 'Why go back to church now that the Waldorf is ours for good?' Hilton tartly replied: 'You can't pray for something you want and forget to give thanks when you get it. Let's go!'

There was still one area which appealed to Hilton's spirit of adventure — the overseas market. He applied the same principles there as those that had made him one of the richest men in America. This rule was useful when he made his first overseas purchase:

> Show due respect towards
> whoever you are dealing with

This principle helped him in his dealings with the Puerto

Rican government, who had approached seven American hotels to open up a luxury hotel in San Juan. None of them were interested, and replied with a curt business letter in English. Hilton wrote his in perfect Spanish. Naturally this struck the right note and the Caribe-Hilton hotel chain was born.

In his business deals abroad like at home, Hilton also relied on three rules:

- Invest your own capital

- Treat bankers like friends

- Give your manager a share in the firm.

This formula met with success wherever he went, since it avoided ruffling the feathers of the people he dealt with overseas. Hilton preferred offering foreign investors a partnership in his hotels. They bought the land and paid the construction costs. Hilton provided technical assistance and helped put the hotel into operation. Then both parties signed a general lease or a general management contract. The personnel, carefully screened and selected on site, were invited to perfect their skills in Hilton Hotels in the United States.

Foreign hotels were beginning to spring up everywhere, so Hilton International Corporation was set up in 1948. This company was independent of the parent company, but Hilton was its president and chairman.

Hilton's overseas operations represented two of his ideals: first of all, it would help Americans get acquainted with the rest of the world, which would promote greater tolerance, and secondly, these hotels would allow the world to discover America and its citizens.

Well-known personalities helped finance Hilton Hotels abroad. The Shah of Iran was the owner of a Hilton through the Pahlavi Foundation. Howard Hughes was also associated with it through Trans World Airlines. In May 1967, Hilton International became a subsidiary of TWA. Hilton, by then, had retired from the business he had built up from scratch.

Hilton finally had the time to enjoy his family and friends in his mansion in California. Although he had given up his inspection tours, he never missed inauguration celebrations. Overseas, always respectful of tradition, Hilton made sure that these gala events included the national customs and folklore of the host country.

Although successful in business, Hilton was less happy in his private life. He and his first wife, Mary Barron, had three sons, Nick, Barron, and Eric. When the youngest was born in 1933, Hilton was harried, exhausted, and crushed under the weight of the hard work he was putting in. His marriage fell apart. He later married Zsa Zsa Gabor, but this lasted only briefly. His third marriage was much less turbulent. In 1976, at the age of 89, he married Mary Frances Kelly. She was 20 years younger and a long-time friend of his.

This man of vision imposed his mark on the world. In 1965, the company formed by Hilton owned 61 hotels in 19 countries; in other words, it had 40,000 rooms and 400,000 employees. Hilton personally controlled 30 per cent of the enormous revenues estimated at over $500,000 million!

This is a clear illustration of the principle:

Have faith in your ideas, your destiny and in God

This formula sums up the phenomenal career of Conrad Hilton, one of the greatest and richest hotel magnates in the world.

TIPS FOR SUCCESS

Like Hilton, you must make friends in business. They will become your allies and will help you climb the ladder of success more quickly than you can imagine. However, be discerning in your choice of friends, especially those connected to your business. Avoid the losers, the manipulators, and those who think small. Let's examine each of these categories.

LOSERS

Start off by identifying these people. The signs of their failure are generally quite obvious. The further you proceed on the road to success, the better your ability to judge people will become. Furthermore, as your mental programming becomes more and more positive, you will begin attracting more and more winners. Above all, don't choose losers as partners, since a winner-loser combination rarely comes up with positive results no matter how strong the winner is.

The loser will cause you an enormous waste of time, energy, and money. Lastly, to reach for the top, the winner will invariably have to take over from the loser in order to re-do almost all his work from scratch. This partnership will always pull in opposite directions and is destined to fail in the long run.

All in all, the winner, despite his good intentions, will have harmed the loser, who won't feel that bad because he is used to failing. It's what he feeds on. But the pill will be harder to swallow for the winner. He will nevertheless have learned a lesson: it will reinforce his judgement in the choice of his future associates and he will never repeat the same mistake again. In any event, these two types will never get along, as they simply do not share the same fundamental values.

SCHEMERS

Their careers may appear successful at first, but are bound to fail in the long run. Those who constantly resort to shady deals and manoeuvres always end up having to account for themselves. The truth always comes out in the end. Their list of enemies keeps on getting longer and longer. Watch out for those who continually backstab associates or employees in their absence. They most likely do the same when you're not around. And anyone capable of playing dirty tricks on others can do the same to you.

SHORT-SIGHTED PEOPLE

Avoid these people like the plague. They will always stifle you because they themselves are limited. They are so narrow-minded that they cannot possibly conceive that others can enjoy a much larger vision of the world than they do. They diminish everything they come into contact with. The only thing they are good at is sapping your enthusiasm and trying to dissuade you from going ahead and embarking on new ventures. They will laugh at you if you aim high. They will label you a madman or a dreamer. Play deaf to them. Go your own way. And above all, avoid any partnership with them. You will waste your energy trying to fire them up and in convincing them to follow you. This is energy you might have used towards your own goals.

By joining forces with a winner, your chances of success will grow. In fact, the success achieved by a two-winner combination will surpass that which each of you could achieve individually. So, if you want to go far, get involved with those who are as far-sighted as you are. There will be unexpected bonuses in this alliance.

Great lessons can be learned and ideas discovered from the head-on collision of the ideas, backgrounds, and personalities of two success-orientated individuals working together. Corporate boards of directors are in fact this kind of group, each member contributing his experience and expertise. Chambers of commerce and sales associations operate in the same way. Uniting people fuelled by the same goal and values is a winning formula. However, avoid large groups. The French philosopher Montaigne put it this way: 'When men are assembled, their heads shrink.'

It is not necessary to be the chairman of a company or a member of an association to take advantage of this principle. Build your own group. Choose people you trust, preferably your friends, but especially people with a positive mental attitude. This is a must. Defeatists can do immeasurable harm to an entire group. For, even in positive people, there is a shadowy area of doubt which can be affected negatively by objections and pessimistic views.

Why not set up a group with three or four members? One that will become your 'collective brain power'? They must have a common goal — that of making a fortune. Get together on a regular basis, preferably at pre-set times. Put specific items on the agenda. The first item should be: how can we find a way to get rich? Don't stifle your ideas. Let your imagination run riot. You will probably be astonished by the number of ideas generated in this meeting. After this brainstorming session, refine your ideas. Try to analyse all the implications, applications, and concrete possibilities. One person's vague idea can be refined by someone else's suggestion and become a brilliant idea. Lay out your plans. Constructive criticism and suggestions from others will help you weigh the pros and cons.

These meetings must not be exclusively dedicated to searching for ideas. Take advantage of them to discuss the problems you have encountered at work. Exchange your ideas on your recipe for success. Discuss a book you might have read that week. Talk about strategy.

If people took the time to look carefully at the way they

generally spend their evenings, they would probably be aghast at how unproductive they really are. If you want to succeed, you must dare to be different. At least once a week, or a month, have a productive, stimulating evening with your group. The results will amaze you. Let others watch TV, you cannot afford to watch TV. Nor have you the time. You are busy getting rich. Instead of wasting three hours a day in front of the television, spend only two and use the hour you saved to put you on the road to success.

LEARN TO COMMUNICATE

We are living in the midst of an information revolution. People who want to succeed must learn to express themselves clearly, firmly, and convincingly. On the road to success you are constantly called upon to persuade and convince people. So, take a public speaking course. Onassis, who spoke four languages, took one. Getty learned to speak Arabic in one month by listening to recorded lessons. Try skipping TV one night and register for a language course. Speaking a second or even third language is an invaluable asset. It will also broaden your circle of contacts.

Take public speaking courses even if you show talent in this area already. Those able to talk in public are admired. What people fail to realize is that anyone can do it by taking lessons and with a little practice. The ability to speak in public, whether to a large audience or to a board meeting, will build your self-confidence, giving you a considerable advantage.

MAKE A GOOD INVESTMENT

Take a course on the art of selling. To succeed you need to be able to sell — an idea, a service, your expertise. Ultimately, you need to be able to sell yourself. Studies have shown that an individual's success is largely based on personality.

You will be called upon to do some selling no matter

which field of activity you are involved in. Lawyers pleading their cases are selling themselves to the judge. Politicians making speeches are selling their government's policies. Administrators defending their budgets are selling them. Then there are those involved directly in sales. In every sphere, being familiar with sales techniques will enhance your performance.

LEARN HOW TO LISTEN

Speaking well is essential in sales. But you must also know how to listen. As a rule, people talk too much and don't listen enough. In almost every business deal, the one who knows how to listen and speaks the least is the one who gets the most out of it. The more the person you are dealing with talks, the more he opens up, revealing his motivations, needs and personality, thus allowing you to spot his weak points, which will inevitably increase your powers of influence over him. By listening attentively to people, you are showing that they interest you and are important in your eyes.

Most people love to talk. Their favourite topic is themselves. Learn to ask the right questions, so that you can show just how interested you really are in them. Observe yourself in action. What is your speaking-listening ratio? If you talk more than you listen, be careful. The other person is probably chalking up more points than you simply because he is learning more about you than you about him. Try to correct this tendency. It's merely a new habit to acquire. Try it out once. Say only the basics. Then listen. People will be delighted to have talked with you and will consider you a fine conversationalist, even though you haven't really said much.

DRESS CAREFULLY

Our world is very image-conscious. Some may think this is a shame, of course, but the fact remains the same. In all human contact, first impressions play an important role. What is the determining factor in first impressions?

Usually, external things, such as a well-cut suit or dress, a warm smile, or a neat haircut. People usually judge others on their appearance. Someone sloppy generally makes a bad impression.

If you wish to succeed, dress like someone successful. If you don't know how, look around you. Get advice. Remember, all human contact contains some element of seduction. Neat, appropriate clothes go hand in hand with this. Clothes do not make the man, so the saying goes. But in business, they help a lot. Remember the care Watson took in selecting his wardrobe. Can you afford to neglect your own?

A HEALTHY MIND AND A HEALTHY BODY

This is one of the oldest maxims in the world. It is still true today. On the road to success, it is vital to stay in good shape. 'When the body is weak, it takes over command. When strong, it obeys,' said the French philosopher Jean-Jacques Rousseau. A healthy body will be your best tool in reaching for success. You will be more energetic — not only physically, but mentally as well.

Exercise regularly. It relaxes your body as much as your mind. Choose a sport that totally absorbs you and allows you to forget your professional worries.

Most of the rich men we studied took some sort of physical exercise that helped chase away the formidable tensions facing them every day. Onassis recommended judo and yoga. In fact, the first advice he gave in his recipe for success was to stay fit and healthy. He himself often went for long swims. So did Paul Getty. At the beginning of his career, Walt Disney was so overworked and neglectful of his body that he had a nervous breakdown. As soon as he was well again, he adopted a programme of relaxation and exercise.

Most great men have added physical activities to their daily routine. The great German writer Goethe went for long walks to stimulate his genius. Nietzsche claimed that all of his great ideas came to him while he was walking and thinking about things other than philosophical questions. Pope John Paul II had a swimming pool built near his living quarters. In response to one of the Vatican administrators disgruntled about this expense, he said that it would be much less expensive than setting up elections for a new pope. Pope John Paul II also goes skiing and often jogs in the Vatican gardens. That is surely one of the keys to his phenomenal physical endurance.

Follow their example and do some exercise on a regular basis.

OTHER PEOPLE'S MONEY

We have already mentioned that success is a team effort. Besides this, it is never achieved with one person's money alone. It is often the product of OPM (Other People's Money). We have seen how Onassis used OPM to finance his shipping activities. He believed that behind each millionaire lies a borrower. He knew what he was talking about. Hilton also went into debt quite heavily.

Taking out loans is a delicate matter, however. For some, large loans can be catastrophic. Fluctuating interest rates can often make nasty surprises. On the other hand, without loans, many companies would never have been able to expand. Take Chrysler, for instance. It was saved by a massive loan negotiated by Lee Iacocca. Furthermore, Honda would never have been able to expand without the support of his bankers. On a more modest scale, many small investors have made handsome profits by investing $10,000 to buy a $100,000 building, resold a year later for $110,000, and so doubled their investment within a year. However, the lives of these 10 men have shown that most did not take out loans at the beginning of their careers. They started off small and grew slowly. Then, they borrowed money.

A lesson can be learned here. It is preferable not to rely on large loans at first. It's best to start out without a luxurious office. Successful people are cost-conscious. Offices are always too large. Bankers and creditors do not want to finance luxury items.

Should you or shouldn't you borrow money? How much?

When? This question is not easy to resolve. One thing is sure, though: if your subconscious is well programmed, you will know whether or not you should use OPM. Caution is always recommended. Some people never dare to borrow money and spend their lives saving up their pennies and tightening their belts, thus missing out on countless opportunities. All rich men have taken out loans at one point or other in their lives. Do as they have. But first analyse your ability to pay it back, and then rely on your instinct and subconscious mind. And don't forget that fortune favours the bold.

YOU HAVE AN INFERIORITY COMPLEX

One out of two people is reputed to suffer from low self-esteem at some point in their lives. If this is the case for you — so much the better! Think of Steven Spielberg and Soichiro Honda. Both suffered from deep inferiority complexes in their youth. But they knew how to turn it to their advantage. They didn't spend their lives bogged down in self-pity. They managed to capitalize on their complexes. You, too, can do the same. Instead of brooding over your shortcomings, you should tell yourself that you are going to become the best there is in your field.

Discover the virtues of creative frustration. The dissatisfaction you feel, no matter where it springs from, can help you go far. In one way, you will have an advantage over those with strong egos. They don't feel the need to better themselves or to change. Convert your frustration and inferiority complex into success. People will admire you. And, as a result, you will lose your low self-esteem.

GIVE BACK PART OF WHAT YOU REAP

These 10 rich men all eventually became philanthropists. Spielberg, the only living member in this illustrous gallery of men, is perhaps still too young to dream of building the 'Spielberg Foundation'. However, he is very aware of this principle and puts it into practice. Do the same yourself.

CHOOSE A ROLE MODEL

All those admired by someone started out admiring someone themselves. Spielberg venerated Walt Disney. Honda held Napoleon in great esteem.

Just like the great and the rich, choose an idol who will inspire you to achieve great heights. All great men had lofty ideals. They aimed high. You, too, are now aiming high. You now belong to this family of achievers. A good example is the best sermon, so the proverb goes.

A ROLE MODEL IS AN EXAMPLE TO FOLLOW

A role model can also help you in another way. When faced with a problem, ask yourself what your hero would do. You can select one of the men we talked about in this book.

Read the biographies of great men. Try to discover what led to their success. Use their example for inspiration. Remember that all those admired by someone started out admiring someone themselves. In the beginning, most of these men were just like you. But they applied rules that most people ignore or fail to use. You now know these principles — it's up to you to apply them and to become someone admired by all!

SELECTED BIBLIOGRAPHY

Bailey, Adrian. *Walt Disney's World of Fantasy* (Chartwell Books, 1982).

Bolton, Whitney. *The Silver Spade* (Farrar Strauss and Young, 1954).

Crawley, Tony. *The Steven Spielberg Story* (Quill Books, 1983).

Ford, Henry. *My Life and Work* (Doubleday, 1926).

Gawain, Shakti. *Creative Visualization* (Bantam, 1982).

Gunther, Max. *The Very, Very Rich and How They Got That Way* (Playboy Press, 1972).

Iacocca, Lee. *Iacocca* (Bantam Books, 1984).

Kroc, Ray and Anderson, Robert. *Grinding It Out: The Making of McDonald's* (Henry Regnery, 1977).

Lundberg, Ferdinand. *The Rich and the Super-Rich, A Study in the Power of Money Today* (Lyle Stuart, 1968).

McCormack, Mark. *What They Don't Teach You at Harvard Business School* (Bantam Books, 1984).

Naisbitt, John. *Megatrends* (Warner Books, 1982).

Peters, Thomas J. and Waterman, Robert. *In Search of Excellence* (Warner Books, 1982).

Schreiber, David J. *Live and Be Free through Psycho-Cybernetics* (Warner Books, 1976).

Sobel, Robert. *IBM: Colossus in Transition* (Bantam Books, 1981).

INDEX